FLOYD'S AMERICAN PIE

D0100775

KEITH FLOYD

☆

BBC BOOKS

*I would like to thank
Sheila Keating for her enormous help
under the most difficult circumstances
both in America and back in England
while we were filming* Floyd's American Pie.
*Without her help and encouragement
this masterpiece might have taken
ten years to write!!!*

FOOD PHOTOGRAPHY James Murphy
FOOD PREPARATION Berit Vinegrad
STYLING Cathy Sinker
BACKDROPS (FOR THE ABOVE) AND MAP
Annabel Playfair

ILLUSTRATIONS Phil Dobson

Published by BBC Books,
a division of BBC Enterprises Limited,
Woodlands, 80 Wood Lane, London W12 0TT

First published 1989
© Keith Floyd 1989

ISBN 0 563 20803 1 (Paperback)
0 563 20791 4 (Hardback)

Set in 11/13 Garamond by Butler & Tanner Ltd, Frome, Somerset
Printed and bound in Great Britain by Butler & Tanner Ltd, Frome, Somerset
Colour separations by Technik Ltd, Berkhamsted
Cover printed by Richard Clay Ltd, Norwich

Ingredients

Prologue

This is not a cookery book – even though you'll find some recipes at the back.

This is a personal and haphazard note of people, music, tastes and things that your average gold-card-carrying cook would stumble into as he wandered from sea to shining sea in search of America, travelling by Lear Jets, stretch cadillacs, chuck wagons and Corvette Stingrays.

And even though it didn't take me four days to hitch-hike from Saginaw, I think I did find America.

Or rather I think I discovered what Americans think is America. And who knows, they might be right. But then, in the end, I thought:

I know you are
But what about me?

Keith Floyd
Ashprington, 1989

How I made my American Pie

'I would like bacon, egg, toast, grapefruit juice and coffee, please.'

'How would you like your egg? Easy over, hard over, sunny side up . . . ?'

'I'd like it well cooked.'

'Sure, but *how* would you like it cooked? Easy over, hard over, sunny side up?'

It's only breakfast, and I'm already bewildered.

'Over hard, please.' I think.

'Hard over. And a side of bacon.'

'I suppose so.'

'Coffee, sir?'

'Yes, please.'

'Regular or de-caff?'

'Regular, please.'

'OK, one cup of leaded coming up.'

On the road with J.J.

'Floyd, you can't drive a cadillac in Florida,' said J.J.

'Why not?'

'Because this is Florida. You have to have a convertible. It says so, here in the affirmation. Listen: "Your travels through life should be in harmony with your surroundings." And anyway, it's about 90 out there.'

(I should explain that no God-fearing American leaves home without their book of affirmations: a sort of collection of thoughts and inspirations to get them through the day.)

'So you see, you have to have a convertible.'

'Well, go and get one.'

'What colour? Red, blue, silver, black, white, off-white . . . ?'

'Anything else I can get you today, sir?' says the waitress.

'Some ketchup, please.'

'Certainly, sir, no problem. I'll get that for you right now.'

'You know, Floyd, you really need some new publicity pictures,' says J.J.

'Oh?'

'Well, pardon me for saying it, but you look a little like a college professor, almost conservative, in these – but you're really wild and loose!'

'Anything else I can get you today, sir?' says the waitress.

'Some ketchup, please.'

'Certainly, sir, I'll just get that right away. No problem.'

'I couldn't sleep last night,' says J.J. 'But I have this thing I do. I try to cram my body into the tip of my nose, and then when it gets there I pretend the tip fell off.'

Help.

'Can I get you anything else today, sir?'

'The bill, please.' Quick.

Eight minutes later, a bright blue convertible draws up outside, with J.J. in peaked cap at the wheel, and the radio tuned to Z93. Nonstop rock and roll.

☆

Cruising down St Pete's Beach (St Petersburg Beach, Florida. Except everyone here calls it St Pete's).

The hood is rolled down, Z93 is turned up. Past the neon signs, past the billboards and traffic lights hanging on wire. Everywhere looks like it will be nice when it's finished. We're headed for Woody's on the beach where they do brilliant chicken wings, dipped in their own special batter and deep-fried. If this is fast food, I like it.

'So what do you think of America, Floyd?' says J.J.

'I don't know. Where is America?' (You see, I don't think it's real.)

'What do you mean, where is America?'
'Well, *what* is America?'
'I don't know,' says J.J.

☆

J.J. is driving with panache, dancing behind the wheel, whacking up the volume on the radio, secretly getting lost, street after street.
'Where are we going J.J.?'
'Well, where would you like to go?'
'I'd like to go to Woody's, the bar we went to yesterday. Actually I thought it was over there . . .'
'Well, I thought I'd take you a different way.'
It had seemed like a good idea to ring up Avis and ask them if they knew someone who could drive me around St Pete's. And now we have this 5 foot 1 inch, blonde, totally off-the-wall person called J.J., who isn't called J.J. anyway.

☆

We were lunching on fried grouper at Woody's on the beach.
'I don't like my name,' said J.J.
'Well, change it.'
'Yes. I will, I *will*. Yes . . . what can I be called?'
We called a witgathering and came up with J.J. It's the kind of thing people do every day over lunch in Florida.

☆

Silence as the billboards slide by.
'You really did come in a spaceship, didn't you?' says J.J.
'I beg your pardon?'
'Yeah, I was just sitting on the beach, and this spaceship lands and says, "Get in," and now I'm surrounded by mad British people, and I don't know who I am any more. Who am I, Floyd?'
Beats me.

'Could you turn the music up, please, J.J.?'

Z93. Nonstop rock and roll – a little rock in a sea of madness. Beneath a big sun.

☆

The Stones' '2000 Light Years From Home' is playing as J.J. pulls the convertible up at Woody's on the beach. Chicken wings with fries is the order of the day. And beers all round. And dill pickles. The pickles here are great. They *are* bottled, but consumed at such a rate, they're always fresh, not left in hot vinegar on the top shelf in some grubby servery.

The sun is streaming down, and there are enormous jars of 'sun tea' cooking on the roof. They put tea bags in water in these huge jars and leave them on the roof, to let the sun do the brewing.

'Coleslaw or salad?'

'Salad, please.'

'What kinda dressing? Blue Cheese, Thousand Island, Ranch, French, Italian, Creamy Italian . . . ?'

'Blue Cheese, please. And some beer.'

'Bud, Bud Light, Coors, Michelob, Michelob Light . . . ?'

Here we go again.

☆

'The Don Ce-Sar Hotel in Pass-a-Grille stretched lazily over the stubbed wilderness, surrendering its shape to the blinding brightness of the gulf . . .' – F. Scott Fitzgerald, *Crack-Up*.

'J.J., I want to go to the Don CeSar.'

'OK. Why?'

'Because F. Scott Fitzgerald used to stay there.'

'Oh. Wow.'

The Don CeSar is a great big pink and white hotel that looks like a wedding cake, in Pass-a-Grille at the end of the strip.

I could imagine the scene in Fitzgerald's time: women in flowing gowns, wearing diamonds as big as the Ritz, draped over lounge lizards

15

in evening dress, sipping cocktails in the cool, high-ceilinged rooms. The sea breeze would waft in from the terrace, an orchestra would play dance music ... I felt sure that the ghost of Scott Fitzgerald, and all those fabulous decadent days, would be there somewhere.

'There was nothin' but snakes and jungle here when Thomas J. Rowe decided to build a great hotel, just like the grand hotels of Europe,' says the lady from the local heritage group. 'He was such a romantic man, a cavalier. Don Caesar was the hero in his favourite opera, *Maritana*, probably the most popular pre-Gilbert and Sullivan opera there was. Rowe changed the name to Don Ce-sar; now it's Don CeSar without the hyphen.'

'There must have been great parties when Scott Fitzgerald stayed here?'

'Oh, sure, he and Zelda stayed here. There's a very interesting story. Mr Rowe's secretary is still alive. And when I brought her here, she said: "Oh, where's Mr Rowe's fountain?" ...'

'How interesting. About Scott Fitzgerald ...'

'Oh yes. He stayed here. You see, Rowe knew Plant, the great railroad man ...'

'Did Scott Fitzgerald write any of his stories here?'

'Oh, you want to hear about Scott Fitzgerald. Well, one time, they came to stay and Zelda arrived with six trunks and about twenty-five pieces of luggage. They were here for two and a half months, and they say she wore the same dress every single day. She was an unusual package, to say the least.'

I eat half a plastic burger for lunch and decide to try again later. Funny, they have plastic food, but they won't take American Express. It's true. No one round here wants to take American Express. An American yesterday said: 'American Express – don't leave home *with* it.'

Lunch over, I ask the hotel's PR lady: 'There must be some good stories about Scott Fitzgerald?'

'Well, I just wish there were. I'd love to know more. I'm always finding out things. In fact just today one of the waiters in Zelda's (the restaurant downstairs) said, "I've just found a man who's got the old menus for the Don CeSar ..."'

'The parties in the twenties must have been fabulous ...'

'Well, usually on our anniversary, we like to do a twenties theme. People just love to dress up ...'

'J. J. call home.'

*The eccentric
Evander Preston.*

Roll down the hood, whack up the stereo…this is AMERICA!

I never did find out about Scott Fitzgerald. Or all those parties in the twenties. The only things she cared about were occupancy rates and profits. But apparently the ghost of Thomas Rowe still stalks the balconies on moonlit nights, dressed in a white linen suit and a panama hat ...

In the kitchen they were making a giant ice-carving of a swan. 'I thought they were putting the finishing touches with a fork,' said Tim, the sound man. 'But then they went over it gently with a chainsaw afterwards!'

'J.J., get me out of here.'

☆

'I called my mother and said the BBC were here,' someone said. 'She said: "Stop stuttering, dear, and tell me what you mean."'

Sitting in the bar at the Tradewinds Hotel, with a plate of deep-fried shrimp and a bucket of bourbon. I don't actually *want* a bucket of bourbon – but everything comes in bucket-sized plastic cups full of ice.

A bucket of Bud
A bucket of Rye,
A dustbin full of Key Lime Pie ...
Well, that's Florida –
But what am I?

The TV screen in the corner is advertising forthcoming attractions at the hotel. Tomorrow there is a morning worship service – followed by cocktails. At least it's better than the real TV, which is running nonstop coverage of the countdown to the execution of a mass murderer.

'Can I get you another drink, sir?'

Don't these people ever stop selling? 'Could I have a *small* bourbon – like, not in a bucket. Less ice, same amount of bourbon?'

'Howzat, sir?'

'A *small* bourbon ...?'

'Oh, you mean a regular bourbon.'

'Thank you.'

There are many women in the bar. All thirty-three, divorced and looking for a way out, but they can't seem to find the door.

'Brains like chicken soup,' I hear myself say.

'But good chicken soup,' says Andy, the assistant cameraman.

But you don't want to mess with these dames. Maybe they sound like chicken soup, but by God they'd eat you quicker than you could open a can of the stuff.

'You the cook from the BBC?' says this tanned blonde in a pink wraparound dress that shows a filmstar's cleavage.

'Yes.'

'You guys having fun?'

'Yes.'

'Why do you wear bow ties?'

'Because . . .'

'You ever had sex on the beach?'

Er . . .

'You should try it. It's wild.'

'Really . . . Won't you get trampled to death by windsurfers and joggers? Or middle-aged ballet dancers pirouetting to poetry? There was one on the beach this morning.'

'You guys are crazy. It's a drink!'

'What's a drink?'

'Sex On The Beach.'

'I think I'll stick to bourbon.'

There seem to be about six of us now. Me, Andy, surrounded by these mad women. I order drinks and back up to the bar so I can see the door. Maybe the rest of the crew will come in. Before the massacre.

'So what do you do, Dolores?'

'Nothing.'

'Don't you work?'

'I just party.'

'Yes, but what do you live on?'

'Alimony.'

And her oval blue eyes stare hard at me. Mae West would have nothing on this bunch.

The room was humming harder as the ceiling slipped away . . .

'Now, guys. Can I freshen these drinks for you all?'

Bartender busy with bottles and blender, long fingers pecking like a chicken over the trays of limes, cherries, bananas, oranges, sticks and straws for this next round of multicoloured drinks. Who says as he serves: 'Are you Australian?'

☆

A black reggae band is busting the carefully aged wooden walls of Silas Dent's restaurant, a place Dolores said provided a great experience of wall-to-wall flesh pressing. I tell her I can't stay late as I start filming tomorrow. But she has gone. Gyrating in the arms of some Florida Adonis. Relieved, I turn to go.

'Good heavens. Keith Floyd. What are you doing here?'

'Um . . .'

'How was Hong Kong?'

'I . . .'

'Was the Mandarin fun? And Jenny – how was she?'

Help. I'm being attacked by another madwoman. But this one isn't American. She's British. Very, very British. And I reel under this barrage of bizarre questions.

'I've never been to Hong Kong.'

'You have. I sent you there.'

I stall for time, hoping she'll give me some clue to who she is before I have to ask. After all, one should never forget a lady's face. Even if one has (I think) not met her before. Perhaps it would be simpler to say I enjoyed Hong Kong. Thank her profusely and run. But now she's introducing me to her friend, an elegant Englishwoman who has something to do with garden centres.

'So what did you think of Ivana?'

The pale light of understanding began to dawn. It was Nina, a consultant who'd 'engaged' me to help Donald Trump's flamboyant wife host a lunch at Mosimann's to publicise her acquisition of the New York Plaza – a snip at several million dollars.

'I didn't go to Hong Kong though . . .'

'What about Bangkok? Do you want to go there?'

I felt a soft arm round my neck. It was Dolores. Hanging from her blond fisherman.

'Dolores, this is Nina. Nina, this is Dolores.'

And to the bartender. 'Where are the restrooms?'

Exit Floyd – wondering whether he is an Australian or a Martian.

☆

Sometimes morning never comes too soon. Today it does. The dirty picture windows of my room in the Holiday Inn rattle with rain and wind and sand scuds up the beach eight storeys below. But the joggers are still there, bent into the wind doing 2 miles an hour, their bodies inversely inclined to the palm trees on this first morning of filming in Florida.

HANGING OUT WITH EVANDER PRESTON

Evander Preston is 6 foot 2 inches tall, an ex-rock session musician who looks like a renegade from the Byrds, with a chest-length beard and matching hair. They say he's fifty plus, his friends call him Moses and he has a fantasy about being looked after by dwarfs.

He has a chihuahua called Ms Pee Wee who wears dresses and hats and sunglasses, and who wants to be driven around in his red and black miniature Model T with 'Let the good times roll' on the front – provided someone answers his ad in the *St Pete's Times* for a driver of cheerful disposition under 36 inches tall.

He hangs out (his words not mine – I prefer 'holds court') in his studio salon in Pass-a-Grille, where he's restoring the building to the way it was in 1916, and where he makes things like model express trains in 18-carat gold, with diamond headlights, and cargoes of rubies, sapphires, emeralds and diamonds in the freight wagons, worth about 400 000 dollars.

There are African masks around the walls and hanging up are jackets which look real but are made out of wood, in between glass cases full of jewellery. And a painting of Bob Dylan and Salvador Dali, inspired by Dylan's song, 'Romance in Durango'. It looks like the strongroom a very sophisticated 7-foot magpie would have in the bowels of his hideout.

He is passionate about food and wine – and his exploits in that area are legendary. He's a man who lends instruments to Pete Townshend and Frank Zappa when they're in town, and then cooks for them, or parties for days with movie folk.

Soft-spoken women spread priceless baubles on a velvet pad, and fit-looking men in shorts and trainers – so immaculate in this cool Aladdin's cave – create golden fantasies. Golden corkscrews less than an inch long that actually work, garlic crushers and erotic rings – all are exquisitely crafted. Would-be customers are admitted courteously after they ring the discreet buzzer on the high-security door.

Steve sets up his lights, Andy and Clive are checking the camera. Tim is busy with sound. Frances is trying to rearrange something for David who's found some Brits playing darts in the garden – I mean yard. But it's the old firm, and that's good.

The kitchen is a studio too, its equipment chosen as much for serious cooking as for quirky aesthetics. Chinese stoves and tandoori ovens cleverly arranged. Big practical pipes bring water and steam. Knives and cooking pots hang in studied disarray. Helpers in white aprons speed slowly with brimming baskets of produce. The blender is whirring, its shrill tone muted by the sound of rythmic chopping.

They are not interested in us. They are working for the Boss. Evander Preston. You can feel his presence, but he is nowhere in sight.

Clive says he's ready to turn over. David says: let's go. Someone says: where's Evander?

Evander says: I'm here.

He has appeared – no – manifested himself in the kitchen. And stands stock still like a magnificent bear, chewing on a hand-made cigar a foot long.

David Pritchard is happy and ready to go. This will be great. You know what to do, Evander. You happy, Floyd? Right, let's hit. Turn over.

Floyd in yellow suit and two-tone shoes before the big over. Evander towering above both. Clive pans up from a groaning table of ingredients to a two shot of Floyd and Preston. Pritchard gives the sign.

'So, Evander, what do you do with armadillo?'

And this passionate, cultured and articulate giant froze. He could not speak.

This was a real shock. I mean, any American can talk the hind leg off a donkey. They are blasé about TV, cool about films and all seem to know Robert Redford. They are masters of the self-publicist's art. Yet, Evander had dried.

We walked in the yard and I tried to hype him up. Predictably, there he opened up like he was giving an interview to *Rolling Stone* ...

'We could lower the waitress from nets suspended above the dining table ... I don't want, I mean *don't* want to publish music ...'

He finished his cigar and said: let me try again. We went back to the kitchen.

'So, Evander, what do you do with armadillo?'

'Well, you take a pound of it, cubed, mix it with a couple of cans of milk and a quarter of chowder mix, three-quarters of a cup of cornstarch, add a little butter, salt and pepper.'

And there you have it: authentic armadillo chowder.

'How about gator burgers?' (Short for alligator, you understand.)

'Well, all you need is a couple of pounds of gator meat, a couple of eggs, some sausage, breadcrumbs, salt, pepper and garlic, mix them all up into patties, grill and serve in a bun.'

Evander made 'real simple things from the land': marinaded conch (a kind of mussel in a shell), quail with black-eyed peas, gator burgers, frogs' legs, armadillo gumbo ('armadillo tastes a bit like chicken'), dirty rice (they call it dirty because of the colour), squirrel sausage, venison with blackjack sauce, smothered rabbit and hind quarters of wild boar barbecued with honey-glazed sauce, egg rolls made with crabmeat, and hearts of palm salad or 'swamp cabbage' (from Florida palm trees), served with stewed collard greens with fried corn kernels and pimento, buttermilk and sunshine biscuits, hush puppies and calamondin chutney, followed by Key lime pie. In between playing the blues on his piano under the picture of Dylan and Dali, and opening bottles of his sangria made with Chablis, Triple Sec and brandy.

Evander collects people. There is Captain Jack who runs fishing trips from Pass-a-Grille and has been known to dress up in animal skins and carve the tenderloin at Evander's bashes. 'Hell, that Evander's had me doin' some strange things,' says Captain Jack.

But he still hasn't found his dwarf.

The lady from the local heritage group is polishing palm leaves with vegetable oil, and there's the English couple who drive cars with 'True Brit' on the front and sell darts to Florida.

'We're so used to American accents, we can't tell Australians from the British any more ... now there's a nice English pub near where we live. It has draught Guinness, Whitbread, Newcastle Brown ... and they serve steak and kidney pie and sausage and mash ...'

Then there's Boss Hogg, with his cowboy hat, checked shirt and a whip in his hand: the rancher who caught the armadillo and shot the alligator. (Actually he's in the clothing manufacturing business – if you ring him at work, you have to ask for 'Men's Upholstery' – but he does have a ranch, too.)

'Armadillos can't hear so well. So you kinda ease up on 'em, kinda pounce on 'em, push 'em over and grab 'em by the tail at the same time. The best bit is the flank. Fry it up and put it in a sandwich,' says Boss Hogg.

'Hell, I just narrowly missed stepping on two rattlesnakes the other day (Note: there are no rattlesnakes at Evander's!) ... Hey, Eddie,' he shouts to someone in the kitchen, 'get us another beer, buddy ...'

Then it was outside to watch Boss Hogg's whip-cracking show. I wonder what Greenpeace would make of this circus ...

Evander promised to make me a fish in solid gold and invited me to join his charmed circle of eccentrics across the world, and said: excuse me, I need to play piano.

Happy to be back in his world as the crew packed up. Boss Hogg, in boots, jeans and stomach that flowed over his silver-buckled belt, leaned against the door jamb, tapping time. While Evander played the blues.

Floyd on the Air

Satellite dishes sprout like mushrooms outside Channel 13. Inside, the lady at reception looks spruce in her business suit – but underneath the desk she's wearing thick woolly ankle socks and sneakers.

I, against all my principles, am wearing a solid gold Florida bone fish around my neck. I've joined the medallion mafia at last. Help.

J.J. is being cheerleader, beating the drum, hyping the hype. Being quite magnificent. Turning the place upside down and telling them Floyd has arrived!

The TV in the corner is locked into a game show, the kind where the husband wins a washing machine if he can tell the audience why his wife thinks she's an alien.

Perhaps that's the answer: America *is* a game show.

Leaflets scattered around the tables in reception advertise forthcoming events: damn, we've missed the pig racing.

J.J. is talking about reincarnation. 'Perhaps I could come back as a human being? Or a British person? No, I couldn't be. Could I?'

I don't want to let her down hard or anything, but frankly she's got more chance of being struck by lightning.

'J.J., you can be what you like. For today. It's your choice.'

'OK, so I'll work on my Japanese...'

The TV has gone into the 'coming shortly, but just before that, and stay with us because after that we have ... right then, let's talk about the next thing we're not going to do' routine, where everything stops before it's started. Coming up – not yet, of course – is the countdown to the execution of mass murderer Ted Bundy. The grotesque timetable reads like an afternoon's viewing on *Grandstand*:

9 a.m.–2 p.m. Psychiatrists and attorneys make
   an attempt to have Bundy declared insane,
   so by law he can't be executed.

2 p.m.–3 p.m. Interview with the only journalist
   to see Bundy today.

3 p.m. More interviews with investigators.

8 p.m.–1 a.m. Bundy meets with his family.

5 a.m. Last meal.

7 a.m. Execution.

And, coming up: 'We have Floyd with us. Well known in England ... If you're familiar with him, you'll be saying: "Good grief, what's he doing here?" Well, he'll be talking about food and American culture, or subculture ...'

Back to an item about a new waxwork of newly inaugurated President Bush. 'And coming up, Burt Wolf talks about cucumbers ...'

'And Keith Floyd will be with us shortly.'

Burt Wolf is standing in a field of cucumbers. 'The Americans eat almost 7 pounds of cucumbers per person, per year. These are the cucumber fields of Michigan. Why Michigan? Because Michigan produces more pickling cucumbers than any state in the country. Over 275 million pounds per year. And experts tell me that 275 million pounds of cucumbers have a street value of in excess of 200 million dollars ...'

'Cucumbers are pollinated by bees. And a bee must visit a cucumber flower seven times in order to get a straight cucumber. That's some pretty serious dating!

'My favourite piece of information about cucumbers deals with the old saying: "cool as a cucumber". People say that because the internal temperature of a cucumber is usually 10 degrees less than the air outside. Watch this . . .

'The reading on the thermometer is 95. Put it into the cucumber and it goes down 10 and I get a reading of 85. Now that's pretty cool. From the fields of Michigan that's what's cooking for today. I'm Burt Wolf . . .'

'Coming up. Floyd and food in America . . .'

'I was trying to think of a designation for you,' says the chat show host. 'I was thinking it's a sort of combination of Burt Wolf and Dick Clark.'

'Well, we take it one step further. Where Burt Wolf was in the field there, we'd have actually cooked there, as well . . .'

We'll start the programme burning down the highway in a '67 Corvette Stingray. Close-up of the tape going into the stereo. 'Roll Over Beethoven'. We're doing 120 – which I know we shouldn't be . . . with my cameraman, Clive, sitting behind my shoulder. And I'm doing a piece to camera, which is: 'If the Florida sunshine, the ultimate state of the art machine – the Corvette Stingray – rock and roll and gastronomy don't turn you on, then switch off . . .'

'That's right, then nothing will . . . let's take a break. We'll be right back to talk with Floyd some more . . .

'We should talk about American food, compared to British food . . . I hear you think our breakfast is quite good . . . ?' says my host. After the break.

'Yes – you see, everything here is to do with sunshine. Food is a sunshine thing . . . all those sweet things at breakfast and crisp bacon. Mind you, I'm having a real problem at breakfast, trying to get my leg over, I mean my egg over, easy, hard, or whatever . . .

'I think American fast food is great. I like the fish and the shrimp and the burgers in the beach bars,' I tell him.

'You like the burgers?'

'Yes, I *do*. Because everything is freshly made. It's what we've all been laughing at in Britain for years and calling American junk food, but I love it.

'You see, in Britain, American fast food is run by English people. I mean, that's a bit like asking Tammy Wynette to sing Vivaldi . . .'

☆

Into the convertible, heading for Woody's on the beach.

'Hey, you were hot, Floyd,' says J.J.

There's an eagle over the sunshine skyway. And on Z93 they're playing the Byrds' 'Eight Miles High'.

☆

'Is it true about the cheese?' says J.J.

'Pardon?'

'Well, from reading your book, there's a lot that makes me think you have a heavy-duty personal involvement with cheese.'

'Sorry?'

'It's true isn't it? You even went out of your way to have little boxes created to put cheese in.'

'Yes ...'

'To give to your customers, right?'

'Yes.'

'I think that's the strangest ... I find that so strange. I mean, nothing personal. But as an American ... OK, it's like ... but you know, I *like* it. I wish someone would have served *me* cheese in a box ... We did have a place in Milwaukee once. They had ropes, and they had boxes. And they'd put the food in them and pulley them across. That's how you got your food. They didn't have any waiters or waitresses.'

I think J.J. deserves a hug. 'You are wonderful, J.J. Do you know that? Truly wonderful.'

'Yeah. Oh good. Well, cheerio,' says J.J., raising her beer. 'Is that proper? Is that British? To say cheerio?'

DOUG GOODMAN

Bombing along the freeway in a winnebago, locked into Z93 with Elvis singing 'A Fool Such As I'. I'm off to film a cooking sketch, in which I cook some chicken in a sauce which I've just invented for a Vietnam vet called Doug Goodman ...

My director seems to be running some sort of private competition with himself to find me the smallest place to cook in. But I will not be defeated. In fact these winnebagos are brilliant: microwaves, ice-makers, Magimixes. This one belongs to a guy called Dan who has another business in Kentucky – a commuting distance of a mere 900 miles.

'I sell them starting from 150 000 dollars, but you get lots of American entertainers putting in about 500 000 dollars' worth of sound equipment. And I remember one that was made for a sheik, which cost a million dollars. It had tyres almost 6 feet tall,' says Dan.

It has taken some thinking – minutes, in fact – to come up with a real Floridian dish to cook for my intrepid friend, apparently no mean cook himself. After all, everything I've eaten since I've been here has been deep-fried: chicken wings, grouper, shrimp . . . and very good it was too. But I wanted to do something a bit more inventive.

So I make chicken fillets with lime juice and pineapple, flamed with rum and doused with a dash of Budweiser, served with rice and decorated with plump Florida raisins. Salvador Dali died yesterday – and he was big in St Pete's Beach – so this is my humble attempt at an artistic tribute to him, to Florida, Z93, and to Vietnam vets.

I offer Doug an American light beer to wash down the chicken.

'Hell, drinking light beer is like taking a shower with your boots on.'

'What kind of food did you get in the jungle?'

'Anything you could get your hands on. When you've got a good imagination, and you know the basics about cooking, you can scrounge around. You see the animals eating a lot of things and you follow suit: leaves, berries, a lot of roots – 'cos you get a lot less impurities in them than you do in the stems on top . . .'

Later, as the waves rolled in and the sun started to set, I walked along the beach talking to this tough yet vulnerable man 'from a small town in America', whose mother had signed him into the services because he wanted to see the world, who had killed people in Vietnam and fought as a mercenary in the Congo – 'and on a couple of jobs I can't name' – but could still crack up at the beauty of a Florida night sky.

So, how do you feel when you kill a man? 'Well, I've always respected my enemy, to the point of almost loving him. When you respect your enemy highly, you do not take him out unnecessarily. If I went to the same watering hole as my enemy, I wouldn't kill him. But if he'd just killed a friend of mine, *then* I'd kill him.

'In the heat of the battle, it's a matter of attrition. Him or me. If you don't take someone out, they take you out. Everything's flying around you, you see your friends getting killed, and when you see that, there's no question about your job. It is a job and it's survival.

'But after eight years down the road I got tired of fighting political wars. I gave it all up, primarily because of Vietnam. Because I just saw so much waste. Not that I thought Vietnam was wrong, because Communism is a real thing, but I made a personal decision.

'I wasn't against my country. I love my country. I'm 100 per cent dyed in the wool American. I believe in fighting for ideals, but I don't like being used. It wasn't based on some great crisis in my life, or nothin'. I just looked around and said: "Hey, they're using me."

'I think all wars since Vietnam belong to professionals. They don't belong to innocent kids, they belong to guys who really enjoy fighting.

'The days are gone when there were citizen soldiers – you went off to war, you fought for a good, solid cause, and you came back. Nations are getting tired of sending off young men with great ideals, who have a chance to contribute to something else other than war.'

It was strange, walking along this quiet, pink and shadow-bathed beach listening to this man talk of sentiment and violence, all in one breath. Of how he'd rather take the money and bite the bullet than have innocent kids going to war.

'The typical American man,' he told me, 'is full of ego – in business and in war, and ego has no place in war. He's full of himself in general. He leaves little room for feeling. Me, I cry at sunsets, and I don't care who knows it – but I might rip someone's face off for making fun of me!

'I'm considered a bit of a dinosaur, because I still believe in things like honour. I believe in those old Samurai concepts.

'You have to have some kind of balance in your life all the time. I always say I have a set of scales and if they don't balance then I'm not being honest with myself.

'Now I live down by the river with my cocker spaniel. My wife lives on the beach. After 20 years we came to a parting of the ways. She kicked me and my cocker spaniel out. Said we were both too big an' ugly!

'I live down there with my brother and my friends. Almost all of them are Vietnam vets. We take care of each other. We have a lot of quality of life.

'You know, there's a lot of people who went through terrible things in Vietnam, and had a lot of problems, but there are a lot of crybabies out there too. I think people tend to over-romanticise what they did. I find that most of them who complain and cry and moan about what happened to them, they're wanting to relive that experience. Otherwise why do they run around in camouflage fatigues, and all that kind of thing? Why don't they get right, get their clothes on, dress like everybody else?

'Men, women, nations, we all try to complicate things too much. I like to sit on the river and relax. Hell, I haven't had so much fun since the pigs ate my little sister . . .

'And I love to cook,' he said, bringing the subject back to where we had started.

'Anyone who loves living, who has loved life as much as I do, and has seen the other side, has a taste for life, a real rage to live – I want to get every bit of taste and nuance out of life, and cooking is a part of it.

'Like you start out with several different choices of ingredients. That's what life is: choices. You can come up with all kinds of different concoctions. You get a feeling about what blends and what doesn't. Cooking is like life. It requires the greatest amount of honesty. You can't lie with food.'

The sun is way down over the sea. It's quiet, it's cool. It is America. The land of the free. 'Would you kill for all of this?' I ask him.

'Always. To protect your way of life – that is the greatest kind of honour.'

FLOYD'S FIRST TASTE OF AMERICAN FOOTBALL

Tonight Miami is gripped by riots and superbowl fever. No place for the sensitive.

In St Pete's the bar is crowded with guys in peaked caps and ladies in tight jeans, wearing 3D glasses, eyes glued to the giant screen in the corner. It is Super Bowl night. The Cincinnati Bengals v the San Francisco 49ers. Most are rooting for Cincinnati, but the 49ers, with their superstar Joe Montana, are favourites.

'Looks like a cross between rugby and stock car racing to me,' says my producer.

'Excuse me, what is happening?'

'Well,' says Mike, 'the jock' (a term used to denote the equivalent of a varsity multiple blue apparently) from St Pete's, 'this guy here is trying to make a down into the touch down zone, 100 yards down. They're both trying to go both ways, each way.'

'Ah ...'

'You see you get four downs. You get three plays to make it either 10 yards or a touch down. If you get 10 yards, you get another three plays until you get to the end zone. You're looking for six points. Then a field goal is an extra point. That's seven points. Like right now they're trying for the first down ... OK?'

'Well ...'

Roars and screams erupt around the bar.

'Now, that wasn't good, that wasn't good at all,' says Mike's mate Mark, from Orlando, shaking his head.

'What wasn't?'

More roars around the bar.

'What's happening now, please?'

'That was a punt!'

'A punt?'

'Right.'

'What's that?'

'Well, where they kick the ball ...' A note of exasperation is beginning to creep into Mike's voice.

'Why is everybody leaving the pitch?'

'Well, Cincinnati's offence is going to come on and go against the 49ers' defence, OK? Cincinnati has three plays. If they don't get a first down, normally they'll go for a punt. Then it'll go back to the 49ers and they do the same thing. You see, every time you get 10 yards you get a first down. That means you get to start a whole new series ... second down, third down, fourth down. So what more d'ya want to know?'

I decide to pester someone else. 'Excuse me, can you tell me what's happening?'

'Are you Australian?' asks the blonde, taking a break from biting her fingernails with excitement. She is called Tammy.

'OK. See, what they have is four downs, and for each down they have to make at least 10 yards to get another touch down. That's why they have to stop. It depends on how far they get ...'

Let's give up on that one, and try a new tack. 'Why are there so many different people in each team?'

'Well, some are receivers who catch the ball and have to pay attention to the quarterbacks. Then there are some that block and protect the quarterbacks, and there are some that block other players so that the quarterbacks don't get tackled, and so the receivers don't get tackled. Anyway there's only eleven. It's pretty much like soccer, isn't it?'

Well, not quite . . .

I ask the bartender for a beer, please.

'You British are so polite,' he says. 'Americans never say please.'

'So why does it all take so long?' I ask Tammy.

'Well, there are four quarters and a quarter is fifteen minutes long . . .'

'But it's been on for at least two hours . . .'

'That's because they have halftime and that lasts half an hour . . .'

'Then there must have been about four halftimes . . .'

'No, see, you have to take breaks for penalties and then the clock will stop with certain plays, whereas it will go on with other plays . . .'

'Why?'

'I don't know . . .'

'Then if they're tied, they'll play a little overtime gig,' says Tammy's friend, Brad. 'Come on, you big flunky, make the big play . . . ! How many minutes left? One, two?'

Just as the tension is at its height they break for an advert for McDonald's hamburgers.

'It ain't over till the fat lady sings,' says Brad.

'See these commercials are so good, you *wait* for these commercials – like last year they maybe just missed a Clio, so they're really trying,' says Tammy.

'What's a Clio?'

'They're the academy awards of commercials. This game has some of the best commercials you'll ever see on American TV. Made just for this game.'

'Everybody's got to make a buck. It's America after all,' says Brad. 'Best country in the world. So what else d'you need to know? I mean, that's it basically,' he says. 'I mean, they have to get from one end of the field to the other in so many plays and if they don't do that they have to turn the ball over. So what they have are downs. Each down, you have to make at least 10 yards. If you don't, then you go on to the second down. OK? Then you have to move it at least 10 yards. If you don't, then you go to the third, then the fourth. But every time you make 10 yards you go back to the first down ... got it?'

Clear as Mississippi mud pie, old bean.

Apparently the 49ers won.

THE MAN WHO WOULD BE
KING OF ROCK 'N' ROLL

The Mercedes – which isn't like any Mercedes I've ever seen – swerves into a parking spot outside the hotel. Past the sign which reads 'Congrats Mike and Margie. It's a Boy.'

A dark-skinned, dark-haired guy with tight trousers and unbuttoned shirt climbs out.

'Hi. I'm Tony Belmont.' The voice is pure Italian–New York.

'The car? It's expected. The King of Rock 'n' Roll promoters – they expect me to either come in on the top of an elephant or in something unusual ...

'This car was built for the Mercedes Company by George Barris, the greatest American car designer, the man who did the Batmobile for the TV series, and the ambulance for *Ghostbusters*. George makes cars for the stars, that's his motto.

'Of course, most of my friends are stars, so I provide a pretty good revenue for George. I tell him Tom Jones or somebody wants a car. So he's a close friend.

'This car was a prototype of what the Mercedes would look like in the year 1993. It's 21 inches longer than a regular 560 Mercedes.

'Well, the car was supposed to be destroyed. Prototypes of all cars of the future are supposed to be destroyed after the shows. This one didn't get destroyed. What happened to this car after that reads like a novel. Drug dealers stole it, tried to get it to Mexico. They were stopped at the border, the car was impounded. The story just got wilder and wilder.

'So George tells me about the car. He said: "It's the most beautiful sports car you've ever seen. It's copyrighted, blueprinted and it's the only one left."

The man who would be King of Rock 'n' Roll... Tony Belmont.

I wish I could have caught that fish…

Desert Island Dish. Captain Jack and me, with Andy on bellows.

'Well, it was what I needed. In my business, as a promoter, you need an image. Otherwise you're one of the crowd. Just like the Beatles had an image: their hair, their dress . . . gimmicks and images are very important. I have nine cars. I have a Studebaker Golden Hawk with a Paxton Supercharger, a '59 Bonneville Tri-power. They're what we call "muscle cars" cars . . . I drive this Mercedes and a stock Mercedes and a '57 Cadillac Fleetwood. All white.'

'So tell me some rock 'n' roll stories.'

'You got four weeks? OK. I manage many, many rock stars. Nearly everybody has worked with me at some time.

'I worked with the Buddy Holly tour in 1959. Buddy was a very sweet, nice, talented man. He was a good guy. Buddy would have been an Elvis. His time was just caught short. He had a lot of charisma on stage. The girls liked him.

'There's dozens of beautiful stories in rock and roll. Like Carole King hires a babysitter. And the babysitter is sitting at the piano fooling around, flipping pages, only to find a sheet of music Carole King has written the night before. She starts playing. Carole King comes in and she hears the song she did as a ballad being played as hard rock and roll. She's astounded. She comes in and says: that's great. I wanna record you. Come down to the studio tomorrow. The babysitter said OK. She was sixteen, her name was Eva. They changed her name to Little Eva. The song was called "The Loco-motion". Hit time.

'I go back to the beginning of rock and roll. A lot of the rock stars call me "The Mystery Man" because I sang with a lot of the groups, I managed so many, and I go back so far. That's because I started so young.

'My father was one of the great guitarists in America. He started managing in 1918 – artists like George Burns and Gracie Allen.

'I went to work for Alan Freed in the mid-fifties. Alan Freed was the father of rock and roll. Back then it wasn't even called rock and roll yet. It was called Race Sounds or R & B. Alan Freed invented the name rock and roll.

'Alan Freed was the only white DJ that was playing original black records, never cover records. See, in the early fifties when a black group put out a record, a white group would put out the same record and sell more. A lot of people said it was terrible, but at the same time it did a lot for the black artists, to bring their talent forward. Because people started saying: "Well, this sounds good. Who really did it?" and go back to the original.

'Alan had a show called "The Moondog Show" in Cleveland, Ohio, and one night he announced this music as rock and roll. And it stuck.

'We had an office in Times Square, New York, right in the beating heart of the city. Alan Freed was the ultimate promoter. He was doing something no one had ever done before: taking the groups, putting them into one show, creating a lot of excitement, wearing his crazy leopardskin jackets . . .

'Rock and roll had some rocky times. You have to remember this was the dawn of a new age, and many of the adults were worried about what it was going to do to the kids. Round about 1959 Alan Freed and a bunch of us were arrested for doing a rock and roll concert. It's inconceivable today, but we were arrested for disturbing the peace and inciting to riot!

'What we were doing was telling the kids to get up and dance in the aisles. The police moved in from every direction and forced these kids to just sit in their seats. Of course, they weren't going to listen to that. They started standing up and the rest was bedlam. Alan Freed was taken away in handcuffs.

'Then in the late fifties there were the payola scandals. They tried to charge DJs like Alan Freed with taking kickbacks to play records, which wasn't really the truth.

'The truth of the matter was it was just a business arrangement. Just like today when Mr Jones gives his client a bottle of scotch at Christmastime.

'Alan Freed was subpoenaed, but instead of cracking, he was very indignant and said: I don't have to tell you anything. So they said: we're gonna make an example of this guy. And they did. The IRS (International Revenue Service) got involved in his private affairs. Finally he died without a nickel to his name in 1964.

'I think it was a vendetta from the industry and society. Rock and roll was new – wild and beating. Kids were jumping up and dancing and nobody was quite ready for it. Alan Freed was the father of rock and roll and the perfect target.

'I carried on the business and eventually changed it to Belmont Promotions.

'I have archives of rock and roll. I have eighty-eight hours of videos and films . . .

'I remember a show at the Peabody Hotel in Memphis. It was an Alan Freed production. The show was packed with stars. Little Richard was one and Jerry Lee Lewis was another. The way it worked was you put your best two acts on front and back, because the old cliché was: they'll remember what they see first and what they see last. Jerry Lee said to Alan Freed: I close the show, right? Alan said: No. You're next to last. Well, that was the wrong person to say it to. Jerry Lee had a big ego.

'Jerry Lee's manager said: look, this is Alan Freed. If you don't go along with this guy, you're dead in the business.

'So he went out second to last, sat down at this big white Steinway piano and began to play rock and roll. The kids were going wild. He was given fifteen minutes, but he wouldn't stop. He finished up with "Whole Lotta Shakin' Goin' On", knocked the piano stool down, and the crowd went crazy.

'He reached into his pocket, got out some lighter fluid, sprayed it over the piano, lit it with a match, and there's a great big bonfire. He walked over to the mike and said: Let some **** follow that act!

'Little Richard came on, completely upset, walked up to the mike and said: that's my piano. At that point the leg crumbled, the piano slid down in ashes ...

'Some cute things occurred. We had a roadie, who used to carry the bags. He also did some song-writing and arranging. He was constantly asking if somebody would listen to his material. He was always brushed aside. We couldn't be bothered with him. Send him out for a pastrami sandwich and he wouldn't even come back with the right mustard on the sandwich.

'Finally he went off on his own. He later did very well. His name was Neil Diamond.'

I think of Sam Phillips, owner of the Sun Studio, the man who sold Elvis's contract to RCA.

'Well, Sam did what he had to do. He had such a small company and Elvis was growing at such a tremendous rate that there really wasn't anything he could do for this man. He was far greater than anything his company could provide. Sam also needed the money.

'I don't think it was a bad move on his part. Hindsight is wonderful, though ... look at all the people who said the Beatles would never make it. Their recordings were sent to this country and people just turned them down.

'You should see my office. Of course, my real office is in Times Square. There are about 1500 glossy pictures there ...'

☆

39

Tony Belmont's office is way across town. But then everything in St Pete's is way across town. There is no 'downtown'. Just a lazy sprawl.

He calls in on his Italian mama living three doors away, who wants to cook everyone pasta, then settles on the couch in his kitchen/diner. 'Frankie Valli slept on that couch. So did Bobby Rydell – they get bored with meetings. There's nothin' like talking to a rock star in the middle of a meeting, and his whole life is depending on it, and suddenly you hear snoring. All my life I've been with snorers – every one of them; Frank Sinatra, everybody . . .

'Frankie Valli called me up one night from a bowling alley in New Jersey. He said: the guy here doesn't like our name (they were called the Four Lovers then). I said: what's the bowling alley called? He said: The Four Seasons. I said: why don't you call yourselves that? Come into the office . . .

'Barbra Streisand turned me down for half a million dollars for an hour. I can't believe that – it's phenomenal. I made my first million by the time I was 27 years old, but I'm amazed by someone who turns down half a million for an hour.

'That's James Dean.' Pointing to one of hundreds of photographs pinned around the wall. 'I met him. I liked him. He was a sweet nice guy. If you dropped something on the floor, he'd pick if up for you.'

'That guy with the butch haircut in that funny yellow picture is Charlie Bronson. He used to hang around Greenwich village and come into the clubs. He used to hang around with Robert de Niro and Dustin Hoffman. Imagine, at one time they shared a little flat in a loft: Bronson, Hoffman and De Niro, putting money together to pay the rent.

'That's Eddie Murphy. He worked for me a long time ago. I hire comedians sometimes to open up shows. We paid him 200 dollars and he was happy to get it.

'I have guys who run around in barrels, get shot out of cannonballs . . . Dick Clark says if they eventually throw Christians to the lions again, it'll be a Belmont Promotion.

'I did a stunt for a wheat company. They needed a gimmick. So we had a three-storey box of puffed wheat and we had a human cannonball fly over the top of the box. We got network coverage all over the United States.'

He's at the piano now, mocking up an old doo-wop number, bursting into falsetto. 'I sang with Dion and the Belmonts in the late fifties. In the days when girls tore off my silver lamé jacket. That was when I was still able to do the splits and things. Phil Spector was my manager.

'Falsetto work – there's nothing about that you can learn from books. That came from the streets of New York, it came from the early black singers, guys like the Drifters.

'I guess my voice stopped in a time tunnel. I didn't develop new styles. I'm somewhere between the crooner and fifties rock and roll.

'I'd like to put on a real doo-wop show again. They were a lot of fun. There's a lot of imagination.

'I put on a rock and roll *Frankenstein* once. You know: "He did the mash, the monster mash . . ." and we had electric wires underneath 350 of the front seats. The audience were sitting in the dark with wind blowing in their faces, and there's this lightning crack and we gave them a little buzz right under their bottoms! The fire marshal went crazy: What are you? Nuts? You're gonna fry 350 of my people . . . !

'Those kind of shows are an adventure. That's what I want written on my tombstone: "Just one more adventure".'

'I've done a lot of walk-ons and appearances in movies. I played a promoter in *The Love Boat* series, for the Temptations. I was one of the characters in the mess hall on *Mash*. And I was in the first rock and roll movie of all time: *Blackboard Jungle*.

'The movie opens up and all you see is from the waist down. Tight jeans and motorcycle boots. And you see the cigarette fall to the ground, but you don't see me. Then as I open the door you hear: "One, two, three o'clock, four o'clock, rock . . ." and the whole thing goes crazy . . .

'I'm really a drummer. We did Berlin about 1960. Ringo came backstage and I signed an autograph for him.

'I've played drums since I was seven years old. I made my debut at 12 years old with Dizzy Gillespie, the great jazz artist, at the Metropole in New York. The Metropole was the mecca of jazz in New York City.

'They put a big hat on me and a moustache, and I looked like a midget.

'The song was "Caravan", and I went through this great big drum solo, with the house lights down. I leaned back, and behind is a curtain, and behind the curtain are metal doors – the Metropole went back to Prohibition days. They used to open the door and slide in the booze.

'Well, somebody forgot to lock the doors. I go through the curtain, through the doors, and fall right into the alley, right on top of a derelict who's sleeping there.

'The house lights come back on. No drummer. Dizzy Gillespie is walking up and down the stage with his trumpet, trying to find the drummer.

'I come round the front. My hat fell off, my moustache fell off. The doorman sees a little kid. He says: "You can't come in here", and chases me away. So I get on a bus and go home. Dizzy Gillespie never did find out what happened to me.

'I write songs too, but I do so many things, I just don't have the time. That's me standing on the top of my train. I own the world's largest railroad car. The famous *Chicago Zephyr*, the train that used to go from Chicago to California.

'You know, Floyd, I really like the show. But I would take it one step further. When you're doing things with a frying-pan, I'd have a false bottom – a Benny Hill type thing. Mix that with cooking and it'd be great . . .'

A wop bop be loo bam boo. Rock on, Tony!

GONE FISHING

'Jeremiah was a bullfrog . . .' Z93 is blasting out. Past the Don CeSar, past the fishermen, each with his personal pelican at his elbow – they say that beside every fisherman in St Pete's you'll find a pelican. Past the mad lady skipping through the waves, fully clothed, singing.

The crew have decided to start a therapy group for people who don't think they need therapy.

Today, the international TV presenter is wearing a brace of wrist watches for time zone credibility.

I need a new lighter. A Zippo, naturally. 'J.J., remind me to buy a Zippo.'

'What's a Zippo?' says J.J.

We pull up at a quiet beach bar for a quick witgathering session.

'Well, I know I am, but what about you?' says J.J.

Quite.

'Have you ever heard of Jeeves, J.J.?'

'No. Should I?'

'I think perhaps you should.'

☆

'Floyd, Floyd! FLOYD! Wake up. The crew is waiting.'

J.J. is standing over me in a sailor suit and peaked cap, duffel bags and cameras slung over her shoulder – and a bottle of bourbon in the survival kit.

I open my eyes, and I'm blinded by the sun streaming down on the waterfront.

Captain Jack has loaded the boats. We're going filming. And the script in David Pritchard's head reads: 'Catch and cook a big fish . . .'

☆

Captain Jack Powell is a gentle man who looks as though he should be putting out to sea in all weathers in a patched-up old skiff with the paint flaking away, but this being Florida he runs a computerised boat he designed himself, with the biggest outboard motor Yamaha can make. He's taken Tammy Wynette out fishing and he was the marine adviser on the movie *Cocoon*.

Underneath the glamour, though, he has a heart and soul as honest as any fisherman I've ever met. 'The water is like a mistress. It'll completely humble you,' he says. 'I've been doin' this all my life. I've been in 14 hurricanes, two typhoons, a tidal wave, and I wouldn't even want to count the gales and storms and squalls and stuff. But I keep going out. I guess there's a certain thrill in seeing Mother Nature at her strongest. And I've never felt I wouldn't make it back.

'I'm a big conservationist. If I'm not going to eat what I catch, I put it back. The biggest fish I've had was a 15-foot shark – but I don't allow anything over 4 feet between the eyes onto my boat.

'I like to go out to Back Bay to the uninhabited islands and watch the fish in about a foot of water. I designed my boat to run in what we call "skinny water", offshore.

'You'll see 20-pounders "tailing" – swimming along with their tails out of the water. Sometimes you don't want to disturb them by throwing a line. You just want to watch them for a while. I love to take people there who have never seen it before, and just watch their reactions.

'Every day is exciting. Each trip there is something which will break you up laughing or have you in tears.

'I like to fish on light custom-made rods. The lightest tackle catches the biggest fish, but the really big ones – jewfish like elephants – always get away.

'I've been within a few pounds of several records. And there are about six I could hold if I would kill the fish. The money would be great – in endorsements on the rod, line, boat, clothes, sunglasses, shoes, motor oil. But I guess I'll wait for the big one, the world record ...'

It had been a lazy, sunny afternoon, and we were drifting quietly in the gulf listening to Captain Jack telling tales of the sea. The game plan had been to catch and cook a big fish. So far we hadn't caught anything exceptional, but there was a grouper which was big enough, everyone was happy with the sequence we had shot, and I was fishing away quietly on the light 16-pound tackle Captain Jack favours, sipping a few beers with the boys, chatting idly and thinking about calling it a day.

Then I got a bite. Suddenly Captain Jack began to get excited. It was a big one, he said – and it was only a matter of moments before we realised just *how* big. Captain Jack's gentle eyes lit up as he estimated that what we had was a jewfish – one of those 'elephants' – weighing in at 150 pounds at least. And if we could land it, this could be his big chance: that world record fish, worth a million dollars in sponsorship. Already, he joked, he could see visions of his new boat, his new house, and his new car, swimming before his eyes.

From the beginning I think we all knew it was a battle I couldn't win – a 150-pound fish is bigger than anyone can handle on 16-pound tackle – but what a coup it would have been to land that fish for the programme. The fact is that every big fish I have had on the line when we have been filming I have lost – *every one*. There have been 20-pound salmon, 18-pound pike – you name it, but they have all got away. This was my big chance to redress the balance – and some!

I heard myself saying: 'Please, God, let me land this one ...' Behind me Captain Jack was joking: 'This is like something out of *The Old Man And The Sea*. We'll come back in three days and you'll still be fighting him.'

I honestly didn't know you could get so worked up over a fish, but as the fight went on and on, it became much more than wanting to film a cracking sequence. It became a matter of honour, something to do with losing credibility if I wasn't strong enough to land that fish. It really was him or me.

By now, the rod was bent almost double. That monster was pulling me out of the boat. I was sweating and trembling, but I couldn't let go.

There was an amazing sense of camaraderie on that boat. I felt that every member of the crew knew just what I was going through and would have thrown down their cameras and microphones to help me, had they not been thorough professionals, and keenly aware that this was a very important piece of film.

Captain Jack came up, clapped a hand on my shoulder, and poured beer into my mouth. I even broke my golden rule and smoked a cigarette in front of the camera. And my old friend Andy did a brilliant thing. Quite spontaneously he knelt down in front of me so that I could push my feet against his back, to stop myself from being hauled overboard.

I fought that fish for an hour, and all the time half of me just wanted to let go of the rod and say: 'Whoops, sorry, it just slipped out of my hand', the pain and the strain were so bad.

But I had to go through with it. Once, I got the monster quite near the boat, and it was so huge that it actually showed up as a fish, rather than a vague blur, on the printout of the fishfinder.

Finally, Captain Jack stepped in for the third time, to add more tension to the line. Andy told me later that at that split second he knew: 'It's going now . . .' and he was right.

When I lost that fish I was still fighting him all the way – it was simply his sheer brute strength which snapped the line.

My legs buckled. Captain Jack sat me down and, I'm not ashamed to say, I burst into tears. I simply couldn't help myself. I have never cried in front of the camera before – but this experience was something else entirely. I remembered Captain Jack saying to me earlier: 'I've taken some mighty beefy, tough guys out and it doesn't take Mother Nature long to make them feel like they are an inch tall.'

I curled up like a baby in the bottom of the boat, as we headed for the treasure island where, in fifteen minutes, up against a sunset deadline, I had to sparkle in front of the cameras, barbecue the grouper and rustle up a perky lime sauce to go with it. But it was the jewfish I was preoccupied with. God, I really wanted to land that fish.

That evening in Clive's room at the hotel, we all gathered to watch the rushes. I watched my face all screwed up with pain on the monitor, and heard Captain Jack say: 'He's running for the rocks, he's running for the bottom.' And as the line snapped I heard myself whisper: 'I tried. I'm sorry. I couldn't do it.'

Later, in the bar of the hotel, no one took a blind bit of notice of the Elvis Presley lookalike gyrating on stage behind us; we were all too drained, and eager to talk about the day. Clive summed it all up when he told me: 'It was heartrending to watch. The whole thing became more and more serious, and I could see you getting more and more distraught. But all I could do was stay behind the camera and do the job I'm paid to do. You wouldn't have thanked me if I'd stopped filming and helped you ...'

'In a way,' said Tim, 'you feel mercenary, coming in close, taking pictures and recording, when someone is really under such great pressure, and clearly in agony.'

'This day the fish won,' said David, 'and you shouldn't be sad about it. It was a brilliant experience. A mix of tiredness, emotion, sadness, courage and endurance.'

Andy, who had been so selfless in helping me as best he could, was philosophical. 'Emotionally,' he reckoned, 'it was a great moment. But there was no shame in it. You felt you'd let Captain Jack and David and the crew down, but no one was to blame. The line broke, it's that simple. But I know how you felt. You really wanted to land that fish ...'

As for Captain Jack, who had seen his dream of a million bucks shatter with the line, he threw an arm around my shoulder, smiled and said sagely: 'You fought him well, for a long time, but you lost him. Fish: one; You: nil. And that's why they call it fishing – not catching.'

☆

'I would like one egg, easy over, well cooked, please ...'

'That means you get it real easy. I guess you mean one over hard ...'

Oh well. Back to the phrase book.

'So what's shakin', Floyd?' says J.J. 'Are you getting acclimated yet?'

'Am I what?'

'Getting acclimated. Acclimated is coming into my space and not freaking out totally ... By the way d'you play snooker?'

'I don't play "snucker", no.'

'Anything else I can get you today, sir?' says the waitress.

'Some ketchup, please.'

'Sure. Anything you like. Anything's possible. That's what Bush says, and I go along with him.'

'You know, Floyd, I'm really confused.'

'Why?'

'Well, only because I don't know who I am, what my name is or where I come from. You know, you're teaching me so much about America. Aren't I the American, though? Well, I thought I was! But isn't that exciting? Because I can just be anything I want, can't I?'

'Can I get you anything else today, sir?'

'Some ketchup, please.'

'Sure. I'll get that for you right away.'

'You know, Floyd, there are some things I want to talk to you about: one is "choice" and the other is "sexuality".'

'But it's only 8.30 in the morning, J.J.'

'OK, I'll save it for lunch.'

'Can I get you some more coffee here?' says the waitress.

'Thank you. And could I have some ketchup, please!'

☆

'*That fish,*' *joked Clive,* '*is probably sitting on the bottom, with its fins wrapped around a stone, telling its friends: "Guess what happened to me ..."* '

One day I was in my pub, the Maltster's Arms, talking tractors, and watching the river flow, and the ducks practising formation swimming. The next day I was in the front end of a jumbo jet, in the first-class lounge, with some nice stewardesses giving me bottles of wine as souvenirs, and falling over themselves to make sure I had sufficient champagne – and would I mind signing an autograph for the pilot? I plugged in the earphones, and they were playing sounds from the sixties, when I *really* knew I had to come to America (of course I'd *secretly* known since I first heard 'Blue Suede Shoes' in 1956).

Twenty-five years on, I was forty-five going on twenty, excited as hell and heading for an adventure. Off to discover America through a frying-pan . . .

Sitting in the Carved Angel in Dartmouth a few days earlier, in that oasis of gastronomy and tranquillity, I was drinking Chateau d'Yquem and eating sticky rice pudding with an old friend, who had said: 'Eating in America is not an event, it's an incident . . .'

But I knew he must be wrong because America is the home of rock and roll, and rock and roll and food are soulmates. They're both about honesty and passion and the two are irrevocably intertwined in my life. When my producer said 'Nashville or Memphis?' I said 'Memphis – or I ain't coming', because Memphis is not only the home of 'soul food', but the home of the Sun Studio, where Elvis cut his first record and forever changed the life of a Somerset lad called Keith Floyd who thought the world revolved around fishing.

I thought of all the food in rock and roll and jazz: the black-eyed peas and biscuits in 'Ode to Billy Joe' . . . Fats Domino's 'Jambalay, crawfish pie, filé gumbo' ... the Inkspots' mustard greens, pork and beans ... and I knew there must be more to American cooking than hamburgers and fried chicken ...

Then they were playing 'Are You Lonesome Tonight?' and suddenly I was, a little. Trapped in lonely luxury. No one had waved goodbye and there was no one to meet me at the other end.

Nothing for it but to have another drink, another canapé, and start making notes on the menu.

The guy up front looked a bit like a young Pat Boone – about thirty-five years old with cruel eyes, cowboy boots, neatly cut pigskin jacket and gold dripping from his wrists. His glamorous Asian wife was equally weighed down by gold.

In between their glasses of whisky and champagne and plates of canapés, they had hand-tooled leather-covered Bibles embossed with gold crucifixes, prayer reviews and copies of magazines with names like *God Today*. It was all too weird. Elvis, and waves of loneliness, and now Bible-bashers drinking champagne in the first-class compartment of a jumbo jet...

The lights of Tampa airport were calling us in ...

I walked for about 3 miles through a waterless aquarium: silent corridor after silent corridor of tinted glass.

'I'm sorry, would you do this again, please?,' they said, after I had filled in the forms at immigration for the fifth time, and all the other passengers were lined up behind me.

And then there *was* someone there to meet me after all. My intrepid producer, David Pritchard, beaming all over his face, even more excited than me, jumping up and down, telling me how wonderful everything was. It was really hot, there were brilliant things to film, the seafood was great, and he had a Chevy outside ...

☆

Welcome to the Chuckwagon.
Off to cook in the Winnebago.

Mardi Gras Madness. French Market, New Orleans.

Making Cajun magic with Paul Prudhomme.

CHAPTER THREE

New Orleans is practising for Mardi Gras

Floyd in *American Pie* T-shirt, still decorated in plastic glitter beads, and hoarse from shouting at the camera from the balcony of Kolbs Restaurant, while the floats rumbled below, majorettes high-kicked and bands all jangled together.

On the heels of the last float come the big yellow trucks with the huge brushes, three abreast, like a conquering army, down the wide streets. Behind them, trucks spraying water. The sanitising of pleasure. Rock and roll, then purge your soul...

Maybe I'm just cynical, but I prefer the barrel-burning at Ottery St Mary on 5th November!

Walking towards the hotel, past the healers in Jackson Square who claim to cure culture shock, heartaches, hysteria and hangovers. The night is still balmy and from the open doors of a bar called Bonaparte's Retreat on Decatur Street I hear: 'All the Way to Memphis...'

There are two guys in the band, called the Shifters, playing the guitars with the cut-outs that I thought were the business when I was fifteen. I order the Floyd Wide Awake Drink – iced Tia Maria shandy – and they are belting out the Beatles: 'A man must break his back to earn his day of leisure. Will she understand it when he's dead...'

A spindly character with white hair and black-rimmed glasses, wearing a pale blue denim embroidered shirt, jumps onto the tiny dance floor and gives it everything he's got. 'That's Melvin,' someone says. 'He's seventy-two years old.'

'Let's dance,' says J. J.

'I don't dance...'

'Come on, Floyd! That's dumb...'

☆

'If I want to stay out till 4 a.m. . . . ain't nobody's business but mine . . .' Billie Holliday on the jukebox in between sets from the band. My voice has gone, my knees are weak. It's been twenty years since I danced like this . . .

'Long distance information, give me Memphis, Tennessee . . .' The boys in the band are back. Melvin spins J. J. round the floor. On the silent TV screen in the corner of the bar a blonde lady is cooking in a sterile kitchen. The band play the Beatles: 'You Can't Do That'.

'Every weekend I come here and dance,' says Melvin. 'The work I do, they think we can't have no fun . . .'

'What do you do?'

'I'm a trainee priest.'

'We're having some fun here tonight, aren't we?' A familiar voice over the microphone. J. J. is on stage. 'I'd like to dedicate this number to *Floyd's American Pie* . . . Jambalay, crawfish pie, filé gumbo . . .'

'Right now I'm Head Brother in the Greek Orthodox Society of Christ, but in eight months I'll be a priest. Then I'm gonna go back to Pennsylvania, where I used to be a chef,' says Melvin.

'See, when I go out I'm a different person. I work ten to five, then I go home and change and come out and dance. They don't mind, so long as I don't get silly, and I don't go out in my cloth.

'Are you English? You know, what I'm really looking for is a tall Englishwoman – with freckles. That would knock me out . . .'

The Shifters are playing 'mad, bad, Leroy Brown . . .'

☆

Angelo the cab driver steers the chariot through the narrow streets of the French Quarter, past the ladies walking home, their faces painted in Mardi Gras colours of green, purple and gold.

I'm still singing softly, almost hoarse: 'I heard the news . . . there's good rockin' tonight . . .'

☆

Day comes slowly to New Orleans. They party till dawn, then stretch and yawn, put on their glad rags and start again at noon.

At nine in the morning Jackson Square belongs to me and the pigeons. The pale taupe-coloured Cathedral of St Louis watches and waits. The wrought-iron balconies are filled with flowers. New Orleans is like a vacant film set waiting for the extras to arrive in costume.

First on the scene is Perri the Hobo, dressed in a red nose, wig, battered hat and pantaloons. He gives me a business card advertising children's parties and functions at low rates, with a telephone number. 'I used to be a mechanical engineer,' he says.

Next are the wandering musicians, playing Dixieland jazz. The square is filling up. The Pontalba Bar on the corner opens its doors and the bartender makes hot buttered rum: dark rum, with a slab of butter, brown sugar, cinnamon and nutmeg, topped up with hot water.

'It's a real big drink up north,' says the bartender. 'A bunch of Yankees set up this bar, so it's a house special.' Is everywhere in America trying to be like somewhere else, I wonder, sipping this drink which tastes like liquid Christmas pudding.

This is showman's city, from the bartenders to the clowns, to the French Quarter with its shops full of Mardi Gras masks and costumes. But all along the narrow streets outside the French Quarter, which reminds me sometimes of Union Street in Plymouth, sometimes of Avignon, there are 'For sale' signs on the houses.

'You could rent an old Creole house round here for 150 dollars a month,' says someone.

If this was any other European city, a quarter like this would have been invaded by the young, the rich and the aspiring artists.

'See,' says the bartender mixing another special: brandy, 'simple syrup', milk and nutmeg, shaken together, 'this town has three main employers: the oil business, which is non-existent; the shipping business, which is *almost* non-existent; and the tourists. The only thing going on here is tourism. There's very little other work here, and the work there is, they don't want to pay...

'But even so we carry on partying. We party late and wake up late. The main problem with this town is: it's never boring. They call this "The City That Care Forgot" – nobody cares! Have a good time!'

PAUL PRUDHOMME

On another lonely New Orleans dawn, with only the pigeons as my witness, I manoeuvre myself past the Richelieu swimming pool and out onto the sleepy streets, heading for WWL TV.

The presenter shows the clip from *Floyd on Britain and Ireland* where I score a try – or pretend to – with Ray Gravell. I talk about alligators and bayous and Cajun and Creole cooking and Mardi Gras, and race back to the Richelieu for breakfast and the compulsory Affirmation For The Day. J. J. clears her throat and reads: 'There is security in knowing our journeys are necessary and right for us.'

'Good morning, sir. What can I get you?'

One egg over hard, a double side of bacon (with ketchup!) and several buckets of coffee later, I am back on the still sluggish streets, heading for the obligatory fish market . . .

☆

Battistella's fish market has been in the family for 150 years and supplies New Orleans' top restaurants with the kind of fish you usually only see at the zoo: sheep's heads, black drum, amberjack, mahi-mahi, red snapper and redfish – a rare sight, since there is now a conservation law against fishing for redfish. (Note to any New Orleans lawmen reading this: Mr Battistella's were frozen before the law came into force!)

Day-dreaming for a moment about the blackened redfish made famous by New Orleans' best-known chef Paul Prudhomme – cooked so that it is charred and crisp and smoky on the outside, and mouthwateringly moist on the inside – I'm interrupted by the sound of a bottle-green monster which looks like a cross between a pick-up truck and the Pompidou Centre screeching to a halt at the open door.

From somewhere in the bowels of this strange craft, a hoist appears, and up comes an almost circular character, squeezed into an electric wheelchair, dressed in white, and wearing a cap decorated with an alligator and a badge saying 'Totally Hot!'

The apparition comes whizzing through the doors, circles maniacally around me three times tooting his horn, then skids to a halt, offers his hand and beams at me. 'Hi, Floyd!' says Paul Prudhomme.

Not at all like a white-clad Mekon. No, not at all.

☆

A showman he may be, but Paul Prudhomme cares deeply and passionately about food. He's a perfectionist, a man who lives by the rule of the freshest of ingredients, cooked with love and immense care. There is no freezer at his restaurant, K-Paul's, because each day his menu depends on what can be bought fresh. Today it includes rabbit tenderloin with Creole mustard sauce, blackened yellowfin tuna and smoked stuffed softshell crawfish with charon – try saying that one quickly!

Each afternoon he holds court outside the kitchen, his electric wheelchair parked behind a huge table, silver-topped cane propped beside him. Chefs with beaded brows rush up with bowls of gumbo and sauces, scrutinising his face while he tastes.

'A hard taskmaster?' I ask one young black cook whose sauce is being meticulously corrected. 'Sure – that's his job,' he says with reverence.

We cook spicy pan-fried trout in a creamy sauce, which, amazingly, Paul serves with English white wine from the Lamberhurst Vineyard – 'It reacts well with this kind of food. In fact, as you English would say: it's bloody marvellous!'

And we make a sunshine dish of vegetables: red, yellow and green bell peppers, onions, okra (or ladies' fingers), and tomatoes cooked with Louisiana sausage and Cajun spices, layering the vegetables to create different textures and flavours.

'You know, people think that Cajun and Creole food is hot – it doesn't have to be. It's spicy, sure, and it should wake up the tastebuds, but it doesn't have to be hot,' says Paul.

'People ask me what is the difference between Cajun and Creole cooking – well, Cajun is old, country cooking. It began in southern France, then found its way to Nova Scotia. Then when the Acadians, as they were called, were transported by the British from Nova Scotia to Louisiana in the eighteenth century, they adapted their cooking to the ingredients they could find in the country and on the bayou: filé powder from the sassafras tree, cayenne pepper ... and they became known as Cajuns.

'Creole food is city food. It began in New Orleans, and it's a mixture of nationalities: French, Italian, Spanish, African, American Indian ...'

Paul has travelled the world preaching the message of Louisiana food, but he would never move away from New Orleans. 'This is a mystical part of the world – we have souls and emotions and voodoo, and things which happen which are inexplicable,' he says. 'We're a very creative people – it's something to do with the weather and the warm water from the Gulf of Mexico, and this wonderful 12-month growing season, which gives us such an abundance of food.

'We like to think of our food as emotional. The tastes change with every bite – you have to pay attention when you eat it. And we also know about cooking with love and joy, and expressing ourselves through cooking.

'I was raised about 100 miles from New Orleans on farmland next to the bayou, in a little community called Opelousas,' he says. 'There were 13 children in our family and we all cook. Our job was to raise crops and give one-third to the landlord. But we were privileged to grow all the food we wanted to live on, so long as we didn't sell it.

'We raised anything we could, and then went into the swamps hunting for duck and rabbit and alligator. We'd get turtles and bring them back and keep them alive, till we wanted fresh turtle meat.

'I was the last of the family so my job was always to help my mother produce the food. By the time I was 10 years old I knew how to kill a hog and reserve the blood, and make sausages, and do all kinds of things … and by the time I was 17 I had my own restaurant, even though I had actually only been in one three or four times in my whole life. We didn't eat out, because it was too expensive, and we needed the money – the maximum money we had in a year was about 300 to 500 dollars, after we paid the bills. But I knew I wanted a restaurant.

'At one time, before I was born, the family lived a lot on beans and rice, and my mother made 20 kinds of bread, but when I came along we were better off for food.

'My mother made jambalaya once a week. She'd take all the leftovers – chicken, alligator – out of the icebox and season it heavily, put a lot of pepper in it and make a really rich sauce, then put rice into it … a one-dish meal.

'And on special days, she'd make my favourite meal: sticky pork roast, dirty rice, candied yams and potato salad – you can keep all your fancy meals in smart restaurants anywhere in the world, that is the food for me.

'You know, ever since the Vietnam war, Americans have started wanting to know about themselves, and writers started travelling and writing about food that many Americans didn't even know about.

'Cooking is a big thing now in America – even the men are moving into the kitchen. When I started giving demonstrations 25 years ago, there would be 100 per cent women out there. Then, about 1983, all of a sudden I started noticing men in the audience. I was in Tampa, Florida, in '85 and there was an audience of about 300, and about 180 of them were guys. I'll never forget that as long as I live.

'Now, many of our psychiatrists recommend that a family under stress should cook together at the weekends, because it's relaxing and enriching.

'Well, in Louisiana we're way ahead of all that – we've been living that way for the last 100 years.'

☆

France has its Michelin stars, New Orleans has beans. Awarded by critic Gene Bourg.

'Food critics here have the same power as critics on Broadway,' says Hillery Moise who runs Hillery's at the Gazebo, at the end of the French market, with husband Ed as chef. 'If you don't have a decent amount of beans, you're just blackballed! He's ruined a lot of people's business – he's very tough! ... If you can make it in New Orleans, you can make it anywhere. The restaurant business is tough here. The last guy left standing will win.'

A sticker on a Cadillac crawling by says: 'The guy who dies with the most toys wins.'

'We all owe a lot to Paul Prudhomme for putting Louisiana cooking on the map,' says Ed. 'He's the big one. He's taken something we all knew about and spread it around the world. He has people who come from Tokyo, Hong Kong and all over the United States to work at his restaurant, K-Paul's, just to get a feel for what he does.

'It's a local cuisine – people here have been eating that way since the Cajuns first came down from Nova Scotia, using French techniques, and applying them to local ingredients. But it's a style of cooking that can stand on its own anywhere. It's good, it's valid. And Paul has done a wonderful job promoting it.

'And he's done the rounds, he cooked in a lot of places. He didn't just come from nowhere. Before he opened K-Paul's, when he was cooking in other restaurants, he'd mix up his own seasoning, and pull packets of it out of his back pocket when no one was looking, because he didn't like the way they seasoned things. He likes robust, country seasoning.

'My food here is a combination of Cajun and Creole, and the French and Italian influences I grew up with. I come from a big, pretty close-knit family, and whenever we got together everybody would cook a different dish and bring it along in a big pot. One aunt married a Frenchman, another married an Italian, so from an early age, I got a taste of all kinds of good food.

'So, I cook what I like really – not strictly one way or the other … You know, I used to have an old black Creole chef working for me, in another restaurant, and on St Patrick's day I asked him to make an Irish stew – I was going to serve soda bread, corned beef and cabbage, to get people in.

'My mother had Irish ancestors, and she used to make it at home. Do you know, he cooked it exactly the way my mother used to make it? I guess all that kind of food has the same roots … Have you met Herb yet? He's our bartender. Hurricane we call him, Hurricane Herb …'

Hurricane Herb fixes a bourbon on the rocks to wash down Ed's excellent Cajun meatloaf with fresh tomato sauce, followed by caramel custard – made to his grandmother's secret recipe.

'It's basic eggs, sugar, milk and vanilla,' says Ed, 'but I'm not going to tell you what *kind* of milk – it's Cajun Magic, as Paul Prudhomme would say.'

Hurricane Herb used to work on the riverboats, up and down the Mississippi. 'You can't gamble on them any more in this city – you have to go 9 miles out to gamble,' he says, mixing Bloody Marys at lightning speed behind the counter.

'Why do they call me Hurricane? 'Cos I'm a bunch of wind! I guess I've always been the kind of guy who likes to spin a yarn. I just like people …

> "I'm just an angel in disguise,
> That has wandered from above …
> A heavenly surprise that came to earth,
> For all the ladies to love …"

'You know I've been all around the world – I was at sea for 21 years – but if I had to start over I'd settle in this city all over again. It's been my home for 56 years and you can have more fun here than anywhere in the world...

'This is the city they say care forgot! We just like to have a good time, and we never stop selling. We sell 365 days a year.

'You know my two other favourite places? Portsmouth and Great Yarmouth. There's a big white house that stays on top of this hill in Portsmouth that I'd like to buy, but it belongs to Prince Charles and he won't sell it.

'You know, that's the one person in this world I would *never* want to be. Can you imagine being born for just one thing? Poor old Charles. I don't care how much money he's got. Know who's my favourite? Andrew! He's great, just great...

'Yes, sir, you can have fun here at the drop of a hat. Doesn't have to be a holiday. Mondays is good. Tuesdays is good ... drop the hat, we're ready!

'Thanks, honey,' he says, winking at the piano player at the Gazebo Bar, as she breaks into: 'More Than I Know.'

'She knows that's my favourite,' says Hurricane Herb, whistling along. 'Mmm ... ain't it just a beautiful day?'

DINNER AT DOOKY'S

To reach Dooky Chase's Restaurant you have to drive through a part of New Orleans which wears a poorer face, where black people pass the time of day sitting on the porches of their wooden houses, a part of town more real than the gaudy gaiety of the French Quarter. The difference is rather like crossing from Belfast's smart shopping centre to the Falls Road.

Inside Dooky's, what was once the whole restaurant is now an all-American, long, narrow bar, with a fast-food and take-away menu to make the lips smack: oyster po-boys, onion rings, Creole gumbo, corn on the cob, red beans and chicken for 5 dollars; and mustard greens with smoked ham or hot smoked sausage for the same price.

Through a corridor and you step into a different world: elegant, discreet, oddly English, with lamplit, rose-coloured walls, dotted with paintings, soft couches and a grand piano – the only giveaway is the buffet of 'Chaurice' (hot sausage), stewed okra and red beans and rice, keeping warm in a row of silver dishes.

Leah Chase, wife of Dooky, greets us (Dooky's real name is Edgar, but Edgar Chase's didn't have the same ring). She is a warm, dignified lady, with deep liquid-brown eyes which sparkle when she talks of the Creole food for which Dooky Chase's is famous. She takes some rare time out of the kitchen, settles herself into a soft sofa, hands clasped quietly in her lap, soft grey hair perfectly coiffured, a scarlet neckerchief topping her impeccable white cook's jacket with 'Chef Leah' embroidered in matching red above her breast pocket.

Leah Chase has come a long way since she was 'as poor as hell' – one of 14 children ('11 lived') raised in the Louisiana countryside on 'greens and red beans . . . and onions. We had onions every which way you could eat them . . . sautéed, boiled, you name it . . . we didn't have much, but what we had was nutritious.

'My father planted a lot, and he raised pigs and chickens. Since I've grown up, some of the foods we were raised on, like quail, are considered fancy,' she smiles, 'but we had to eat what there was to kill.'

On 'Dooky's Authentic Creole Dishes Table d'Hôte' are gumbo, jambalaya, catfish and shrimp Creole. But it was the red beans cooked the way Leah has always cooked them and served up with steamed rice and hot or smoked sausage, fried chicken, or pork chop, which really took my fancy.

'People think black folk eat red beans every day,' Leah jokes. 'In fact it was a Monday dish, cooked while the washing was on the line.'

Laundry day food it may be, but Leah's red beans are truly delicious, spiced up with garlic and a little fresh parsley and thyme.

'I like to cook red beans with pork fat. We always had that in the country,' says Leah. 'Nowadays people look at it and say: "No, no, we can't eat that. Too much cholesterol." I say, don't worry . . .

'People worry so much about what they put in their mouths – I say you should pay more attention to what comes *out* of your mouth, than what goes in. Don't worry about what you eat – live a life where you don't say anything that's gonna hurt anybody.'

This lovely lady's passion for life is still every bit as strong as it was on the day she persuaded her mother to let her come to 'the Quarter' to find work in a restaurant as an 18-year-old, back in 1942.

'There were no restaurants in the black Creole community then –

you ate at home,' she remembers. 'Most of the other black girls worked in clothing factories. Well, I liked to sew, but I couldn't see myself making pockets for pants every day of my life, so I went to work for a wonderful white lady in a restaurant in the Quarter, and I learned to love restaurants so much I always wanted one of my own.

'Then I met Dooky, and his parents *did* have a little restaurant. I thought I was going to be a nice little hostess – I just love to wait tables – but I also knew the sort of food I wanted to serve, and we didn't have anybody in the kitchen then, so I started cooking the Creole dishes I'd known and loved all my life. And I never got out of the kitchen!

'My mother- and father-in-law – he was Dooky too – were so popular. This was the only place black people felt good eating out in. They weren't trustin' of other people putting food on their plate.

'I don't think food was meant to be anything artistic, it's that *love* that is important. People here in New Orleans take real pride in their cooking – every little lady in her home will create things with food, and talk about it with all the love in the world.

'In New Orleans we have good cooks in every home. That's why the restaurant business is so hard: there's so much competition.

'There's a warmth in New Orleans homes. The people are just beautiful, they're always ready to welcome you. They genuinely want to feed you. The first thing they do is prepare you some food. You go elsewhere in this country and they won't offer you anything to eat – that's terrible.'

Since the early days of Dooky's, Leah has seen big changes in this part of the Deep South. 'Black people started to grow,' she says. 'We had judges, lawyers . . . and they wanted their wives to go out and look good in a place that looked good . . . Black people started going to places they couldn't go before. They'd go into hotels and come back here and say: "Leah – they have this, that and the other. You gotta have that!" It was a learning experience for everybody.'

So Leah expanded the restaurant into the bustling business it is today, and she decorated it the way she had always dreamed of. 'I like pretty things,' she says, almost shyly. 'Black Creoles are great carpenters, and I had a cousin who did all of the wooden panels – it was just a pleasure to see him work, and he was so proud to create the things I wanted.

'I started collecting paintings by American black artists, too. I like all art, but the best thing I can do is buy from my own people, and show their work. Otherwise nobody would see it. We have no black galleries here. I wish *I* could have one,' she says wistfully.

'It warms me up to see what people can do with colour. I can't do a darn thing myself, but I love to see what they do. All these works are done by friends, and I feel like I have a little bit of them in my life.

'Sure, it's been a struggle. It's always a struggle. It's still a struggle if you're black in this country, and if you're a woman it's a *big* struggle ... all I do is take it one day at a time. When I get up in the morning I say: "Let me make it through the day. Let me do all of the things I gotta do." If I don't fill in my days, and give it all the gusto I can, I'm not complete at the end of the day. But if I've given everything I've got, then I feel good.

'Money ain't everything, just learn to live. And you can't live without helping people. When I was coming up, my dad always told us we couldn't pass one single day unless we did something for someone else, whether it was running to the grocery store, or whatever ... and I think that's important.

'Me, I'm happy. I *like* living. To me life is just beautiful. I see all the pretty things around me, and some of the most beautiful things don't cost you anything. I think everybody should love living.

'Art and music and food – all those things warm people up. Listen to the music, look at the art a bit, eat good food ... it'll work out.'

Warmed by Leah Chase's words, I head back through the shabby streets to the bright lights of the French Quarter and the Richelieu. Fast Eddie, the bartender, fixes me a bourbon on the rocks. Someone has put Louis Armstrong on the jukebox...

> 'I see friends shaking hands
> Saying "How do you do?"
> They're really saying: "I love you"...
> .... and I think to myself
> What a wonderful world...'

FLOYD COOKS CAJUN

'Excuse me. Are you Hugh Heffner?' says the passer-by.

'I don't think so.'

Fresh from guesting on Chef Buster's radio phone-in on WWL – Buster is a great guy, looking deceptively staid in spectacles and a grey mohair waistcoat, who produces a funny, lively show, peppered with sensible food chat and rock and roll.

I want to be a DJ. I am the morning DJ....

Past Coops Bar on Decatur, where they make brilliant Southern fried chicken, blackened fish and jambalaya, and into the French market, where a sign says: Makin' Groceries. There are stalls laden with mangos, kiwi fruits, collard greens, mustard greens, sticks of sugarcane 8 feet tall, wrapped in silver foil at both ends, like the majorettes' batons at Mardi Gras.

There are shrimps being packaged in dry ice to last 24 hours, for tourists to take home; stalls full of Mardi Gras masks (this season's 'in' mask has peacock feathers); there are hats made from palm, that they reckon you can wear under the shower, and they'll still keep their shape. Someone is selling jamabalaya in tubs. There are purses made from eelskin, and everywhere there are clowns and the sound of music. The singer at the Gazebo Bar reckons he was trained by Louis Armstrong and sounds just like him.

The Mardi Gras colours are draped everywhere. 'Where *do* the colours come from?' I ask someone.

'Well, when they decided there should be a King and Queen of the Mardi Gras, a long time ago, they needed an outfit for the King. And the only one they could get hold of was from the local theatre, where they were doing *King Lear*. The costume just happened to be green, purple and gold...'

I buy ingredients for the filé gumbo I am about to cook at Joe Cahn's New Orleans School of Cooking: crawfish, crab, shrimp, oysters, filé powder made from ground sassafras leaves, andouille (smoked pork sausage), tasso (a highly seasoned ham), Creole seasoning, smoked pork ... and my *pièce de résistance*, a Cajun boudin – a sausage stuffed with crawfish – very stylish, the kind of thing the French *nouvelle cuisine* chefs puff up their chests about...

☆

'Louisiana Cooking is like cooking with jazz,' says Joe Cahn. 'You do it from the soul ... throw in a bit of this, a bit of that. The difference between our cooking and French *haute cuisine* is like the difference between Fats Domino and Mozart...

'We have a passion for eating in this city. And a passion for life. Cajuns and Creoles ... we all love to cook. That's why it's hard for restaurants. They make a gumbo, and people will say: "My grandmother does it better than this, or I do it better than this ..." Everybody loves to cook.'

Big Bad Joe is a clown, whipping out cans of Dixie beer from a holster under his apron, strangling me with Mardi Gras beads ... but this is a serious cooking sketch, and I am pulling out all the stops to make a *real* filé gumbo ... rather like a French *bouillabaisse*, but with hot sausage, ham and spices...

☆

'Run fast, zigzag, and don't look back. Remember these babies can outrun a horse over 25 yards ...' Sitting on the porch at the Munsons' place near Houma. My Cajun friend, Chris, is telling me how to escape from an alligator.

'As a kid in the swamps, one of the first things you learn is how to zigzag if an alligator comes at you,' he says. 'There used to be an old Indian guy who lived down here on the bayou – he lived in a cave, with snakes. He taught me about snakes and alligators. Alligators are fun, you can enjoy them, but they're dangerous too. The meanest creature in the world is a female alligator with babies.

'An alligator has two positions: when he's swimming downstream, he's resting, enjoying himself. But if you see an alligator at a 45 degree angle, he's looking for food. And a big one can come 4 feet out of the water and snatch you right off the bank.'

Outside the little bar is the light plane – wingless because of the hurricane season – which Jim Munson's brother Bill landed after ten attempts onto the pontoon boat Jim was driving, to get into the *Guinness Book of Records*. 'Well, we didn't have any other excuse for a party that weekend,' says Jim.

Jim grew up on a houseboat on the bayou – 'wherever the fishing and the trapping was, that was home'. Chris was raised here too – half French, half German, his grandfather had a general store, supplying trappers and fisherfolk. Then there is Pierre the fisherman – half French, half Indian; and old Fitch, or Un Dent (One Tooth), who is 89 – he thinks – and has lived on the bayou all his life.

There are baby alligators in the pool – hence the advice. 'Where's the crazy one?' asks Chris.

From New Orleans we have driven deep into the country, through scrubland where boards pinned to trees offer hot pork, chicken and biscuits, 'over-stuffed po-boys' and corn-fed hogs for sale.

A lonely gas station sells everything you need for a day out in America: Winchester rifles, death ray guns, crossbows, hand-made arrows, bear traps, live bait and beer in a bucket packed with ice.

The sun is beginning to sink over the bayou, throwing the willows, white oaks, pecan and gum trees into sillhouette. 'Those willows,' says Chris, 'grew up in hurricanes, with winds of 100 miles per hour. I've seen them double over and bend, but never break a limb.'

The oak trees are hung with great beards of moss. 'In the days before electricity they used it to make mattresses, pillows and blankets,' says Chris. 'Moss has a natural insulation factor. You could wrap yourself in it and it would fold around your body like a glove. You could insulate your house with it.'

He talks about his grandfather's store, how the trapping season ran for four months and the hunters camped out and ran up their tabs sending for supplies. Then, when the season was over, they settled up and sold their pelts and hides to Chris's grandfather, and he sold them to the dealers. 'You could live like that in those days,' says Chris, 'because no one was going anywhere.'

'See, the difference between Cajuns and Creoles is we all have our origins in France and Germany, but Creoles are city-dwellers, Cajuns live out on the bayou.

'People think Cajun is a nationality. It's not. It's a lifestyle. If you're hungry, we feed you. If you're cold, we warm you. That's how it is on the bayou. Cajuns have two lifestyles: they play hard and they eat a lot!

'The Cajuns lived off what they could pick or kill in the swampland: racoon, otter, nutria, alligator (whose meat is a little like chicken, with white and dark meat), spiced with wild thyme, basil, green onions and bay leaves – look at the size of this bay leaf,' he says waving a leaf as big as the palm of his hand.

'We like to get some shrimp or catfish fillets, dip them in seasoned flour, wrap them in one of these big bay leaves and deep-fry them.'

*Hot chilli peppers,
cold Dixie beer.*

*'It says here, "Serves 42" –
is that enough?' asks Joe Cahn.*

Filé gumbo, Floyd fashion.

Party time on the Bayou.

As the sun finally goes down, Chris and I cook jambalaya by the bayou, with chicken and spicy sausage and the Louisiana 'trinity' of onions, celery and green bell pepper – the basic seasoning group that flavours all Louisiana cooking.

'The Cajun philosophy is that anything that walks, crawls, swims or flies – and you can catch – you can put it in the jambalaya!' says Chris. 'Jambalaya comes from two words: *jamón*, which is the Spanish for "ham", and *balayez*, which means "everything".'

While we eat this brilliant spicy dish – rather like a good risotto – he and Pierre tell tall tales of life and parties on the bayou. 'Down here,' grins the irrepressible Pierre, 'we party five times a week and double up on Saturday – then it's a bucket of iced water over your head in the morning!

'There's 25 per cent men to 75 per cent women – and all them women want to go out on a Saturday night!

'The only way you know what day of the week it is, is by what food you eat – everybody cooks the same food on the same day: Mondays it's red beans, Fridays white beans and shrimp balls . . .

'It's wonderful – even jail is wonderful,' he winks. 'They have a lil' ole cell specially for me, with an iron bath, colour TV, a games room – you can even drink a beer. I call them up and say: "Gee, I can't make it home – you gonna give me a motel room?"'

Women and small children appear from nowhere. Everyone knows everyone. Everyone looks out for everyone else. 'When other people are warring about racial problems, we don't have any,' laughs Chris. 'We're all part French, German, Mexican, Indian . . . what is there to fight about? We're too busy eating catfish, drinking a little beer, dancing and listening to the music.

'That's how Cajuns are. We'd rather give than receive – we have all we need down here.

'The biggest fights you get in Cajun communities are within families. There's only one cop on the bayou and he doesn't carry a gun. If you do get a guy going wrong, the people just pull him aside and say: "Straighten out or we're gonna eliminate you! There's a lot of alligators around here!"'

It is late when we finally leave the bayou, and Chris and his Cajun friends invite us back the next day to fish for catfish, share a Cajun feast, and dance the Fais-dodo to some Cajun fiddles under the stars.

☆

Next morning, we are welcomed like old friends. There is coffee and king cake waiting: made specially for Mardi Gras, with sweet dough, plaited in a ring and dusted with sugar in the carnival colours of purple, green and gold. Traditionally there is a tiny plastic baby somewhere inside each cake, and whoever finds it must throw the party next time. J. J. finds it.

☆

Heading deep into the swamp. Jim is at the helm.

Egrets and ibis flutter and call, a grey heron with the wing span of a Boeing 707 rises up in front of us, dead tree trunks claw their way out of the water like fingers. Louisiana irises in Mardi Gras colours of purple and gold bloom on the banks and there are hyacinths and spider lilies.

The skeleton of an old oil well stands like a crucifix in midstream. Every log looks like an alligator, and every twist and bend of the bayou looks the same. I feel a man could get lost here for years, but Pierre assures me he has a map in his head.

The colours all turn muted: palest pink maple leaf – the first to bloom in spring – blends with soft grey moss. There are turtles and water moccasin snakes curled on branches, camouflaged until Pierre's keen eye spots them.

Deeper and deeper into the swamp. There is a nutria rat and another and another, swimming towards the boat.

The story goes that Mr McIlhenny – the man who makes Tabasco Sauce – first brought nutria rats over from Argentina. One day there was a hurricane and the cages were knocked over. The rats broke loose and they've been breeding like rabbits ever since. Pierre hurls doughnuts at them to bring them closer. 'All Cajuns carry doughnuts,' he beams.

There are more water moccasin snakes, black and brown – one with a red belly. 'Can we make him jump?' asks my producer. Pierre hurls another volley of doughnuts.

A racoon slips out from behind a tree. Pierre calls him the Lone Ranger because he looks like he is wearing a black mask. Charmingly, he reaches out with his paws, carefully picks up a doughnut, holds it genteelly to his mouth and nibbles.

There is an alligator somewhere in these swamps $13\frac{1}{2}$ feet long, weighing about 650 pounds – they call him Big Jim and there are teeth marks on the engine where he charged the boat one day.

'I don't know what got into him,' says Jim. 'Maybe his girlfriend jilted him. We always call him out and feed him, and he'll come right up to the boat. This day my nephew took the boat out, Big Jim was on the bank. He slid into the water and next thing he was round the back of the boat and he jumped up and grabbed the motor – four or five times!

'Alligators are attracted to white – one lady was leaning over the boat one day, with a white cap on, and I hollered just as that gator came out of the water at her.

'In the summer, alligators are like Cajuns,' says Pierre. 'They stay out all day and all night. From December they sleep in caves along the river bank, then come out to play again around March time, when the water warms up.

'There's about half a million alligators in Louisiana, and about 29 000 get killed in the hunting season in September,' says Jim. 'Every hunter has to have a licence, and you can't kill a gator unless he's over 4 feet long.

'The way to tell the size of an alligator in the water is to look at the distance between his eyes and the tip of his nose, when he breaks the surface. Every inch equals roughly a foot in length. So if it's 4 inches or less between his eyes and the end of his nose, you have to let the gator go free.'

Suddenly the scenery changes again. We are in the Forest of the Dead. A weird landscape, where thousands upon thousands of silver-grey stubs of trees wiped out by salt hurled in a hurricane, stand like spindly tombstones. This, you feel, is what it would be like if they dropped the big bomb.

In Florida I cried on camera for the first time, but I have never had my breath taken away quite like this before.

The only sound is the cawing of vultures overhead. 'Cracker birds. They come all the way from Washington DC for my doughnuts,' jokes Pierre. Then he spots an armadillo.

'An armadillo? Wow, that's wild!' says J. J. Everyone cracks up.

Then Pierre motions for silence. Perched on the bank right up ahead is an alligator. At last. The moment he is aware of us he will take to the water. Clive already has the camera on him. Tim is homing in on the eerie sounds of the swamp. We hold our breath, willing the smiling gator to stay a while longer. Closer and closer ... we are almost alongside him. Very slowly he moves a limb, turns a keen eye on us, then slips into the water.

We scud back, full-steam ahead, through wider grey-brown water-ways, which are like a cross between the Camargue and the Somerset Levels. The grey monochrome is tinted by a pale yellow sun, and the boat throws up waves like the kind of sludge that is churned to the side of the road in wintry weather after the snow and the ice have melted.

☆

'Mud Bug Boogie' is playing on the jukebox inside the bar, where Marco is mixing up the 'Roi du Bon Temps': filling small glasses with half Amaretto and half Bacardi 151°, then lowering them into tumblers half filled with Budweiser and flaming them.

As you tip up the tumbler to drink, the beer douses the flames and all the flavours mingle. 'It's the original Dr Pepper's,' says Marco, whose father was a 'dislocated Mexican', and whose mother was part Irish, German and Italian. 'But I was born a Cajun. Gotta be – I eat crawfish for breakfast!' he says.

Outside, Chris is hypnotising a crawfish: 'You just sit it on its backside, stroke its back and talk French to it.'

Jim is boiling up water in a pot the size of an oil drum, throwing in two bags of Zataraine's Crawfish Crab and Shrimp Boil Seasoning – 'get it so it's foaming real good' – and chopping up and tipping in about six bell peppers, 5 pounds of onions, three heads of garlic, two stalks of celery, twelve corn on the cob, 10 pounds of potatoes, a dozen lemons, some oranges for colour, plenty of chunks of smoked sausage, a 40-pound sack of crawfish, as many shrimps and a dozen crabs.

'After 10 or 15 minutes we turn the fire off and put some ice in to cool the fish down, so that the seasoning can soak in,' says Jim.

Women are arriving in their best skirts, beers are passed around and newspapers spread on the big table. Chris is dusting bite-size pieces of catfish in cornmeal, seasoned with paprika and black pepper and sizzling them in hot oil. Jim drains the shellfish and the vegetables in an enormous net, and tips the feast onto the newspaper, where eager fingers pluck a crawfish, a piece of spicy sausage, a potato. 'Hot chihuahua!' says Pierre – 'That's "very good" in Cajun!'

Fiddles are striking up on the porch, feet are tapping. Pierre has changed into white wellies for the occasion.

'You can have Beaujolais – that's the white impression of Cajun

76

music; or Zydeco – that's black Cajun music,' says Chris. 'Sometimes you get a combination: Zydeco-Beaujolais – and that's the best Cajun music there is. Like old time rock and roll jammin' with Celtic fiddling. There's no set pattern. One guy kicks off and the others jump right in. You listen to one of those bands play and you just wanna get up and dance. Can't help it.'

Andy and I sit on the steps by the bar, sipping beers, watching the shadows and listening to the music and laughter, and, carried away by the moment, we make up this song:

'ANDY'S SONG'

(From the album
Louisiana Days and Cajun Nights
yet to be released!)

Sittin' by the bayou
Tappin' my shoes,
Got a bar by my side,
Ain't got no blues.

There's gators in the pond,
Bananas on the tree,
I didn't know Louisiana
Was waiting for me.

Catfish are bitin'
There's herons in the sky,
And when that ol' sun falls down
It makes me wanna cry

Andy's out back
Hummin' the blues,
I'm sittin' on the front porch
Thinking about alligator shoes

There's a Cajun moon rising
To set my soul free,
How long has Louisiana
Bin waitin' for me?

Andy and I pretending to be songwriters.

Some time after midnight we head back to New Orleans, resisting the offers of these happy people to stay the night, the week, the month ... It has been a remarkable two days in which this small, close-knit, open-hearted community have taken us in with gusto, and wrapped us with a warmth as welcome as those old Cajun blankets of moss.

☆

My heart rips with the pain of a special loneliness as the car pulls away from this magical place that I don't want to leave, and heads down the dark road to tomorrow ...

CHAPTER FOUR

Time to Check Out?

The cab, swaying and swishing on soft tyres in the high wind, was about half a mile from the Mississippi Bridge when the driver handed me the paper.

The headline on the front page leapt out at me. It was 30 years ago today, on this February Friday, that Buddy Holly's plane crashed into an Iowa cornfield – the day they thought the music died. And now I, with a force ten migraine, thought I was dying too.

The words of Don McLean's 'American Pie' haunted my brain, tangled up in a cacophony with Chuck Berry's 'Long Distance Information, give me Memphis Tennessee . . .', uncannily blasting from the radio.

I hauled myself back to reality. 'Is this *the* Mississippi Bridge?' I asked the driver.

'No, sir.'

It didn't matter. It was Memphis, and I was here to find the real core of my childhood soul. I was here, after 30 years, to discover whether, as a kid in Wiveliscombe, I was right to sell my treasured fishing rods to buy the first ever Elvis Presley record from Furze's Bicycle Shop.

The driver (who wore a fringed buckskin jacket and sunglasses, even though there was no sun) was telling me about General Jackson, one of the triumvirate who named Memphis after the Egyptian town because they thought the Mississippi was the American Nile. And did I know that women outnumbered men in Memphis by three to one? (Taxi drivers the world over, like fishermen, tell the odd fib.)

He chattered on, but it was information of a different kind that I craved – like where did it all begin? Where did Elvis, Jerry Lee Lewis and Carl Perkins cut their first records?

'Right here, sir.'

We eased to a halt outside an insignificant shop, in a row of non-descript stores and parking lots. In the empty window a neon sign glowed. It said simply: 'The Sun Studio'. That was all.

'Do you want to go in?'

Not yet. I couldn't tell this cheery character with his head full of long-distance tourist information that the moment was not right, that I was too tired from the flight, that my head hurt – dammit, that I was just too nervous. 'Not now,' I said quietly. 'Take me to the Peabody Hotel, please.'

I knew that what to me was like finding the Holy Grail could mean nothing to this friendly guy – why, he'd had Jerry Lee Lewis in his cab more times than he cared to remember.

How could he understand? There are only *two* recording studios in the whole world. One is Abbey Road in London, made famous by the Beatles; but *the* studio was here in Memphis: this unobtrusive building in this unobtrusive row.

Memphis was iced over and mean as we headed for the hotel. There was little traffic and nobody walked the streets this afternoon. My right eye was closed down by the migraine and I needed a hot bath and a drink.

'This is the hotel, sir.'

Heartbreak Hotel, I wondered, as the porter held open the door. Maybe.

☆

'This is the hospital where they brought Elvis,' I heard someone say genially, as they strapped me to the trolley and wheeled me towards the place where they did the brain scans.

What supreme irony, if I was to check out on my first visit to the States, here in Memphis, where another great hero, Dr Martin Luther King had been killed, on the anniversary of Buddy Holly's death.

Had I really seen three crows in the sky on the drive here, I wondered, completely paranoid by now.

You see, the headache hadn't got any better. 'It's that blast of icy wind,' someone had said. 'You're tired, under pressure,' someone else had said. 'It's just a migraine,' I said. 'Perhaps you should see a doctor – just in case,' someone else had said.

Well, there *was* a heavy filming schedule ahead, so I agreed. But it was just a migraine.

Seconds later I heard sirens screaming outside the hotel. The paramedics hurried into the hotel – three of them pushing a stretcher on a trolley.

'It's only a migraine,' I said.

'Well, your blood pressure's OK. Are you stressed, tired? What is your lifestyle like?'

I couldn't think where to begin.

'We think you should get a proper check-up at the hospital. Just to be on the safe side.'

'But it's only a migraine.'

'It's only a migraine,' I repeated to the hospital receptionist, rather limply by now.

'National Insurance Number?'

'Actually, I'm English ...'

'Insurance policy, please ... what are you doing here in the States?'

Good question. 'Well, I'm a TV presenter ...'

'What's that?'

Oh dear ...

'City code?'

'Well, actually, I live in this very small village ...'

'Zip code?'

Help.

It seems American computers aren't programmed for little villages in Devon. This one wasn't anyhow, and my very English, rambling address wasn't going to fit into her programmed slots. No way. Eventually even she had to laugh.

Which was more than I was doing two hours later when I found myself dressed in a sort of short frock, alone in a room full of scary-looking equipment, waiting to be wheeled off for a brain scan. I'd already had every test ever devised by the medical profession, and seen every expert on the workings of the brain that the Memphis Baptist Memorial Hospital could muster.

'Couldn't I come back tomorrow?'

'We're ready for you now, sir. Yes, sir, it probably is only a migraine – but you can't be too careful, you know ...' grinned the latest expert, wheeling the trolley towards the lifts, crashing merrily into walls. The lift doors closed ...

Two and a half hours later, the top man at the Baptist Memorial Hospital smiled at me across his desk and told me reassuringly: 'We've checked you out thoroughly, sir.

'It's just a migraine.'

The Peabody Hotel

The foyer of the luxurious Peabody Hotel, just 200 yards from Beale Street, was deserted. The playerless piano tinkled maddening above the hum of the air conditioning. Two waitresses in pink and cream, one with her leg coquettishly kicked back, lounged against the inlaid marble bar, red lips flashing in soft, but animated conversation.

A black maintenance man in a white tailored boiler suit ambled around the mezzanine, and leant over the balustrade to gaze down at the ducks manically chasing each other round and round the fountain. I made a resolution not to ask anyone about the ducks.

And I pretended not to notice when a bell boy rolled out a red carpet from the fountain to the brass-doored lift some 50 yards away.

The King Cotton March heralded the entrance of the Duck Master, a distinguished black man of some 80 years, in immaculate morning coat, who called the ducks to attention on the edge of the fountain, then marched them in single file to the waiting lift, which swept them up to their luxury duck penthouse in the sky.

Off to hot and cold running water, wall-to-wall carpet and all the lettuce and corn they can eat after a hard days' grind chasing their tails to the delight of curious guests who applaud enthusiastically as the lift doors glide shut.

The bartender offered to freshen my half-empty glass.

'Thank you,' I said. 'Another Kentucky Fried Gentleman would go down well.'

He served me the bourbon without a flicker of comprehension. Well, I thought it was funny – but I suppose watching ducks swim around a fountain all day can take its toll on a man's sense of humour.

The bar began to fill with businessmen freshly showered after flying in from Dallas, New Orleans, Pittsburgh and New York. Waitresses with trays held high swayed through the tables dispensing cocktails. A human being sat at the piano now, but the music was the same.

Me, I was wondering what time this place gets to New York. I wanted to get out for a walk, but the bartender said: take a cab, it can be rough out there.

'You're safe as far as Beale Street,' someone said.

'After that you might get ripped apart,' someone else said.

'A black man in this city aged between 18 and 25 stands a one in nine chance of death by homicide,' he said.

'Sure. This is the murder capital of America,' said someone else.

'But it's also the cleanest and the quietest city.'

I felt trapped in claustrophobic luxury, hemmed in by the relentless drip, drip of the fountain, the desperate tinkling of the piano, and the ducks chasing each other compulsively round and round the fountain. Round and round . . .

Did Elvis feel like this, trapped inside that ostentatious pile that is Graceland, a prisoner of his fame? A man who started out full of hope and bursting with music in this city of musical dreams, who only ever wanted to be a rock and roll singer, but ended up desperate and lonely.

Do you believe in Rock 'n' Roll?

One day, when I was about 13 and my life still revolved around those two great boyhood loves of fishing and fiddling around with bikes, one of the kids in the village asked me: 'Have you heard about Elvis Presley?'

'No,' I admitted, feeling extremely uncool. 'Well,' he said, 'there's this wild new music. They call it rock and roll.'

Until that moment my life had been quite tranquil and very ordinary. Mr Furze's bicycle shop at Wiveliscombe was the hub of life. It was an alluring place, full of exciting mechanical things. You could buy John Bull puncture outfits and cowhorn handlebars to customise your bike, or tyres to turn it into a dirt track machine.

Bikes were fun, but they were also essential, because you had to have a bike to go fishing. And fishing was my idea of heaven. Give me my rods, my bike, a packed lunch of bread and cheese, and a new lake or river to explore for each day of the school holidays and I was as happy as a sandboy. Then someone said: 'Have you heard about Elvis Presley?'

I don't believe that any other generation has been so completely overwhelmed by music as mine. For me, and for every other teenager in the fifties, life was never the same again. Rock and roll changed everything.

Until then the only music you heard on the radio was on the *Billy Cotton Band Show* or *Housewives' Choice*. There might have been a bit of skiffle slotted in between 'St Therese of the Roses' or 'Mona Lisa', but I never bothered to listen. Mr Furze at the bicycle shop had just begun to stock a few records but I knew they were Bing Crosby or Jimmy Shand or The Stargazers and I had no interest. Then someone said: 'Have you heard about Elvis Presley?'

I ordered my first Elvis record from Mr Furze. It was 'I'm Left, You're right, She's Gone'. The flip side was 'How Do You Think I Feel?' and it was on HMV.

I bought a mahogany-cased, wind-up, 78-speed gramophone with a horn on it, and a little radio, which crackled and faded. But at night, under the bedclothes, you could listen to rock and roll from a station called Radio Luxembourg.

On Sundays, I used to go to Bible class, run by an evangelist doctor. One Sunday he gave me a very heavy, chromium-plated, electric arm pick-up, which my father, who was a good electrician, fitted to my wind-up record player.

Rock and roll cost money, so I bottled up in the village pub, swept up outside the newsagent's shop, washed up and prepared vegetables in the local hotel, and soon I had a Dansette record player and a whole collection of records: not just Elvis, but Buddy Holly, Little Richard and Chuck Berry too.

For someone who had never given fashion a second thought (you wore school clothes during the week and flannel shorts for fishing), there were suddenly other major considerations in life. I had to have a haircut like Elvis, which naturally wasn't acceptable at school, so I had it cut in a way that could conform during the week but look really cool at weekends.

When my mother was out we would fetch her sewing machine and taper our trousers before we went out, carefully unpicking them when we returned.

Passions like fishing went out of the window. The rods had to be sold to buy crêpe-soled shoes, and more records, of course.

I collected every magazine and newspaper to find out everything about Elvis. I knew that he came from somewhere called Memphis.

Memphis sounded like a magical place. I imagined it must be full of cars with long fins, and really groovy people clicking their fingers and strutting to the music. I imagined there must be music everywhere. There would be soda fountains and milkshake bars and Coca-Cola machines and jukeboxes ... everything that was absolutely alien to a teenager living in a Somerset village with a population of 2000 people. I knew it would be a bright, happy, sunshine place ...

☆

The eternal flame by Elvis's grave was out. 'It's gas and it isn't working, I'm afraid,' said Stacey, our personal Graceland guide, in her singsong Southern accent.

A teddy bear, some plastic flowers, and a smaller bear with 'Nebraska' written on it and a sprig of holly sprouting from its head, lay forlornly by the headstone which read: 'Elvis Aaron Presley, January 8, 1935– August 16, 1977'.

The inscription, by Elvis's father, Vernon, signs off with Elvis's logo: the letters TCB inside a lightning flash – meaning Taking Care of Business – in a Flash.

Propped against the railings which enclose this semi-circle of graves in 'The Meditation Garden' (Elvis's parents and grandmother are buried here too) were a garish selection of red and white hearts made from fake flowers, ribbon and lace.

Stacey whisked us past the pool ('Elvis didn't even like swimming, but he *had* to have a pool'), and rattled through Elvis's collection of flashy wheels: among them the '73 Stutz Blackhawk made especially for him with gold-trim dashboard and gold key, a '75 Dino Ferrari, the pink jeep from *Blue Hawaii*, and a Harley Davidson bike. Sometimes, says the Graceland literature, he would drive all around the grounds in a tractor, pulling his friends in a wagon behind.

All I could think was: imagine having all those cars and all that money, and no garage. Elvis never built a garage. Why didn't anybody say to him: 'Why don't you build a garage?' ...

I didn't want to come to Graceland. I knew I would feel alienated by the people who would show me round and present the Elvis package tour. And I was right.

Graceland is tacky, unkept, unloved, surrounded by gift shops and plastic guitars, cheap mugs and teddy bears. No one seems to care about Elvis, just where the next buck is coming from.

'Between 3000 and 4000 people a day come to Graceland in the summer,' Stacy is saying. 'Thirty per cent are not from America. Between 7 and 8.30 in the morning they can walk up to Elvis's grave. Otherwise they have to go on a tour. Elvis bought Graceland in 1957 for 100 000 dollars . . .

'This is the dining room. Elvis always sat where he could watch TV.

'The 24-carat gold leaf piano was a surprise gift from Priscilla.

'By 1984 Elvis had sold one billion records worldwide. Laid end to end, that's enought to wrap around the earth more than twice.

'We're expecting another batch of gold records from RCA just any time now, and we just don't know where we're gonna put them all.'

Now *this* is something special, staggering even – the hall of gold records marking those endless, endless sales . . .

Stacey is still flinging out facts. 'Elvis's 1973 TV special "Aloha from Hawaii" was seen by more people in America than man's first walk on the moon . . .

'Elvis couldn't read music at all, but he liked to play the piano, and he was quite good at it.

'The stained-glass peacocks were added when Elvis redecorated in 1974. The peacock is a symbol of eternal life, which Elvis liked. He had 14 of them at Graceland at one time – until they scratched the paint off his Rolls-Royce.

'Sorry, you can't see the upstairs rooms. They are private.'

Elvis must have been screaming in pain and loneliness in this ostentatious, gloomy house – so much smaller than I ever imagined – held prisoner by so-called 'mates' who kept him locked up here, feeding him peanut butter sandwiches, because they didn't want the good times to stop. Unable to go to the movies or to a supermarket unless they were specially opened up for him, late at night.

'Elvis had three televisions which enabled him to watch all three major networks at once,' says Stacey.

'And this is his gym, with the piano he played just before he died . . .

'Elvis was 6 feet 4 inches tall, his shoe size was 12D . . .'

The facts and measurements go on and on. This was his gun collection, here are his sheriff's badges . . . Where is the soul of the man whose singing magnetised millions?

'Does anybody sell blue suede shoes in Memphis?' I asked Stacey, as we drove out through Graceland's musical gates and on to Elvis Presley Boulevard.

'Not that I know of ... I don't even think Elvis had any. I guess he had everything but blue suede shoes ...'

☆

'Where were you the day that Elvis Presley died?'

'On the golf course,' says the barman, polishing glasses idly. 'I'll never forget it.

'Elvis Presley Boulevard was nothin' before he died, you know – nothin' there but a bunch of car dealers, but since he died there's the Elvis hotel, Elvis gift shops ...

'I mean, I like his music, an' all – but you wouldn't catch me at any torchlight vigil at five o'clock in the morning at Graceland.'

Everyone in Memphis has an opinion about Elvis, or a story to tell. The hotel's public relations officer tells me her husband was a car dealer and Elvis used to ring up for three Cadillacs in the middle of the night.

☆

Even the Duck Master looks trapped and sad, a parody of himself, just as those ducks are a parody of the American desire for novelty. Memphis has hit me like a big grey blanket. I can't put my finger on it, but it seems tense, joyless.

> Memphis blues, turnip greens,
> Guess I shouldn't have come here
> Know what I mean?

'Are there any famous writers from Memphis – apart from William Faulkner?' I ask the barman. 'I'll just check with the concierge,' he says.

Upstairs in my room I had the TV on while I showered. The programme was all about the fact that it was 25 years ago today that the Beatles had hit America.

Yet another anniversary ...

The Meditation Garden, Graceland.

The story starts here: the Sun Studio, Memphis.

'...then why can't my dreams come true?'

The March of the Peabody Ducks.

☆

This morning, there was a story in the newspapers about a move to stop the post office from printing Elvis stamps. After all, the man died a drug addict . . .

☆

'I came here in 1940, from Pennsylvania. I'm a Yankee,' says Edward D. Pembroke, the Duck Master. 'I'd been in a circus all my life, doin' everythin' that had to be done. I come here crippled up and sick. They gave me the bell captain's job.

'Then I took on the ducks. I bin a lot of places with them ducks. You have to scold them sometimes, like kids. Them ducks are all different. The drake is the boss, and if somethin' goes wrong, he'll call 'em to him.

'They've all got their own ways. They look upon me as their leader and their protector. When they come here, I clip their wings, and from then on they're *my* ducks. If they're misbehavin', the minute I speak to them, they stop.

'We don't keep them ducks for more than four months, 'cos they get too fat to walk from the elevator to the fountain. An' if they get sick, the oil leaves their feathers and they become like frizzy chickens, so I send them back.

'People come to see me stop the ducks. When I stop and start the ducks everybody laughs.

'It's my livin', that's all,' says Edward D. Pembroke. 'Ain't nothin' holdin' me here but the job. I eat the world's best ribs over at the Rendezvous Restaurant, and I drink vodka, but I'd leave tomorrow and go back to New England. Ain't nothin' holdin' me, but the job.'

☆

I step outside into the iced Memphis streets and head for the Sun Studio. I walk through the shop where you can buy T-shirts and sweatshirts emblazoned with the famous gold motif, push open the creaky door tentatively and stand in silence inside the cool, white room.

This is a monument. More important than Graceland. I had a dream, and this is where that dream began.

On the walls are black and white pictures of 'the million-dollar quartet' – Elvis, Jerry Lee Lewis, Carl Perkins and Johnny Cash – the Traveling Wilburys (almost) of 1956. One picture shows Elvis performing – wearing his dad's trousers. He was that poor.

There are Martin guitars propped against the wall, a drum kit, a piano ... but the important thing is the microphone. The silver-topped microphone that appears on two of the original Elvis LP covers.

I have never collected autographs, or ripped pieces of people's clothes, or any of the weird things that fans are supposed to do, but standing in that room I felt like a kid again.

It was something to do with the fact that all my life I have wanted to be a communicator and I felt that if I had been in Memphis in 1956, I wouldn't have been a cook or a writer, I would have been a rock and roll singer.

I knew what Ringo Starr felt like when he stood on the spot where Elvis recorded and said: 'This is it. This is our Mecca, where it all began for us.' Meaning the Beatles.

I knew what Bob Dylan felt when, like a child at a shrine, he asked for a Polaroid picture of himself in this room ... Because for him, as for me, rock and roll, and therefore life, started here.

I knew why a band like U2, who could have their pick of the most sophisticated studios in the world, should have come here, to this simple white room, to record.

'It's the tiles on the wall that give it that unique sound,' says a voice behind me. Gary Hardy, the man who gave Sun Studio back to the people after it had been closed for so long, offers his hand. He's a stocky, deep-voiced, 38-year-old ex-musician turned record producer, whose sister took him to see Elvis and Jerry Lee Lewis on stage as a kid. A man who cares so much about Sun Studio that no one who doesn't instinctively show the proper respect is allowed to record within these hallowed walls.

'They don't have to bow down and kiss the floor but I wouldn't even entertain the idea of doing a recording with anyone who made fun,' he says. 'How could I open up a place that means so much to so many people, to someone who didn't respect it?

'You know, this might sound a bit off the wall, but this studio is dead on the Chickasaw Indian trail – I think there's something special about this spot. There's been a lot of special activity here for a long time ...'

He talks about Sam Phillips, the legendary producer who ran Sun Records and let Elvis go to RCA because, says Gary, he was far more interested in Carl Perkins and Jerry Lee Lewis – a decision which, in retrospect, was about as clever as that of the theatre manager who passed up Fred Astaire on the basis that he wasn't much of a hoofer.

Sam Phillips is in his sixties now – and they say he isn't bitter. 'He's his own man,' says Gary. 'Greatness requires you to be eccentric. You have to live with that craziness which goes with it. That's the price a genius pays – otherwise he'd just be an ordinary person.

'Sam was a director. On out-takes, you can hear him telling Elvis: "Now don't get too damn close to that microphone." His great talent was letting artists play until they played what he wanted to hear ...

'Sam left a lucrative job with a radio station to record what they called "race music" on the Sun label – black music played by musicians who had left the Mississippi Delta and were playing blues and rhythm and blues on Beale Street.

'After World War Two, America's social and ethnic views changed. America was forced to accept that black people were a part of our culture, and for the first three years Sun Records was almost exclusively black.

'But Sam didn't have the success he had hoped for, so in the end, where his genius came through was in bringing together white country and gospel music with black music – and that became rock and roll. Black music, coming through white artists.

'I like to dispel myths – like people say the first time Elvis came here, he was a truck driver. Well, he was working for a machine shop, the *second* time he was a truck driver. He came in all dirty from head to toe with machine oil and grease. For 4 dollars you could come in and make a demo. Elvis came in and did "My Happiness" and "That's When Your Heartaches Begin".'

Gary chats, feet up in the control room, looking out at the microphone, the photographs, the gold discs, those famous wall titles ... he's happy just to sit and feel the atmosphere.

'This place is home to me,' he says. 'The Sun Studio, to me, is like the White House to the President.'

Gary Hardy believes in rock and roll. I believe in rock and roll. Do you believe in rock and roll?

FOOD, MUSIC AND RELIGION

Everyone in Memphis eats barbecue. They go to the Rendezvous Restaurant, or to take-out joints like the Cozy Corner Bar-B-Q, where Raymond, who looks like Fats Domino and used to want to be a saxophone player, plays Duke Ellington and Patsy Cline, and barbecues baloney, rib tips, Boston butts (the centre of a shoulder of beef), corn hens and slab ribs, coated in his dry mix, over charcoal, hickory chips and cherrywood. The old-fashioned way.

'When a person reaches in that barbecue, he's gotta *feel* and *know* the temperature. He's gotta *know* an hour from now whether to add more charcoal, how much more cookin' ...

'I can't think of a more perfect meal than a $2\frac{1}{2}$-inch sirloin steak, cooked over charcoal medium, with gravy, baked potatoes and garlic bread. Play a bit of Duke Ellington in the background and that's good eatin' ...'

☆

Me, I go to Sleep Out Louie's on this cold Memphis night, where the fire is burning and they serve real beef stew with a side order of cheese on toast.

☆

Saturday evening at the Peabody. Ladies in taffeta frocks with flounced net skirts and boned bodices (all cut to one pattern, only the colours change) crowd around the bar on the arms of well-heeled chaps in tuxedos and cowboy boots.

Everywhere you look they are closing in, surging through the doors, clustering around the ever-tinkling piano, larking perilously close to the duck fountain. One blonde is already in tears at the bar. A girlfriend comforts her and her boyfriend pretends not to notice. It's dance night at the Peabody.

Someone takes the stool next to me. He says: 'Hi, Floyd. I really like your programme. I used to play with Eric Clapton. We wrote "Layla" together – I'm just drifting through, cutting a record.'

I'm confused. Am I a cook? Who am I? It doesn't matter any more. I'm just an adventurer, on a journey. And after all, food and rock and roll go together. They had the *Presley Family Cookbook* on sale at Graceland, didn't they?

I order a lime daiquiri and decide that food and music are soulmates, because they are about giving, not receiving. The adulation you get from being a rock and roll singer doesn't compensate for the heart you pour into it, just as the platitudinous bouquets you get from food writers can never repay you for the love you put into a meal. Just ask the Reverend Cutter. He knows about food and music. The faithful go to his Baptist church to praise God, to sing and to eat ... another trinity.

☆

The slow Southern fan in the Reverend James Allen Cutter's simple kitchen turns and turns again.

The Reverend is talking to Miz Callie, swaying slowly in her rocking chair – he's teasing her that she's 100 years old if she's a day. She chuckles and throws up her hands in mock protest. It's an old ritual and they both enjoy it. He's been her pastor for 20 years, and she is a favourite at his church.

'The Lord has blessed her real good,' says the Reverend. 'It's true that she must be close on 100. And she's seen a lot of changes in this city of Memphis.'

'I used to cook for a lot of rich white folks. Now they all left and died so I cook for the church,' says Miz Callie in her singsong voice that cracks only slightly.

'I was married when I was 14. I wanted to go to school, beyond the eighth grade, and this man said if you marry me I'll send you to school. But he lied.

'I got pregnant and I had a child, but my husband, he wouldn't work. He was very good-looking. He didn't like to work. Din' feel he had to. So I went back home.

'That's when I started to cook. I said: I'm gonna cook for someone in a great big house. So I cooked for the white folks. I'd cook salmon, and I'd bake a whole ham. I'd make up a great big bowl of biscuit dough and wrap up that ham and put it in the stove, turn it down real low and let the crust get hard.

'I never cooked for any coloured people. They din' have cooks. Memphis used to be very segregated. If the white people liked you, they'd treat you nice. But still there were so many things you couldn't do, and places you couldn't go.

'You couldn't go up and get on a bus first. You had to let the white folks git on first. They'd push you back: "Get on behind". You had to go sit at the back of the bus, an' if you were sitting down, and the bus was full, if the white people came on, they'd say: "Git up and let the white folks get a seat".

'People took it till they got tired of it. I remember one morning goin' to work, one woman whacked a white man with her umbrella. He had kicked her 'cos she was gittin' on the bus in front of him. They arrested her for disturbin' the peace – but he din' have no right to kick her.

'In Mississippi it was worse. If they din' like you, they just threw you in the water and drowned you down there.

'Boss Crump – he was the boss of the town, and he was a mean ol' man. He din' like black folks.'

'He didn't like black folks, but he used them,' says Reverend Cutter, sitting down beside Miz Callie. 'He was a vicious individual. He bought people and controlled them. He used to tell blacks from Arkansas: you come to my town and you get out alive if I want you too.

'He was the boss. This was Boss Crump town. He was never elected for any public office, but he placed into office every politician in Memphis. Even the mayor could not be elected unless he got the OK from Boss Crump. Senators in Tennessee could not be elected unless they got the OK from Boss Crump. Down on Beale Street they used to sing a song that went somethin' like: "Ain't gonna have it, If Boss Crump don' like it ..."

'There used to be a time when the South was a terrible place to live. Now, Northerners are coming South because we're getting it straightened out.

'But Memphis don't have the opportunities that Atlanta has for minorities, particularly blacks – in Memphis you can have two doctorates, two masters, and a PhD, but you ain't got no sense. It doesn't help you at all. It's not what you know, but who you know – but we're getting away from that now.

'I was one of Martin Luther King's lieutenants in the Southern Christian Leadership Conference. I was with him one March in Memphis and we had to get him away. I remember we put him in a green and white Pontiac '56, and we pleaded with him not to come back.

'When he went to Morocco and some of the Arab countries, he frightened America, especially the FBI. J. Edgar Hoover hated Martin Luther King with a passion. He vowed that he would never allow a black man to become a power to threaten the political system in America: like Jesse Jackson is doin' now.

'Martin and I disagreed on some things and after that I didn't go on all the marches, but I respected him.

'If you knew Martin, he had a charisma, somethin' that just drew people to him. He was kinda like Gandhi. He made sense out of difficult, frustrating situations. And even when I hear his speeches now, I'm almost in tears.

'He opened the door and awakened something in most Americans, but we still have things to carry on, that Martin did not accomplish.

'I tell you – one of our presidents had that charisma: Lyndon B. Johnson. That man was more like Martin Luther King than anyone I've ever seen to this day. He could have ran for president again, but he died of a broken heart. The very people he was trying to help turned and rioted. It broke his heart.

'There was tragedy in Martin's family. I know his widow, Coretta, and I knew his father. His mother was shot down while she was playing the organ. Some young, deranged man came in and shot and killed her, at the organ, right there in church. And his brother was drowned in a pool under mysterious circumstances.

'Now, Jesse Jackson, he and I keep in touch, and he done somethin' for American politics this year that was really great . . .'

The slow fan keeps on turning, and in the heat of the kitchen, David Pritchard and the crew are filming me cooking chitlins (the small intestines of pigs), yams, black-eyed peas and turnip greens for the Reverend and his striking wife, Portia.

Yesterday, at Buntyn's Restaurant, where they churn out plates of yams and turnip greens and glorious coconut pie faster than you can blink, and where the owner says that Elvis's grandmother used to go and eat, I took some sound advice. 'When you cook chitlins,' he said, 'do it with the window open, and a bottle of bourbon handy.'

Last night, in her long green gown, Portia sang with the gospel choir

97

at the Reverend's Greater Faith Baptist Church. It's a stark and modern building, but it rocked with joy once that choir started singing and swaying and clapping. Then the Reverend preached, his voice rising and falling with passion, light with humour, heavy with his message ...

'... You won't find any person depressed that's praising God. You won't find them layin' on a psychiatrist's couch either ... I tell folk all the time you are not saved because you look good – 'cos if that was the case I would've bin saved a long time ago ... you can go and be *saved* tonight!' Two ladies with wide grins, wearing glorious hats, nod: 'Yis, Lord, yis, Lord'.

'We ain't talkin' 'bout saving your body, because that ain't worth much. But there's a soul that's got God's image in it ... You can go home *saved* tonight, and by saved I don't mean Jesus saves green stamps, licks 'em and puts 'em in a book ... I'm talking 'bout God setting your spirit free ... Jesus loves you tonight ...' (The choir is singing softly behind him: 'Come to Jesus, while you have time ...')

'Thank God for all of you comin' and I'm gonna get ready for the food now ...'

Out back is the smoker where Reverend Cutter smokes ham and turkey, ready to eat after the service. 'I put in a bay leaf, some soya sauce, and, I'm not ashamed to say, some red wine and put it in the smoker for three to four hours. Then I go off and do the Bible class while it's smoking,' he says.

In Louisiana they had their gastronomic trinity. Here in Memphis there is another one: food, music and religion.

'I come from a family of 13 and we all had to learn to cook, and clean and sew,' says the Reverend. 'I was in the Chaplain corps in the navy and I used to cook for all the officers once in a while. I can make just about everythin'. You name it, I can make it.'

There were barbecued ribs, fried chicken, mustard greens and turnip greens. Miz Callie and members of the church, all dressed up in their best bonnets, brought chocolate cake, pound cake and chess pie. Everyone tucked in, chattering, smiling. 'My grandson, he says to me: "You goin' to the eating church?",' grinned Reverend Cutter, framed in the doorway, where a sign says 'Let it Shine in '89'. 'Last year we had "Get It Straight In '88",' he says.

Back in the Cutters' kitchen, with its pecan orchard outside, I'm playing out-takes from the Sun Studio – Elvis and Jerry Lee Lewis and Carl Perkins jamming and busking their way through the same gospel music that soared to the rafters of the Reverend's church.

Portia is talking about singing. 'They just put up with me till I got better and better. That's how most of our rock and roll and blues singers start off. You check with any of them, and they'll say they got their training singing in the church.'

'Elvis Presley sung in Brewster's Baptist Church off Elvis Presley Boulevard,' says the Reverend. 'Dr Brewster was the man who wrote all those gospel songs. Elvis used to go there every Sunday morning and listen to the choir, and then get out there and do the same things they would do. He got hold of the blues right out of that Baptist Church. He got all that rhythm from that church.

'Elvis was a great person – you know, girls and ladies used to put themselves in big old crates and boxes,' he chuckles, 'and mail themselves to him, get themselves delivered, to try to git to see him.

'Each year Elvis Presley used to give away brand new Lincoln cars to poor people. One lady, he gave her a brand new Lincoln an' her daughter was crying: "You got a car now, and I don't have one …", so Elvis went back and got another Lincoln and gave her daughter one. Ain't no wonder they called him the King. He done a lot of community work.

'He was driving in his car one night and he saw some white guys harassing a black woman. He stopped his long limousine, got out, beat the guys up, took her in the car and took her home.

'He and Dr Brewster would come by my office sometimes. He was just a regular fellow.'

No white person I met in Memphis spoke so highly of Presley.

Nervously I filled plates for the Reverend and Portia with my chitlins and yams and black-eyed peas and turnip greens and waited for their opinion. Someone was on my side, because they were full of praise. Miz Callie ate heartily, and I was proud when they carefully filled freezer pots with the leftovers, ready to eat another day.

REVEREND CUTTER'S
TABLE BLESSING

We thank Thee, O Father, for the food on our table, for the mother who prepared it with love, for the father who serves it with faith, for the children who, by your grace, eat it with love and gratitude. Amen.

A RECIPE FOR A GOOD LIFE

A large portion of gratitude for 24 hours to be alive
A daily portion of worship and devotion
Generous amounts of good common sense and honesty
Large amounts of genuine appreciation of others

Mix thoroughly into a good Christian home. Toss in a generous quantity of a sense of humour and sprinkle the whole mixture generously among your friends and neighbours.

PRESERVING CHILDREN

1 large grass field
6 children, all sizes
Hot sun
3 small dogs (rat terriers preferred)
Narrow strips of brook (pebbly, if possible)
Flowers
Deep blue sky

Mix the children with the dogs and empty into the field, stirring continuously, sprinkle the field with flowers, pour the brook gently over the pebbles. Cover all with a deep blue sky and bake mixture in hot sun. When children are well browned they may be removed. Will be found right and ready for setting away to cool in the bath tub.

The Lorraine Motel

I had a dream, a dream of Memphis, but what had become of Martin Luther King's dream?

I had another reason for coming to this city: to see the place where Martin Luther King had died. Not out of morbid, touristic curiosity, but out of respect.

This man had had such a profound effect on the United States, I thought there would be nothing that would interfere with the right kind of memorial, the kind of tribute he would have understood.

Instead I found a tiny, clear-eyed, black opera singer called Jacqueline Smith camped outside the Lorraine Motel, where Dr King stayed when he came to Memphis, and where he was assassinated in 1968.

She huddled with her portable TV and her cat under a tarpaulin on a pavement that was filmed over with frost. Her friends brought her food. She had been the last resident of the motel, evicted in January 1988.

She had been there for 389 days to protest against a tawdry, city planning, profiteering scheme to turn the Lorraine into an 8.8 million-dollar 'Civil Rights Centre' with Ku Klux Klan exhibits and sound and light shows, and a laser 'sculpture' tracing the path of the bullet which killed Martin Luther King.

'If they do that,' explained Jacqueline, 'the property values will go up and they'll push the poor people out in favour of the rich.

'Dr King was killed in the ghetto when he came here to help the poor sanitation workers. Now that ghetto is turning into the rich man's paradise, and the poor people are being forced out.

'Memphis has the highest poverty rate of any city in the United States, and I would like to see the Lorraine renovated as homes for the poor, the homeless and elderly. I think this would be the greatest tribute we could bestow on Dr King – to give the people something that would carry on his dream.

'I think it would be a bad message for Memphis to give the world that they are trying to make money off of Dr King.'

This gentle, dignified, principled lady who was in high school at the time of the civil rights marches, who studied French and acting and sang with an opera company in Chicago, was all set to play Almeris in *Aida* until the rather large diva in the starring role refused to sing beside her, because she was such a slip of a thing. Singing is her great love, but 'all that has been put on the back burner' while she makes her lonely protest.

'After Dr King was assassinated one of my teachers would tell me about what he was trying to accomplish, and I'd come down here, walk around and look. I didn't plan any of this. I just feel we have to let the world know what's going on here,' she says.

'I feel we will be victorious. We must, because obviously we haven't yet learned the message Dr King tried to leave with us: that of serving mankind and that of love.'

In the collection of newspaper cuttings and letters of support she keeps inside her tiny tent is one from Gandhi's grandson, a journalist in India, printed in the city's newspaper, the *Commercial Appeal*.

'I believe Dr King was among the very few people who really understood the philosophy of my grandfather, M. K. Gandhi,' says the letter, 'and if it is possible for his soul to see what is being done to commemorate his memory, it must be as restless as the soul of Gandhi.

'More than 30 million dollars were collected on the death of Gandhi in 1948 and almost all of it was spent on erecting museums and monuments that make a mockery of his teachings . . . By erecting such lifeless and senseless monuments to dynamic men like Dr King and Gandhi, we are not perpetuating their memories but insulting their intelligence.

'They were men who dedicated their lives to serving the poor and the downtrodden, and the best monument to them is to ensure that the dream they died for becomes a vibrant symbol for the emancipation of the oppressed . . .'

Arun Gandhi.

The trouble with meeting people like Jacqueline is that you wind up feeling as cheap as the minibus-loads of Japanese tourists who came, took photographs, and charged off to the next destination on their itinerary even as I spoke to her.

I felt cheap because I was in Memphis to make a programme for the BBC and, as part of that programme, I was required to let her speak for roughly 1 minute and 30 seconds.

But 10 minutes later, when I was still kneeling there, talking to her, with my knee frozen to the pavement, and the director was getting impatient, and saying things like: 'You've finished now', I told him: 'No, I haven't finished.'

I didn't want to be like that busload of Japanese tourists. I didn't want to be a part of those people who came and took a little bit of her, paid lip service to her cause, took their holiday snaps, and then left her there in the icy wind.

The Fourways Grill

When Jesse Jackson comes to town he eats catfish over at the Fourways Grill, where Irene Cleaves, her greying hair caught up in a net, runs the business that has earned her enough awards to cover every inch of wall space. And where I had come to create a special sauce, with smoked bacon and corn, and a drop of bourbon, to go with her splendid Southern fried chicken.

Only some of her awards are on display. Like the Black Business Association Award, 1988, and the Preservation of Black Heritage Award for Black Cooking in the Style of 'The Way Mama Cooked It', 21 February 1985.

Elsewhere the wall space is taken up with newspaper cuttings, a sign which says 'No Loitering! No Soliciting! No Profanity!' and photographs of Martin Luther King, Gladys Knight and the Pips, Isaac Hayes ... all of whom have come to eat Irene Cleaves' soul food.

Her husband, Clint, who was Boss Crump's chauffeur, borrowed 1500 dollars to start a restaurant 43 years ago.

'When I first went into business I din' know if I was gonna make it or not, but I just kept workin' and workin' and addin' on and addin' on. We started doing regular home-cooked soul food: Southern fried chicken, ham hock ... on Sundays we'd have turkey and dressing, duck and dressing, meatloaf, baked ham ... we'd have broccoli with cheese sauce, string beans, potato salad ... and for dessert we'd have peach cobbler and banana pudding. Then we started doin' breakfasts: hot biscuits and ham and rice, steak and rice, beef liver with rice, country ham. On and on ...

'I wanted to have somewhere where people could appreciate bringin' their whole family: their wives, their children, their grandmothers. Where they wouldn't mind dressin' up and comin' in for their dinner.

'In the beginning we didn't have many whites. And if we did, we had to let them eat in the kitchen, because they wouldn't allow you to serve white people out front. But now I serve anybody I want to, anybody who has money to spend. We get a lot of white folks now.

'At the beginning of desegregation, people would come here and eat breakfast, then set out on the marches to listen to Martin Luther King and then they'd come back and eat here.

'Martin Luther King would eat here too. He was a kind person, not hard to serve. He'd just eat whatever was on the menu.'

JASON D. WILLIAMS

Memphis had to have a Jason D. Williams. And only Memphis wouldn't take enough notice.

Sitting at the bar in a Memphis hotel, reminiscent of a Holiday Inn outside Milton Keynes. The audience look like rent-a-crowd from Bournemouth. Women with coiffured blonde hair and blue rinses, with names like Flo and Rita, swap photographs of the skinny, pale-faced kid – a cross between an adolescent Bob Dylan, John McEnroe and the young Jerry Lee Lewis – who is ripping this joint apart with rock 'n' roll as near as dammit as sharp and witty and exciting as when it first shook up this city.

This guy is no mimic, no plagiarist, the music is raw. I think I am seeding a reincarnation of all those fifties greats.

'Otis Blackwell wrote it, Jerry Lee Lewis recorded it – *I* am going to *perform* it,' announces Jason D. with his mock-cocky grin, launching into a riotous 'Great Balls of Fire'. For the next two hours he is everywhere: under the piano, on top of it, bashing out rock 'n' roll classics with hands that work like high-speed pedals (the left one underpinning the whole act), playing with his feet, his backside, almost every piece of his anatomy: fast, furious and funny.

The next evening he wanders into the Peabody to say hello, raunchy in a black cap and leather jacket. Crazily, this is where he started his career, tinkling the ivories in the Mallards Bar. (Everything round here is to do with ducks. This place has more ducks than Slimbridge!)

He's a country boy from El Dorado, deep in Southern Arkansas, and he's been playing piano since he was three. 'I have a real strong left hand – you noticed that,' he says in his country drawl. 'I'm ambidextrous – I play with both feet too,' he grins. 'That strong left hand comes from blues artists. People say I play like Jerry Lee, but he was one of the last influences and inspirations I came across.

'I learned from black blues piano players. A dear old friend who died not long ago, Memphis Slim, taught me a lot about left-hand blues boogie-woogie style. The left hand holds it all together. The rest is just icing on the cake.

'I can't read a note of music, but I play classical piano – Horowitz is my hero – and I write my own freestyle jazz. I play guitar too, and the harp – the heavenly kind, not the mouth harp.'

The resemblance to the young Jerry Lee Lewis is so startling there was a rumour that Jason D. was his illegitimate son. Jason didn't dispute it – it was good for business. And he *is* adopted ... he has no idea who his real parents are.

'There's a slight possibility it's true – well, more than slight,' he reckons. 'But I hope our characters are a bit different. It's good to be compared to his music, but his lifestyle, no way ... I'm wild on stage, but in real life – I'm a choirboy,' he winks. 'I don't drink – I never smoked before tonight!' he says, lighting up a fat cigar. 'And I like bird watching ...

'My adopted parents are Baptist missionaries – they kind of help balance my life out, and I balance theirs.'

As a kid, like Elvis, he sat in the black churches where they sang gospel music, and drew inspiration. 'Our white church music was too sterile for me,' he says, 'so I used to go across town. That's where I really learned to play blues-gospel. They called me the Great White Speck!'

MEMPHIS BLUES

'Beale Street was the street of escape. All week long the boss man's on your back: do this, do that. Come Saturday, you're free as a bird, and you fly to Beale Street. And as long as you got money to burn, you was King. When your money ran out: goodbye.

'You had to work all week to get some more money to come back and do the same thing all over again.'

Abe Schwab in his apron, round pink face smiling, sits behind the counter in the store on Beale Street that has been in his family for 100 years. And has barely changed in all that time. But Beale Street has . . .

I walk down the street where they say the blues was born, sliding on the ice, shivering against the wind. There is a statue of Elvis at one end, and W. C. Handy, the man they call the father of the blues, at the other. Even the famous Rum Boogie Café on the corner is closed – due to the weather, says a handwritten sign on the door.

But Abe Schwab is remembering Beale Street in the thirties. When the street came alive on sweltering Saturday nights. 'The way I look at it, there were three groups of people came to Beale Street,' says Abe, 'the country people who spent the day shopping and left before dark, the evening group of people who were the city workers who'd get off work and come down, and the night people, the real drinkers and nightclubbers.

'Most country folk back then didn't have any money until the cotton crop came in, in the fall. If they owned some land and had a bit of clout they borrowed money from the bank, then when they had their first bales of cotton they paid off the bank, and whatever they had left they'd blow. They'd come here and shop and get new clothes, go to picture shows.

'You could smell Beale Street, smell the food cookin'. They cooked a lot of buffalo fish and catfish and made fish sandwiches.

'And everywhere there was music. Before integration Beale Street was almost all black. The workers would sing the songs they sang on the railroads and in the fields, chopping cotton from daylight to dark. It got monotonous. The back got tired, so they started singing: blues and spirituals. With the blues you curse everybody and with spirituals you praise the Lord. Music was an escape.

'Many of them had been told there were a lot of jobs in Memphis – they'd been told that for 150 years, but it wasn't true. But they came here expecting to find work, and they didn't find it. So they'd sit up in the doorways of the rooming houses and sing the blues. Another group sat on the sidewalk, between stores, sitting on boxes, with their hats in front of them, for people to drop a nickel in. There was others in their rooms singing, and you had beer halls, with jukeboxes blaring away.

'Years later Elvis lived about eight blocks from Beale Street, and as he got old enough he'd come down here. He was able to move with black people. Some whites just *cannot* do it, it's part of our culture of segregation, but if you're used to movin' with black people, you don't know what the big stink is about. It don't make no sense.

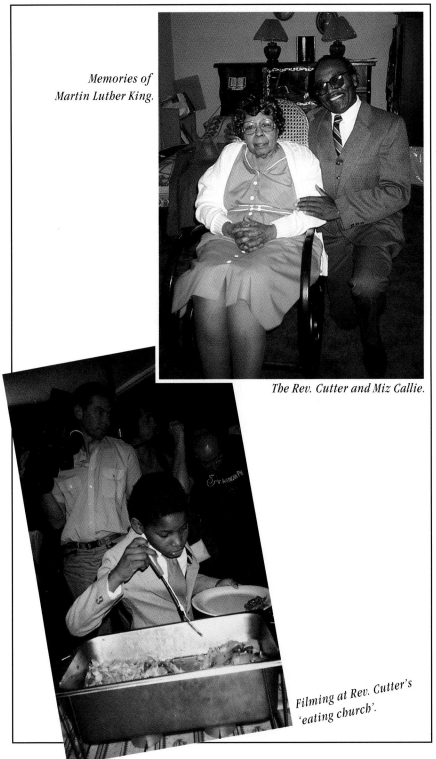

Memories of Martin Luther King.

The Rev. Cutter and Miz Callie.

Filming at Rev. Cutter's 'eating church'.

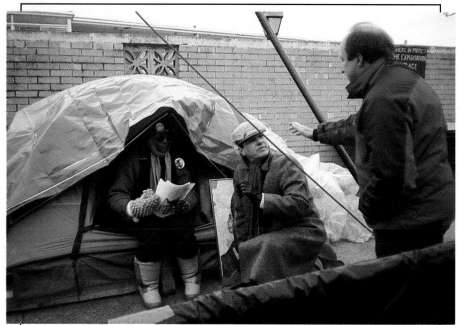

'We had a dream, Jacqueline Smith and I…Sorry, David, did you want to make a TV programme?'

I bet Jason D. Williams has got blue suede shoes!

'In the summertime, the rooms would get hot, because they ain't got no windows, and people would live in Handy Park: they'd eat and drink, play the guitar and the mouth harp, and sleep out there. They'd play for their own entertainment and they'd draw the crowds. This was blues white people had never heard. Elvis would come down the street and hear that music. And he imitated what he heard. His gyrations were part of the dancing which had been goin' on for 100 years.

'His music was Beale Street music, his dancin' was Beale Street dancin'. Sure, he added his own flavour, but it was blues, except you couldn't call it blues, because blues refers to blacks.

'Right up to the end, as far as I know, he bought his costumes from Lansky Brothers, right here on Beale Street.

'In those days, Memphis didn't recognise anythin' special in Elvis. Memphis doesn't recognise its own people for some stupid reason. I bin' trying to figure out why that is, and I reckon you have to be better than the best for Memphis to recognise you. There's so much talent here you have to jump off the highest building to get noticed. We can't see the forest for the trees.

'Beale Street had its own laws. It was always what I call an "open" street – the liquor laws, the women laws, the gamblin' laws, they don't count on Beale Street.

'A man was killed outside this store one time, because he broke one of the Beale Street laws ... There was this man and a woman in the café down the street, and they got to arguin' about something. She came up here and bought a pocket knife. She was going to kill him.

'She goes out front and he's out there waiting for her. He slaps her down. Now I guess she took his money, and the rule is if she took his money, he's entitled to one shot at her. Everybody's watching and nobody said nothing. Then he went back and kicked her. When he kicked her, they killed him.

'He was entitled to one slap, he paid for one blow. But after that he should have gone about his business. That's Beale Street, you don't go back and kick her.

'There was the "shopping block" and the "fun block" where all the gamblin' and the women and the liquor was. If someone was drunk in this shoppin' block, he'd be arrested, or told to leave, but if he was passed out on the pavement in the fun block, the same policeman who ran him off the shopping block would just step straight over him.

'There'd be card games going and people made their livin' off the street, people was always trying to con or gip somebody. They'd say: I'll sell you my diamond ring for 10 dollars – but they only paid 98 cents for it. If you could catch a sucker it was all right. W. C. Fields said there's one born every minute. But nobody ever got hurt on the street, unless they broke the laws.

'Beale Street is different now. You still have a lot of musicians, but in those days, music wasn't commercial. People would walk down the street playing the mouth harp, and they'd just sit in a beer hall and play and drink beer. If they got up and left, a whole group would get up and follow them to the next beer hall. But nobody paid them. Ninety per cent of the music on Beale Street was free.

'On Saturdays, people used to come in here and listen to records. We sold blues here on the Bluebird label, put out by RCA Victor. Because of segregation you couldn't sell blues on a black label.

'We used to sell them for 35 cents, three for a dollar. We'd play the records and a lot of folk would just come in and listen. We'd get such a big crowd the customers couldn't get through, so we'd put on a spiritual record.

'No one would want to hear it, so they'd all go away. Then we'd put on a blues record and they'd all come back again ...'

But tonight as I walk down Beale Street, nothing moves, and the bronze statues of Elvis and W. C. Handy freeze in the sodium streetlights.

☆

Why is it that the people who bring the ice are black and the people who serve the drinks are white?

Why is it that when I hear white people saying 'We're not racist. We've overcome that now' it doesn't ring quite true? Why do I feel that if this was Florida, they'd have therapy groups on how not to be a racist. You'd get up each morning and say: 'Right. I'm not going to be a racist today.' One day at a time.

Of all the comments I heard, there was one that really disturbed me. That of a university-educated Memphisonian in the media business who told me: 'Elvis, to me, was a white nigger.'

He had said it all. Somehow summed up this undercurrent of racial tension and unease which I couldn't quite put my finger on.

☆

The way to beat the Memphis blues is to go to Lou's Place and listen to the real thing – Sonny Blake blowing the mouth harp.

By ten o'clock at night, to quote Fats Waller, the joint is jumpin'. The bar is doing a good trade in Lou's special cocktails: there's a kind of pink pina colada called Ma Rainey – they say that's what she used to drink; a Billie Holliday made with rum, brandy, triple sec and sweet and sour mix; or Lou's own concoction, Lou's Blues – champagne, orange and pineapple juice, mixed with blue curaçao. And there's barbecued ribs, chicken and catfish . . .

Bearded Lou, in a navy fisherman's sweater and peaked cap, looks like he'd be more at home on a trawler than running this jazz joint. His first club was the famous Blues Alley. As 'a Yankee', he admits: 'It all started as a business, but then I learned about the blues, to enjoy it, to love it . . .'

The band, a happy mixture of black and white – including Memphis favourite Bob Tally on piano, and Tot, the big saxophonist, who studied music at college and can play any kind of music you like – are playing old blues favourites like 'Ain't Misbehavin', and 'Crazy', and a soulful version of Otis Redding's 'Dock of the Bay'.

Then Sonny Blake appears – a spindly figure in mud-brown trousers and checked shirt, with a heavy belt proclaiming 'The King' strapped around his skinny waist – and plays his 'Mississippi Delta Blues'.

That legendary blues artist, Sun House once said: 'Them blues make you wish you was dead sometimes', and that's true, but the blues can send your soul soaring too. It's something to do with hope and despair all wrapped up together. And it has a lot to do with the way this city made me feel.

Since I know food and rock and roll go together, it doesn't surprise me to find out that by day Sonny Blake is a deputy chef in Arkansas – 'work by day, play the blues at night' – and that the kind of food he likes to cook is 'simple food, some folks call it soul food: okra, peas, corn, turnip greens, barbecue ribs . . .'

Like the Reverend Cutter, he has his trinity: God, music and food.

'People don't understand about the blues,' says Sonny, accepting a bourbon and coke after his first set. 'Blues and religion, I've cried over them both. I get the same feeling for both, but I get a good feeling when

I sing the blues. The blues is here to stay. The blues ain't never gonna die. I love it. I play nothin' but the blues.

'People think you have to spend a lot of money to have a good time, but that's a mistake. If you have a little band and you really *feel* what they're doing, you have a great time.

'They gave Memphis the credit for bein' the home of the blues, but I can't see it,' he says. 'The blues came out of the Delta part of the Mississippi, back in slavery time ... when a person had worked all day in the cottonfield in the hot sun, for 35 cents a day. They got by, they raised all their food: corn and hogs and chickens, and when they finished working it was the greatest time people had in a day. That's when they played the blues. The blues was just two people with a harp and a piano, or a guitar – this here, what we're playin', is rhythm and blues.

'Even a baby, he got the blues. He'd be hollerin' – he don't know what he's hollerin' about, but he's got the blues.

'Me, I learned the blues from listening to records, to people like Muddy Waters. They can't teach you how to play harmonica – no way. You have to teach yourself. I'm a very slow learner,' he grins, 'but once I got it, I got it!'

'We got a whole lot of black history here. I'm 66 years old, and I figure if I live another five more years I'll wax something, I'll put my blues on record and tell the world about it.'

☆

CHAPTER FIVE

Forget Manhattan –
I'll take the Austin skyline any day

On a clear day, the city's skyscrapers look like cubist mirror sculptures, stepped like pyramids, high above the contrasting Capitol building which looks like a miniature White House in soft, serene, pink granite. Even the '*Uncle Tom's Cabin* houses' on the outskirts of town, with their Southern porches, pick-up trucks and two or three rusted cars in the garden, blend happily into the grand, architectural design of things.

Austin, Texas, is a university town – a light, airy, clean place with pleasing, pastel colours, wide, wide streets, lots of 'no smoking' signs and hundreds of people in high-heeled snakeskin boots and jeans with wide leather belts and silver buckles ...

Obviously the way to discover Texas is to go to the biggest shoe shop in the world and buy yourself two or three pairs of cowboy boots from the lines and lines of hundreds, standing to attention. Or, better still, have a hand-crafted pair of 'cockroach killers' (pointed toes) stitched and sewn with your personal emblem by Noel Escobar Junior, the man who once ran up a pair of Texas Joggers – tennis shoes with boot tops and an inlay of Texas and spurs – to Willie Nelson's design.

Next, see Manny Gammage who has hatted everyone from Prince Charles to Burt Reynolds. Manny reckons the right hat can completely change your personality. (Incidentally Texans wear hats because of the unpredictable weather – they are instant umbrellas in a storm – and they all wear boots, well, just because they're Texans.)

RANCH-HOUSE CUISINE

The first day's filming in Texas. Floyd poised posing at the top of the sweeping staircase beneath the chandelier in the mock-*Dallas* ranch house, in shiny new boots, pigskin jacket and mink hat.

Down the staircase – crew feeling their way backwards – into the kitchen to mix Margaritas, grill some steaks and conjure up a barbecue sauce. All in one take.

'Let me tell you about hat etiquette,' says Larry Beard, who owns the Lariat B Ranch. 'Outside, in hallways or open areas, you may wear a hat. Inside your home, or your office, you should remove it . . .'

I dutifully remove my hat.

'I was wrangler on the movie *Lonesome Dove*,' says Larry (it seems *Lonesome Dove* is to Austin what Elvis is to Memphis). 'A wrangler is someone who is in charge of livestock – horses, pigs, chickens, whatever . . . you furnish 'em, corral 'em, use 'em, train 'em, whatever it takes . . . you're the wrangler.'

There's 170 acres out front, and Larry helps run cattle on another 1000 acres behind, there's a jacuzzi and a gym upstairs, even a second kitchen, so it's a little bewildering when Larry says: 'Two years ago I woke up one February morning with 100 dollars to my name.

'I did not have a job. My wife didn't have a job. We had a nine-month-old son and a foreclosure notice on every piece of property I owned and they were going to cut off my electricity 'cos I couldn't pay the bill.

'I said to myself: "You're walkin' around down here, thinking what the hell are you gonna do for a livin'? You gotta get up, get a job, get going – I mean you gotta put food on the table here, boy."

'That old Texas pride comes out in you. When the going gets tough, the tough get going.

'See, in 1983 the real estate boom really came on strong in Texas. All of a sudden people were just buying land from everywhere. Course, me being born and reared here, I knew what land was selling for, what I could get it for. I knew the people that owned it and said: "Hey, how about selling it?" and I'd broker it for them. Both me and my wife were involved in real estate.

'I made several million dollars in a couple of years. Then, all of a sudden: turn out the lights. Goodnight. The real estate boom had just bust. Overnight.

'Literally all the banks just closed. No more loans. I went bankrupt.
I lost everything.

'I was able to hang on to my ranch, simply because the bank couldn't
sell it, but my trucks were towed off, my tractors were towed off. I had
seven full-time employees – I had to lay all of them off.

'We went through very, very hard times, and very depressing times.
Everybody, when they get to that point, thinks about jumping off a big
wall somewhere or putting the big gun to your head, but I'm a Texan
and I had faith in myself.

'Anybody that's down, they can get back up. It's always too soon to
give up. Thomas Jefferson tried 900 and something times to get electricity
. . . he din' give up!

'See, Texans take pride in the fact that we're different. The attitude
of Texans is that we are the only state that still has written in the
constitution that we have the right to secede from the United States.
Because we were a nation on our own, we believe we're different to any
other state.

'You know, what happened to me is just like the life and times of
most Texans. Most successful businessmen in Texas bought real estate,
and they're either bankrupt or going bankrupt. Guys like me, we were
blowing and going, making hundreds of thousands of dollars every time
we turned around. Couldn't spend it fast enough. Now we're just getting
back on our feet.

'There were tough, tough times. Many times I wondered where the
next dollar was coming from, and everybody else I knew was broke.

'But we're fortunate that we are in the land of opportunity. Where
the sky's the limit . . .

'I had a God-given idea. I invented a new curry comb – a self-
cleaning curry comb for horses, and I went and found people and said:
this is a good idea. This'll work. They agreed. They said: let's put the
money behind it and make it go . . . I started to pay my creditors again, I
got out of bankruptcy.

'We lost it, now we're getting it back . . .'

Floyd in the kitchen, making a barbecue sauce for the 16 ounce Texas
steaks. If only I could get some stars on them, to match the stripes from
the grill . . .

'You know, recently there's been a lot of argument about the injection
of hormones to stimulate the growth of beef – but in Texas, most beef
raisers, such as myself, we don't inject anything. We just feed 'em good,'

says Larry.

'Me, I'm raising a cross between a Charolais and a Brahman. We've found that cross-bred cattle do better than pure-bred cattle in terms of beef gain.'

'No Texas Longhorns?'

'Well the old Longhorns are real hard to put a lot of weight on. They're best suited to range country, because they can roam the country-side for two or three weeks without water, and go for long periods without any substantial protein in the grass . . .

'Now mind how you cook my steak – I don't like my steak so red that I think I could put a tourniquet on and save it,' says Larry, polishing his Colt Frontier Six Shooter 44-40 and a rifle for an afternoon's target practice.

'That's a Winchester 30-30 rifle,' he says. 'The one that won the West.'

THE BEST BARBECUE IN THE WORLD

Highway 183 south to Caldwell County is a lazy, undulating road that looks like it goes on for ever, way out through the Texas countryside, past fields of old, broken-down cars, fields of tyres . . . until you reach Lockhart, the town that time forgot, where the Comanches were beaten in the Battle of Plum Creek, and where every street looks like the one Gary Cooper walked down in *High Noon*.

A man gets thirsty travelling, so I stroll into the nearest saloon, looking for a whisky.

'No, sir, we don't sell whisky in Caldwell County – just beer,' says the bartender.

What is this? Seems every county in Texas takes a vote on whether to be 'wet' or 'dry', save for beer, and Caldwell County said dry.

Oh well, down the street is Kreuz's Barbecue and Meat Market, where they say they make the best barbecue in Texas, the USA, and therefore, by definition, the world.

'We had one gentleman who flew in from Los Angeles, picked up some beef and flew back,' says Don, who runs the place with his brother Rick.

We get all kinds of people in here, politicians, celebrities . . . when

they filmed *Lonesome Dove*, Robert Duvall and the crew came here to eat.'
(I really must see *Lonesome Dove* some time.)

Behind him, people are queueing for slabs of beef: prime rib, shoulder
'clod', pork loin and sausage, smoked over oak, and seasoned only with
salt and pepper, served with crackers or white bread, wrapped in thick
brown butcher's paper.

'Our father had a saying: "It's not what you put on the meat, it's
what you leave off",' says Don. 'We do it real simple, just choice meat
and basic seasonings. We don't have a sauce. Wouldn't even know how
to make a sauce.

'Time's kind of passed this place by. At one time it was maybe junky.
Now it's unique. It's the same as it's always been. We don't even have
forks.'

In the big eating hall, with bottles of hot sauce on the long trestle
tables, Sam Closserman is eating barbecue and crackers off brown paper.
Sam used to be Mayor. He's 85 now, and he's been eating sausage in
Kreuz's since 1906.

'He's our oldest customer, far as we know,' says Don. 'Unless
someone else steps up.'

'When I was about four years old we were very poor,' says Sam,
wiping his chin with a big white handkerchief. 'I used to get a nickel and
come over here and get half a sausage and crackers. And the sausages
were 50 per cent bigger than they are now.

'But I got lucky. I went to the University of Texas, I got rich, I got
to be Mayor, I have a clothing store – I work every day at the store – I
have an automobile agency, an oil business, a banking business.

'Lockhart was a pretty wild town when I was a boy. I remember one
night when I was about nine years old. My dad had a food store, biggest
one in the county. We used to put watermelons out in front of the
store. It was about eight o'clock just getting dark. I was bringin' in the
watermelons, and all of a sudden I heard some shots.

'People were running, so I ran down to the corner, and there was
the sheriff: somebody shot his brains out. Yes, it was a pretty wild town.

'They never caught the killer, but everybody thought they knew who
he was. See, the sheriff – he was a tall, handsome man – had had an
altercation, a gunfight, in the courthouse about a year before with a
councillor. They both shot at each other and the sheriff killed him on the
stairway.

'Most everybody wore guns – except my father. My dad was a very religious person.

'If you see pictures of the early 1900s you'll see most of the men are wearing coats. They wore coats for a reason. They had guns underneath.

'People would come into Lockhart on a Saturday night, with their wagons and horses. There must have been 8000, 10 000, 12 000 people around the square on Saturdays. There were two saloon bars on each side of the square – I think one side had three – and there used to be a house of ill-repute just down the road.

'People would come to Kreuz's, get barbecue, drink soda, beer and have the best time.

'But there'd be a shooting scrape every Saturday, and a murder about once a month.'

DON'T IT MAKE YOUR BROWN EYES BLUE?

Floyd sipping bourbon on the rocks, sitting at a table next to the tiny dance floor where the band is playing moodily in this country and western club. Kelly is tossing back her milky blonde hair and saying, in that honeyed, girlish voice: 'When you hear that music, doesn't it just make your heart bleed? Doesn't it just reach down inside you and rip at you?'

'Why is it all so depressing?' says J.J.

'Oh, honey, you haven't *listened* to country. I'm gonna get them to play a jitterbug. Show you it's not all depressing ...

'When I hear that music it just makes me wanna dance. My uncle taught me to dance when I was four years old. He just stood me on his feet ... yeah, play it. Let's get wild, now ...

'There's a guy round the corner who dances real old, old country. Old country is like ballroom dancing. New country is three step. Guys over 40, they don't know how to do a three step. It's a new country dance, but God it's good ...

'I'm gonna tell you, my favourite TV station is CMT, Country Music Television. Like, it's a country music video station. My TV stays on that. I *sleep* with it on. I *never* get tired of it.

'See that guy over there? That's Rusty Wier. Did you ever see the movie *Urban Cowboy*, with John Travolta and Debra Winger? He wrote and performed one of the hit songs, called "Don't it Make You Wanna Dance" '.

The band has hotted up. 'Let's go and dance,' says J.J.

'Oh, hon, we can't do that,' says Kelly. 'Everybody would get upset if two girls got up and danced. They'd probably run us out of here. That's the way it is. In a rock bar it doesn't matter. No one knows who's dancing with who in a rock bar.'

J.J. is looking perplexed. 'Well, can I go and ask a man to dance?'

'That's OK. As long as he's not with a woman. As long as you don't leave with him, or drag him over to the table and start kissing and hugging him, that's OK. So long as you just dance with him, and leave him alone . . .

'There are some things that are just unwritten. You just don't do it. Like, it's OK for a woman to come in alone, as long as she doesn't sit at the bar. Well you *can* sit at the bar, but people would wonder what kind of a girl you are. Unless the bartender's your boyfriend, and everybody knows it.

'You have to be careful, you know. You don't want to get a reputation. They don't come after you and beat you with a stick or anything, but words are worse than sticks.

'Once you get a bad reputation you can't go back into a place. Nobody'll talk to you. It's kinda old world type thoughts. That's the way it is.

'I come here almost every night with friends. They all know me, they know who I'm dating, so it's OK. The other night my boyfriend came in and I left with him, but that was OK, because they all knew it was my boyfriend.

'Rock and roll in this town is different. But mostly people who come to these places are raised by the old book.

'Like, you don't leave with a man if you came by yourself. Unless it's your boyfriend or your husband come lookin' for you and everybody knows that.

'What you do,' she says, tossing that blonde hair, 'is tell them you're leaving and where you're gonna be, and then in a half hour, *they* leave.

'That's the way you do it.'

BAR TALK

The foyer of the hotel is an enormous glass-roofed atrium where tiny fairy lights sparkle on trees in tubs around the bar and the lifts are glass boxes which shoot up and down the marble walls on long snaking coils. Everyone can see where everyone else gets out. Surveillance of the people, by the people, for the people.

The shoeshine boy sits idly, waiting for business, and in the corner is another playerless piano.

The lady with long white-blonde hair, sipping white wine, joins our conversation. 'I guess I'm on my third career. I had a nursing career, a dancing career, now I'm going to law school . . .'

Her friend joins her. He is black, with a gentle face and a soft voice. A Federal judge. Today he has been admitting new American citizens to the country: Iranians, Vietnamese, Argentinians, one Englishman.

'They just keep coming,' he says, 'hundreds, month after month. The Asians keep coming, the Hispanics from Colombia and Bolivia. The migration doesn't slip. The Federal Government makes the law determining who comes and who doesn't, and so long as the Immigration and Naturalization Service says these people qualify, they've passed their tests, and they are certified to me, I admit them . . . They come because of the freedom this country offers. The opportunities, the jobs.'

I tell him I don't think there is such a thing as America. You can't come here and find America any more than you can travel through France, Germany, Italy, and Spain and say: 'Right, that's Europe.' Florida, Tennessee, Texas are as different as it is possible to be.

'But, you know, as Texans we *tell* the world that we are different from most Americans,' says the Judge. 'We are a republic unto our own. We are distinct. Texans are always saying this.

'When we went through our struggle with Mexico, we also seceded from the Union, set up our own constitution, and we still have that attitude. Texas is unique.'

'J.J., this is the Judge.'

'How did you all get to know each other?' says the Judge.

'We don't! We really don't!' says J.J.

'Or we think we do, but we really don't' – now she's got *me* at it!

'See, I'm viewing America all over again, through their eyes. Every time I think I understand, I don't. I really don't,' says J.J.

☆

Sixth Street at happy hour is a joyous place. Light and frivolous. Car horns honk, the pavements are crowded with hopeful folk heading for the next bar, where, for *three* happy hours, the bartenders serve drinks in bucket sizes and you help yourself to the buffet.

'How about Sex On The Beach?' says the lady drinking tequila and sangria from a three-quarter-pint bucket at the bar of a light, airy joint called Jazz.

Here we go again. 'What *is* Sex On The Beach?'

'Vodka, blueberry liqueur and melon liqueur – it's like eating snails, doesn't sound like a good idea, but when you try it, it's great!' says the bartender who is wearing a 'Pinch me, feel me, eat me' T-shirt.

A model Louisiana alligator dangles across the bar, behind his head, and on the walls are pictures of my friend Paul Prudhomme, best-known exponent of 'Louisiana Cooking'.

Girls in slinky dresses tuck into cocktails and young businessmen in their uniform white shirts and ties drink jugs of beer and pile up their plates with 'Louisiana food': red beans and rice and pan-fried chicken from stainless steel serving dishes over spirit lamps. Waitresses dance between the tables.

'We serve real authentic Louisiana food here,' says the bartender. 'Our chef is trained by the head chef at K-Paul's in New Orleans, and we pay to use Paul Prudhomme's recipes.'

'Are you English?' says a voice next to me, coming from under a hat with a badge shaped like an eye pinned to it, blonde wisps of hair escaping.

'My best friend lives in England. She makes G-strings for topless dancers.'

'Oh?'

'Is it true that England swings like a pendulum do? And what about Twiggy gaining all that weight. What about Justin, her boyfriend? Does he still like her just the same?'

'Well, I don't think they're together any more . . .'

'Oh, I had a time warp . . . My friend in England thinks I'm crazy. I say: "You make G-strings for topless dancers – you think *I'm* crazy?"'

'And what do you do?'

'I'm a topless dancer . . . Isn't Sixth Street great? Guys wanna play, girls wanna play, forget about tomorrow, be born tonight. Every day is a new day to love, a new day to live . . .

'You know, the cowboy thing rules in this town. There's a lot of macho stuff. I don't date cowboys. I'm a little left-wing for cowboys . . .

'You can make 300 to 500 dollars a night on Friday and Saturday, topless dancing, if you can take the mental strain. Course, if you have to have your boobs lifted, that's a 1000 dollars a boob.'

There must be some kind of way out of here . . . 'Must be going – sorry, what was your name?'

'Schizzi Mizzi, the Midnight Mermaid.'

Floyd heading for the door, ready for the next ride on this merry-go-round of madness.

☆

Toulouse on Sixth Street looks like a laundrette with its rows of cocktails turning over crushed ice in huge vats with round glass doors. My beautiful alcoholic laundrette.

'We mix them up in big tubs and pour them in through the top,' says the bartender, who looks like he plays for London Scottish, picking up hundredweights of ice under one arm. 'Are you from Australia or New Zealand?'

The cocktails have names like Chernobyl (vodka-based), Purple People Eater (made with Everclear – 190° proof grain alcohol), Love Potion No. 9, and – surprise, surprise – Mardi Gras.

I settle for a Nutty Irishman – Bailey's, vanilla liqueur and Frangelica.

'We do better business in frozen cocktails than anyone else in this city,' says the bartender.

'We're patterned on the bars in the French Quarter in New Orleans. We sell Cajun food from Louisiana twice a week . . .'

☆

Past McKlusky's Steak Bar where they bring out raw slabs of meat and shine torches on them for inspection before you eat, then ask everyone to cut them in unison when they're cooked, just to check them again. The beat goes on, and the *meat* goes on . . .

And so to Maggie Mae's where happy hour food is chicken wings, lasagne and quiche – as much as you can cram on one small plate for every drink. Does anybody in Austin ever go home?

'In Texas, I'm responsible for how drunk you get,' says the bartender. 'If I serve you too many drinks and you go out and kill someone, it's my fault.

'What would happen is that victim's family would take the bar to court for letting you get drunk. If you'd been in here for happy hour for three hours and I'd served you drink after drink, I would be responsible.'

Margarita Madness, Morality, Money and Litigation . . . the American Way?

☆

'Power Hour' (breakfast) in the glass atrium of the hotel, with the glass lifts whizzing up and down the walls. Today it reminds me of a pleasantly decorated grain silo.

'Good morning, sir, and what can I get for you this morning?'

'I'd like one egg over easy, two side orders of bacon – and hold the fruit salad, please. And some ketchup.'

'It's a pleasure, sir.'

Breakfast comes – prettily decorated with slices of melon and strawberries.

'Anything else I can get for you today, sir?'

'Some ketchup, please.'

A QUICK NOTE ON TEXAS FASHION

Last year horsehair trim for hats was in. This year it's plaited braid. Feathers are definitely out.

Black and white hats for women are in.

Shirts with 'regular buttons' are out – 'snaps' are in.

When showing your horse, an off-white hat is best, as it doesn't draw too much attention away from the horse.

Sorry, but this is Texas!

Longhorn Lady. Shelley of the Lariat 'B' Ranch.

*Churning out thousands of rings of sausage a day
at Kreuz's Barbecue, Lockhart.*

ON THE TRAIL OF THE LONESOME ROSE . . .

The Lonesome Rose stands in 8 acres close by an Indian burial ground, a wagon trail and several rattlesnake pits. The fragments of flint lying on the ground were once Indian arrowheads, and at night a pack of wild coyotes call . . .

Inside, in the designer kitchen, where I'm slicing scallops thinly to make a ceviche, followed by a stew with Texas beef and potatoes, Debbie, pretty in red – wearing a badge which says 'Never try to teach a cow to sing – it wastes your time and annoys the cow' – has just finished her guided tour of the soap-opera standard house she designed herself, in this 'estate' full of soap-opera standard houses. It should be worth a tidy fortune, but isn't.

'The market's gone here in Texas,' she says. 'A couple of houses have foreclosed here. They get auctioned off for half the value, and it sours the market for everyone.

'It was all greed. Everyone tried to get on the real estate bandwagon, while the getting was good. When they did good, it was great. They spent their money, they borrowed against everything they owned, then they bailed out and filed bankruptcy.

'I work in the real estate business, and my husband is manager of a restaurant, and we're just hanging on. We don't take vacations or go out to dinner much. We stay home and I cook, and have friends over. We're kinda laid back and take it easy now.

'During the boom everybody partied, the attitude was "There's no end to this money". But we'll never again see it like it was in the early eighties.'

FIRST MAKE YOUR TORTILLA

When Texans aren't barbecueing steak, they eat Mexican food, with its essential flavours of tomato, onion, garlic and hot pepper.

The first thing to know about Mexican food is that it all starts with the tortilla: either the corn tortilla, made from corn masa (a kind of dough) and water, originating from southern Mexico, or the less usual, and less typically Mexican, flour tortilla made with flour, shortening (fat), salt and water, from the north.

The dough is divided into balls and flattened to make little pancakes – rather like Chinese pancakes for Peking duck – and cooked on a griddle for the briefest of moments on either side.

Once you have your tortillas you can deep-fry them, to make nachos (crispy corn chips) for scooping up salsas (dips made from various combinations of peppers, onions, tomatoes and seasonings).

Or you can wrap them around a filling of chicken, beef, or chilli, to make tacos, or turn them into enchiladas by dipping them in chilli sauce before frying them and rolling them around the filling (rather like Italian cannelloni). Top them with cheese, put them in the oven so that the cheese melts, and serve them with salad, jalapeño chillies, radishes and sour cream, rice and black beans.

The next most important thing in Mexican cooking is the chilli pepper, or 'chile', as they spell it here. There are all kinds of different peppers, varying in size and intensity, but the most common are the poblano, a big chilli, the size of a bell pepper though narrower, which can be mild or hot (there's no way of telling until you bite into it); the jalapeño, little and hot; the serrano, which is even smaller and quite hot; and the cascabel, which is small and reddish-brown.

We're filming at Seis Salsa, a small, colourful restaurant, filled with cacti, where they favour the poblano. Bunches of them, dried by the sun, hang on the whitewashed walls, between the woven hangings.

'Chilli peppers are full of vitamins,' says Irene Montemayor, whose son, Luis, runs the restaurant with his American partner.

'Poor Mexican people, they raise their children with fresh tortillas, beans and chilli sauce, and you see those kids so healthy ...

'We make here chilli rellenos, with poblano peppers. Because some peppers are mild, and some are so hot you can hardly eat them, we grill them whole, rub off the skins, make a slit and take out the pips, then soak them in hot, salt water for 10 to 15 minutes.

'Then I cook some ground beef, add some raisins, pecans and cloves, fill the peppers with the mixture, pin them together with toothpicks, cover them with egg batter and grill them. This is chilli rellenos.

'Or we make another kind of rellenos – with cheese. We fry some onions, put them into the chillies, cover them with white cheese and sour cream and grill them the same way.'

In the kitchen two young girls make tortillas from 50 pounds of dough each morning – putting the little balls of corn dough between sheets of greaseproof paper and then into a press to flatten them. The flour dough is rolled by hand, because it would stretch if put in the press.

They also make gorditas, mini-tortillas, made with corn masa and shortening, which are topped with beans and cheese or chicken and garnished with peppers, tomatoes and jalapeños. Gorditas means 'little fat ones' – 'not for the weight conscious', says Irene.

Under Luis's brisk guidance I make chicken fajitas – sizzling strips of marinated chicken, served with poblano peppers, onions, spring onions and tortillas. Along with red snapper, it is a speciality.

'Then we have re-fried beans,' says Irene. 'We cook our beans in lots of water with bacon pieces, pork sausages, tomatoes, onion, garlic, salt, black pepper and coriander.

'When the beans are soft, and have soaked up the flavours, we take them out and mash them, then fry them in bacon fat. Real re-fried beans are fried twice, so that they become a little drier, but for health-conscious people we only fry them once.

'For parties we serve mole (pronounced molay) – made from seven different dried peppers, almonds, peanuts, sesame seeds, pumpkin seeds and a little piece of chocolate, ground together. (Traditionally you use an old Indian metate, a stone grinder made out of volcanic rock from the Piedras Negras, or black rocks – we have another, called a molcajete, like a mortar, for making sauces.) Then you boil it up in a big pot with chicken broth to make a sauce. Sometimes you add pieces of chicken, and you eat it with corn tortillas, rice and beans. And you drink cold Mexican beer.'

☆

Meanwhile, back on a midnight Sixth Street, which thinks it's in New Orleans, the pick-up trucks, the convertibles and the Chevies with their windows down, music playing, horns honking, are jammed bumper to bumper.

The bars are throbbing, and the happiest crowd of people you are ever likely to meet are doing that old Spanish thing of walking up and down, up and down, telling jokes, doing deals, in this charmingly vacuous city.

☆

CHAPTER SIX

The vineyards stretch for 330 acres – rolling hills with the vines standing stark like crosses on a field at Ypres.

Over the brow come two horses: a grey and a bay, their hooves the only sound on this misty soft California morning. On the bay is an elegant, blonde young woman dressed in pink coutured jeans. Her partner is dark and suave. An expert horseman.

They pull up gracefully in front of the camera. Joy smiles her brilliant smile. 'We'll see you at the house,' they say, and canter off . . .

☆

I think I must be in the Dordogne. An enormous table on the terrace is laden with the fruits of the vine and the land: wild quail, freshly caught salmon, a loin of lamb . . .

There are baby leeks and asparagus, garlic and sage . . . alongside fresh breads, a French fougasse, French sticks . . . There are fruits: kumquats, Meyer lemons (a cross between a tangerine and a lemon), and bowls of exquisite mushrooms: cinnamon caps, baby blue oysters, pom pom blanc and shiitake.

Then there are the cheeses: a big white double cream Jack, and a dark-skinned Vella Dried Jack – made in the same way, but soaked in cocoa and dried for seven or eight months, until it becomes like a Parmesan – crusty and delicious. There are goat's cheeses and a snappy Sonoma County cheddar.

Wild flowers and edible flowers decorate the table ... Forrest, the dark rider on the grey horse from the vineyards, pops the cork of the winery's sparkling wine ... the fields are green, the fruit trees are laden. This surely must be paradise.

Forrest says it's God's chosen corner.

'It's such a unique climate – right between the coolest grape-growing region and the much warmer region. It's coastal, so it can change very rapidly, thanks to our big air conditioner out there on the ocean.

'In summertime the grass is all straw gold, against the big green oak trees, because there is no rain.

'We talk about the bounty of Sonoma County – well, it's always had wonderful fruit and nut crops, but in the last ten years it has just blossomed: the cheeses, the mushrooms, the different vegetables. It has just exploded. It really is the Provence of America. And we're close to the ocean, so we have wonderful seafood ...

'It has become a food producers' Mecca. All the chefs from the Bay buy their food from here ... It's a little off the beaten track still, but we've already got four world-class restaurants opened up here – and there'll be more, based around the idea of great, natural ingredients.'

My enviable task is to select my ingredients from this wealth of fabulous produce, and conjure up a meal on the barbecue, in front of the cameras, worthy of my elegant hosts at the Iron Horse Vineyards – Barry and Audrey Sterling, their daughter Joy, and their partner, Forrest Tancer.

☆

Barry Sterling is an urbane, well-travelled man. An ex-lawyer, with a penchant for gracious living.

'I won't deny it. I was a very successful securities lawyer,' he says. 'I got out of law school at 22, and that was young, for an American. And I was fortunate in that I went back to Los Angeles – where I was born – and in those days it was wide open.

'In San Francisco in those days there was a more staid population. The same lawyers represented the same families and companies. I felt I'd be 65 before I became a partner.

'But Los Angeles was more freewheeling. If anything it was youth-conscious – perhaps because of the motion picture industry. The electronics industry was just starting and the oil industry was going on. I had some good clients and good business.

'But by the time I was 30 I decided I wanted to live in Europe. So I merged my law firm with another one on condition they opened offices in Paris and London.

'I guess we sort of dictated what we wanted to do, but it was a lot of luck, to be able to do that.

'It was a dramatic change for two Westerners finding themselves in an old-world style of life ... We acquired a big old nineteenth-century apartment in Paris – it came with three *caves* which could hold 5000 bottles of wine.

'I'd thought I was pretty big in wine in California because I had 150 bottles – all my friends thought so too! – but getting to Paris I realised that a nineteenth-century gentleman thought in terms of thousands of bottles.

'So I closed up two of the *caves*, and concentrated on filling one. My wife and I travelled through France, tasting and trying and buying. Making some mistakes and some good decisions. My wife studied French art and furniture and culture, and we became involved in food and entertaining. After all, food and wine and good living *is* French culture.

'At the same time, I was going back and forth to England and had a home and offices there, so it gave us another sense of the old world.

'The more we learnt about wine, the more interested we got, so we started looking for a property of our own – initially in France. We wanted an estate-bottled set-up.

'We almost bought a Cru Bourgeois in Bordeaux, but I realised I would have been stuck for the rest of my life never being able to be more than I had bought – there's no class society more established than the classification of wines, specifically in Bordeaux, and I would have been locked in it.

'So, instead, we returned to the United States and did it on our own home territory, where there are no limits. We have no history to tie us ... Because we have no rules that say: you have been classified 1, 2, 3, 4 or 5 or below that – and maybe because we don't know any better – we sail ahead, we keep trying, and as a result I think we are able to do some marvellous things here in California.

'We met Forrest – he was a San Franciscan, who had inherited 40 acres of vineyard over in the Alexander Valley, which is part of our operation. His mother was an American opera singer, a fabulous woman, who lived and sang in Europe, and that set the style of her home and her way of life. So Forrest also had a taste for European style. We hit it off straight away, and he became my head winemaker and partner.

'Joy, my daughter, was educated at Yale and worked as a news journalist and anchorwoman on TV. She covered the Olympics, political campaigns, the first space shuttle landings in California ... but we wanted one of our children to carry on the business, and she was ready for a change, so she became a partner too.

'I think of myself as an enlightened Californian. I'm a native-born Californian, so I have strong ties here, but I'm perfectly at home in England and in France, my children were educated there, and we still live three months of the year in France.

'We have a home on the ramparts of a fourteenth-century village. You can look out at the sea or up at the Alps. And we go off with our shopping bags and buy food in the *marchés* in Antibes or Cannes or Nice, and come back with our cheeses, breads and vegetables. Or we drive the four hours to Milan to the opera, or to see an art show in Florence, or into Barcelona.'

☆

'I was a child of the sixties, and I fell in love with the land,' says Forrest. 'I was a political science major, but to me this is the most creative thing there is. Every day I wake up and think, this is a really exciting thing we're doing. And that's not unique to myself – we all have that enthusiasm which begets commitment to a great product.

'Look at the place – it is fabulously beautiful. It needs to be protected and treasured, like the great vineyards of Bordeaux and Burgundy.

'It's a great challenge, and the potential of what we can do is only equal to our imagination.

'I spend 11 months of the year dreaming about the first day those grapes arrive at the winery. I know we are going to be better all the time and it's so exciting. We all have this common goal that there are still greater wines out there to be made.

'And the great advantage of being a family is that we tighten our belts a bit in those years we don't make that much. That is what farming is all about – and wine *is* agriculture. It's really all about going out there and watching those little grapes grow.'

☆

Martha, the housekeeper, is in the kitchen, making lunch for the crew: roasted chicken, shredded and tossed with Italian pasta, tender blanched asparagus, sautéed peppers and mushrooms, olive oil, Italian Balsamic vinegar, salt and pepper.

Forrest opens bottles of Chardonnay, Pinot Noir and Cabernets.

'You know, California has been producing quality wines since the nineteenth century – really wonderful wines – but many of them were not seen outside of the state or outside of America.

'Then, of course, the thing that slowed us down was Prohibition. The wine industry never really bounced back until the mid-sixties when there were a lot of new plantings.

'The boom was the seventies, the period of great expansion. Oilmen, doctors, businessmen, artists all started producing wine. And in a very short space of time we've gone from producing this rather interesting provincial wine to making wines that are judged on an international standard.

'People no longer say: "Well, they're from California." A great Californian Chardonnay is considered in the same light as a great Meursault.

'We don't really compare ourselves with Europe, though. Our style is California. We're dedicated to producing a style of wine which is really world class, but reflects this piece of dirt.

'But our technique is from wherever we grab it around the world – which is a very American thing.

'The idea is to make world-class wines. And that's what I think California does. We're no longer a curiosity.

'They called this vineyard Iron Horse because the man who bought it in 1940 built a mile and a half of railroad through it. And at one time it was a Palomino ranch. One of Roy Rogers' Triggers was raised and trained here – not the one that's stuffed!

'It isn't such a strange name. After all "Cheval Blanc" is "White Horse", and "Clos des Mouches" is "The House of the Flies".

'I think it's very catchy, and it symbolises there is some strength in the wines. The rampant horse has a lot of spirit – and that's the way I think of us in our approach to wine.

'We're very aggressive. We want to keep shooting for the stars!'

☆

The winery, built 11 years ago, is surrounded by palms and blossoms.

'Gardening is my hobby,' says Barry. 'I have about 10 acres of gardens around the house: orchards, blossom cutting gardens, lots of rhododendron areas, bearded iris, foxgloves . . .

'I don't believe in planting vines on the flat land, where the grapes sit in damp soils, so on the flat areas we grow vegetables commercially: French Charentais melons, French lettuces, French tomatoes, and American products like golden beets. We sell them to the luxury restaurants.

'In the Rhône and Alsace, you put the vines close to the ground where they can absorb the sunshine,' says Forrest. 'Here it is much steeper terrain and our climate is much warmer, so we want to get them up and have the air flow beneath them.'

The vineyards stretch below, with strips of mown grass in between – 'to control the soil'. If temperatures drop during the night, a sprinkler system sprays the vines with warm water to protect them from the frost.

'The Californian wine industry is very innovative and very future-thinking. A lot of the technology was developed between here, Australia and New Zealand and it's being exported throughout the world. A lot of it is going into France.

'We have a multinational team here: I have a young Frenchman from Champagne, an Australian, a second-generation Mexican . . .

'I think we're open to new technological changes as necessary, but I think our product is more natural than any other place in the world. The French still pour a lot of stuff in, but we don't use chemicals, we don't add sugar, there is minimum handling, minimum filtration.

'The Chardonnay is fermented in French oak barrels – personally I find American oak a bit too aggressive – and left *sur lie*, as you would find in Burgundy – as is our Sauvignon Blanc, which is very unusual, and not done in Europe.

'In the old days, Californian wines tended to be oak-aged to excess. Today they are oak-aged just enough to complement the essence of the fruit – what we are trying to do is capture the individual vineyard quality.

'We used to be faulted in California for making wines that were too heavy, that didn't have enough acidity. Now, I think we're making great wines. But we're not content. We feel very much that we're only seeing the tip of the iceberg in terms of what we can do.

'We're entirely estate bottled. For us it's an absolute commitment to making the best wines possible, and in order to do that we have to have total control over the fruit.

'There's no complacency here. No sense of: this is the tradition of what we've always done; this is the way it should always be. If you think that way, you've already been left in the dust.

'We don't have any traditions that limit us in what we can do, or what we should grow. It is strictly the quality of the wine that dictates what we do.

'We have the classic French grapes: Cabernet Sauvignon, Cabernet Franc ... but we also blend things strangely sometimes. There are a lot of us who think that in the future we will be making Cabernets with Sangiovese from Italy, because our climate is so much more similar to Tuscany than to Bordeaux.

'The wine will continue to evolve, but also, I think that if you line them all up together, from the Méthode Champenoise – which is drier than Champagne, but I believe has just as much flavour, delicacy and finesse – to the Cabernets, you'll find an over-riding theme that tells you it is Iron Horse.

'I think there is an amazing consistency which reflects the essential aims of my winemaking: to capture the fruit, to give a nice mouthful, but also have good acidity and a long finish.

'The only interest we have is making the greatest wine possible. In ten years we have gone to some amazing places ... I had the vision, but we've gone further than even I imagined. Now what we can do is make it better.'

'But when I talk about wine, I never sit there and say: "Well, we only use 214-gallon stainless steel tanks", or the pH was this, or the acidity was this ...

'We never lose sight of the fact that wine is a sensuous experience; always has been, always will be.

'The wonderful thing about it is that it attracts so many people from so many walks of life, from all over the world, from the arts, from politics.

'It's great when you get a letter from George Bush saying: loved a bottle of your Chardonnay, but couldn't get the label off – could you send one? It's a point of pride.

'It's a common bond of loving the vine and the food that comes off the land, and enjoying the chemistry that creates good conversation and good living ...'

☆

'Robert Louis Stevenson lived here and wrote about wine. The sheer beauty of the land has attracted writers and artists for hundreds of years,' says Joy, sipping sparkling wine in the light, gracious living room. 'We really do think of it as God's County. Everything grows here. It's phenomenal ...

'It's ironic. In the early seventies this kind of cool climate was considered ridiculous. Everybody wanted to be over in the Napa Valley, where it's hotter and they made those big, fruity wines. Even the so-called advisers said: "You'll never get anything to grow here ..."

'One of the things that is beautiful in this business is that on the one hand it is farming. It is good and honest and full of integrity, and on the other end of the spectrum it is very glamorous.

'We make an expensive product and our customers are the best restaurants and hotels in the world – and we frequent them!

'I put on some slinky silk dress and walk into the Savoy in London and say: "Here we are!" We can look as glamorous as any Count and Countess from Europe.

'What we do in our winemaking is we compete, not only with other Californian wines, but with the wines of the world, and it is very important for us to taste everone else's wines, and taste our own wines in the context of how they are served, to see how they stack up.

'Things are happening so fast in the Californian wine industry that if you are not on top of what is happening, you get left in the dust. Yesterday's tastemaker is yesterday's history.

'And it allows us to be in big cities and see fabulous art ... I was lucky in that from the time I was little I travelled all over the world. So I had a sense that the world was completely accessible – you can, and should, go to every corner of it.

'When my parents moved to France, that really opened the door for us to food and wine and gracious living. Say what you will, the French know how to live ...

'If I couldn't travel, it would be stifling for me. Being able to go to Paris and to London means that coming home, back to the land, is all the sweeter.'

☆

The ashes of the vine roots have died to the correct white embers on the barbecue. I thread kumquats, garlic cloves, sage and cinnamon cap mushrooms on to tiny skewers and marinate them in raspberry vinegar and olive oil, along with tender, primeur asparagus. I select some baby leeks, cut the lamb into scallops, dip them into the olive oil, and put them on to the barbecue . . .

'I love to cook with the utmost simplicity,' says Forrest, watching and approving my efforts. 'I'm a very impromptu sort of chef. I wander in the garden, see what's great, and we eat it. I love to pick fresh vegetables and make pasta primavera with wonderful, homemade, local pasta.

'One of our favourite dishes is free-range chicken, with fresh roasted potatoes from the garden and asparagus. Everything is grown and produced here or by our neighbours. We even make our own olive oil.

'The wonderful thing is we can grow everything from Mexican to Thai food here . . . If there's somebody out there who has decided they want to grow Japanese Daikon radishes, that's fine. Like the wine, there isn't anybody saying: OK – because this is Sonoma County, these are the things you have to grow.'

☆

'We're what we call casually formal in our dining here,' says Forrest. 'We call it Sonoma style. We're not coat and tie people, we're not dressy, but Audrey sets a fabulous table that would be as fitting in Paris as here.

'When we lived in Paris in the sixties,' remembers Barry, 'you entertained at home, so part of what you were doing all the time was making menus and matching the wines – a very serious business in France. This was Paris and it was tough.

'If we had a worry over what to serve with a particular dish, we'd even call up the major restaurants and discuss it with them – what do you think of this year, that year?

'You were really judged that way. Each dinner party was like a contest – especially if you were an American!

'One time I remember a very famous French gourmet and politician, a marvellous man, was a dinner guest, and afterwards he toasted my wife and said this was the best Parisian dinner party he had been to in years – and naturally it was given by an American!

'My wife felt that that was one of her finest moments.'

☆

Barry and Audrey's house, overlooking the vineyards, is nineteenth-century and filled with French antiques. 'It's what I call carpenter Gothic. Very old for California,' jokes Barry.

'During harvest time we have about 50 or 60 people a day for lunch.

'A great deal of our life is dedicated to making and tasting wine, but at the same time we realise that it is a fun subject. Food and wine shouldn't become so serious that it is a bore. They are pleasures, something people can relax and enjoy.

'We're not inventing a cure for some disease, there's not a Nobel prize for making wine.'

'If there was, you'd get it,' says Joy. 'You know, when you look at Iron Horse, you don't create a place like this unless you want to share it. We are part of the hospitality community: food and wine and the land. It's not just the wine. It's wine in a context.

'You know,' she says, 'you always have a home here in California, here at Iron Horse.

'There's nothing phoney about anything here. It's complimentary when people say it's like the Dordogne. We're not touchy about it. We love France too. But then we want to say: hang on, this is *us*. This is America, and I wouldn't live permanently anywhere else. I'm Californian through and through.'

☆

The Meyer lemons make an exquisite sauce, whisked with eggs and butter, for my scallops of lamb. It is possibly the best egg liaison sauce I have ever made.

The brochettes of mushrooms, kumquats, garlic and herbs are ready; so are my primeur leeks and asparagus. I decorate the plate with edible flowers and serve this wonderful spring meal to Forrest on a table set up with white cloths and silver in the flower-filled meadow below the balcony.

'Isn't this one of the most beautiful places on earth?' says Forrest. 'Let's raise our glasses and say: this is what it's all about – good food and good wine. Let's preserve it. We need a little bit of calmness and tranquillity in the world, and a glass of this wine and this wonderful, fresh food can help to create that ... a good glass of wine, to me, has always been the bond of friendship.

'You know, our sparkling wine was served at both summit meetings between Reagan and Gorbachev – and I can't think of a greater thing. A toast to world peace, and they're toasting it with our wine!

'It gives you goose bumps.'

☆

Anything Gorby and Reagan can do…toasting international relations with Forrest Tancer, at Iron House Vineyard.

Sonoma County Bounty.

CHAPTER SEVEN

The Washington Square Bar & Grill

Tony Bennett left his heart in San Francisco. I left mine in the Washington Square Bar & Grill. Where the solid mahogany bar, with its brass rail and mirror, and rows of shining bottles, like candles at an altar, beckon. Where the corned beef hash is the best in the whole world – real beef brisket marinated for days, cooked for hours and mixed with potatoes, onions, fresh dill and mustard. And where Ed Moose, a big, handsome man in Jermyn Street braces, looking like Cary Grant, but reminding me of Jack Lemmon in *The Front Page*, tells long, long Hemingwayesque tales of Prohibition and American journalism in the days when men were men and men drank bourbon.

'If I didn't own this place, I'd be happy to come here. It's a pretty honest place,' says Ed. 'Phoneys don't do well here. Somebody like that – I'm not going to give them the time of day. I'm probably gonna treat 'em like a dog.

'We have a strong base of newspaper men here. I used to be a sports journalist. I know a lot of people in the business: players and announcers, and a lot of them come in here. I like them. That guy over there, wearing the earphones, he's a broadcaster, actor, writer. Mr Renaissance.

'I like actors, I like writers, I like sportsmen, generally speaking. We get some heavyweights in here too – judges, politicians ... These people all do business together. At least, they used to.

'That guy who just walked in – he's a judge: a funny, funny guy. The old guy with him served time for murder, during Prohibition. The judge got him off – he said he may have killed *somebody*, but he didn't kill *that* guy.

'San Francisco has a rich history of newspaper people. It used to be a very good newspaper town – it's not any more.'

On the wall are framed photographs of some of the city's famous newspaper men, like Damon Runyan and Herb Caen, who wrote *Baghdad-by-the-Bay* – 'an unabashed love letter to San Francisco'.

There is Prescott Sullivan – or 'Sully' – 'rarely seen without his battered hat and unlit cigar clenched between his teeth', says the pen portrait underneath. A guy with a 'satirical bite and gentle humour, reminiscent of Mark Twain ... he could dismantle any overly serious situation with his deft comic touch'.

Then there is Tad Dorgan – whenever you use the words 'baloney', 'bonehead', 'speakeasy', or phrases like 'chew the fat', 'putting on the Ritz' or 'as busy as a one-armed paper hanger with the hives!' says *his* pen portrait, you're talking 'Tad'.

'You know, there was an excitement around those guys,' says Ed.

'The new breed of sportswriters are more interested in a psychosexual analysis of somebody than talking about what happens. They fairly all come in with college degrees, they feel very knowledgeable, they're serious. They may come in and have a glass of white wine but I know the kind of guys who can sit down and write a really literate 800-word column after having five or six martinis. That takes practice!

'The fun of sport eludes a lot of these new guys. And sport now has become very serious, because the money is so incredible. Much as I love baseball I have a hard time relating to it when I see some guy making 2 million dollars standing around not doing very much.

'And professional football with all the paraphernalia associated with it, the TV, the eight-minute commercial breaks ... I can't relate to that. It's a very money-oriented, TV-oriented phenomenon. Only a part of it has to do with sport.

'I agree with Mary McGrory, the writer, who said: "Baseball is what we *were* – football is what we've *become*."

'The other big professional sport is basketball. The average player this year is making 600 000 dollars. The difference seems to be in basketball you're dealing with a different kind of guy – they're very exuberant, practically all black, and they have a lot of spirit. They play with great abandon, they're all out to have fun ...'

☆

It's Sunday brunch in the Washington Square Bar & Grill. Later there will be jazz, spilling gaiety onto the sunshine streets of North Beach, where the Italians settled in the gold rush of 1848.

Dennis O'Connor, the bartender, is mixing his famous martinis – 'the most civilised drink in the world'. The corned beef hash arrives – an oval patty, half an inch thick, fried on both sides so that it is crisp and burnt just enough – with poached eggs and hash browns. And there is ketchup on the table.

On weekdays the menu is a mix of Italian and American: fettuccine or New York Strip steak sandwich.

'I was stationed in Rome when I was in the army, and when I worked for the Associated Press I was there for the Olympics,' says Ed. 'That's when I got to really understand what Italian food was all about.

'I was always fairly interested in the bar side – my neighbourhood was a place where a lot of people made liquor during the Prohibition. My father made beer and sold it illegally. One guy made whisky, another made gin.

'This was a Prohibition-type place. All stuccoed over. Nobody could see in or out.

'Prohibition was an integral part of America, and an integral part of my life – I know a lot of people, especially women, became heavy, heavy drinkers because of Prohibition, and that heavy boozing idea was a part of American culture right up to the sixties. It affected people's lives. A lot.

'It's all changing very fast. Places like this are, in a sense, obsolete. We're an anachronism in a sense – but there are a lot of people still looking for a place like this, who don't like the new scene. There are still people who like to drink.

'And women feel they can come in here on their own and not be hassled. The women who come here are usually people who know something, they've been somewhere and they do something. Intelligent women don't want to go to a singles bar. A woman can come in here and the odds of her finding an interesting man are three times greater than if she went to a singles bar. It's old-fashioned. If you like somebody, you talk; if you don't, forget it.

'If I was a woman, I'd come to a joint like this. Women like to be around real men.

'My definition of a real man? Well, somebody who isn't a flake. Whatever his limitations, however screwed-up he may be, he's probably honest. You're not dealing with a phoney. Or if you're dealing with a phoney, he's probably such a blatant phoney that he's funny.

'If you don't know the difference then you have a problem, but I would think that any smart woman can tell a real, flat-out phoney.'

FREAKING OUT IN SAN FRANCISCO

'California is really a hotch-potch, a pot-pourri. It's very rootless. Things happen very fast here,' says the cab driver.

'San Francisco is a town of polarities and excesses. It's always had a history of having weird groups: beatniks, hippies, gays, an endless stream.

'It's not quite so gay as it was. At one time it was roaring. Now everything is much more subdued. Unfortunately it took AIDS to do it.

'There's a whole subculture of hippies still here, though. They're a little mature now, but they're here . . .'

Driving up and down San Francisco's movie-carchase hills, pulling up at the hotel after the flight from Albuquerque on a plane which had seats facing backwards and peanuts called Lovebites. The steward quipped: 'If the air pressure drops, pull on the air supply masks and secure with a Gucci headband. Kick off your shoes – if the person next to you can stand it – and if you have any problems, ask the blonde, we're breaking her in.'

Flying over the desert with trails criss-crossing like lines on the palm of a hand, and rocky outcrops standing up like welts. Over the Grand Canyon and into San Francisco, with J.J. landing the plane, eyes closed, hands outstretched.

'You know, I landed it. I really landed it. I could feel the power. I was right there on the tail,' says J.J.

'It was better than when I got us down in Albuquerque – then I was so busy keeping the wings steady, I forgot about the runway!'

☆

The Peabody ducks would have had nothing on me in San Francisco where I had my very own glass duck palace, 9 miles high on the top floor of the hotel, looking down over an almost 360-degree sweep of the city.

J.J. is mixing margaritas behind the bar, the Rolling Stones are on the stereo, the room is filling up.

'Hey, Floyd, when I was driving along, coming to collect you today, a man jumped out right in front of me,' says J.J.

'I pulled up because I was kinda shocked and his friend said to me: "Oh, he does that all the time. He's a professional accident victim."'

'And then ... I met a man in the supermarket who asked me out to dinner!'

'That's OK. People do that here,' says a lady in red. 'I went to Atlanta with a guy I met in the supermarket the other day. I met him at the strawberries and by the time we got to the lettuce I said OK.

'The only reason I answered him was because he had a whole bunch of artichokes and celery in his trolley. Nice clothes, good vegetables ...'

'The checkout guy was having a gas,' says J.J. 'He said to me: "People have gotten married in this checkout alley ..."'

'Hey, there was an earth tremor this morning, did anybody feel it?' says somebody.

The tall lady with tumbling dark hair refuses a drink. 'I'll come straight with you guys. I'm celebrating my fifth birthday.'

'You look a little older than that ...'

'I've been off the booze for the last five years, and out of the cocaine. I've been reborn ...'

It's the seven-minute syndrome again: American women, from a standing start, revealing their hopes, their fears and the price of their boob implants in seven minutes.

'A friend of mine got a bad shock the other night. He met this girl in the bar, and on the way home in the taxi she turned out to be a man,' says the lady in red.

'Hi, I hope you don't mind,' says a woman no one has ever seen before, 'but we came by telescope ...'

I turn up the Stones on the stereo: '19th Nervous Breakdown'.

JEREMIAH TOWER

Stars Restaurant is big and light, urbane and cheerful, with a serious, mirrored bar down one side, selling a fine selection of 38 malt whiskies, as many beers from around the world – including draught Guinness – and cocktails with names like Cary Grant, Jeremiah's 747, Spruce Goose and Mark's Silk Pyjamas.

On today's menu the appetisers include oysters on the half shell with shallot and black pepper sauce, fresh pasta with salmon gravlax, roast red beets and dill cream. There is also an avocado and Belgian endive salad with lobster vinaigrette and grapefruit; and a clear fish soup with prawn won ton, ginger, garlic and tree oyster mushrooms. The main courses include roast salmon with red pepper, 'mash' potatoes, buttered spinach, turnips and sage hollandaise; and grilled fillet of beef with caramelised onions, Swiss chard, bacon and grilled potato brochette.

At the head of the menu, Chef Jeremiah Tower suggests: 'Tonight, why not enjoy a martini with the rarest and finest vodka from Russia, Stolichnaya Cristall?' Why not, indeed?

Tomorow's lunch card, still being finalised, suggests a glass of Bollinger champagne with appetisers such as steamed mussels with Chinese black bean sauce, followed by a dish like fresh pasta with spit-roast suckling pig, garden vegetables and herbs.

But being an egalitarian sort of establishment, there are also half-pound hamburgers with tomatoes, red onions and fries; chicken tacos with marinated red onions and tomatillo salsa; and the Stars' hot dog with sauerkraut, mustard and coleslaw.

Jeremiah Tower is a sophisticated, well-travelled man, who looks like a young Lord Lichfield. He was educated in England, studied architecture at Harvard, and is being fêted as one of San Francisco's brightest and most innovative chefs.

'I love the complexity of cooking. It's like being the director of an operatic production. The curtain goes up twice a day. It's all-consuming, demanding, dangerous, and when it's working, it's wonderful,' he says.

'Every day I get butterflies – that feeling that this is going to be the night it's not going to work, but when it does, it is the greatest feeling in the world. When you have 200 people in the restaurant, happy, with smiles on their faces, it has to be the same feeling as performing an opera in front of an audience all on their feet.'

These days, San Francisco hostesses court him as a dinner party guest, he stays at the Savoy when he's in London and the Ritz in Paris, but ten years ago he had 10 bucks in his pocket and was headed for Hawaii – 'I figured if you're gonna sleep on the streets, you might as well be in Hawaii!'

'When I'd got out of Harvard I went back to England as fast as I could. I worked for quite a famous wine company in London, then the managing director told me: this is a family firm and you won't get anywhere. This is England.

'So I started work as an apprentice for a firm of architects. I was so poor that I lived in a rooming house in Epsom, full of jockeys. It was winter, and the only heating was from the stove, and I slept in my overcoat.

'I'd saved about £50 and then I had to go to the dentist. The bill was £50 and I saw the handwriting on the wall. I came back to America and went to Harvard for another four years, in architecture school.

'Then I tried to be an architect, but I was just as poor as when I was in England and didn't know what I was.

'So I was headed for Hawaii, and someone said: there's this chef's job going in Berkeley. It was a little café I'd been to once or twice, called Chez Panisse, and I thought: I can do anything if I've only got 10 bucks in my pocket!

'I used to do dinner parties every Saturday night when I was in college, for amusement – if you can cook well in college, it's amazing how many friends you've got! So I'd been cooking a lot – but only for eight people!

'They asked me to do something with the soup. I put in a little white wine, salt and cream and they said I was wonderful! So I was a chef the first day. It couldn't have happened anywhere else in the world, except in 1972 in Berkeley, California, United States of America. They didn't know any better, and neither did I.

'I had one assistant. I did all the shopping in the morning, then I cooked lunch by myself – the dish washer would do the potatoes.

'The menu changed every day. My total inspiration in those days was Elizabeth David: *French Provincial Cooking*, because it was a sort of regional French country restaurant. And I started doing "regions of France" – special dinners every month.

'The restaurant became internationally famous within three or four years. I sold my interest to the others in 1978 (none of us had any money, so we had just declared ourselves equal partners).

'I tried doing cooking schools, couldn't make a living. Then I moved to England to do *The Good Cook* series with Richard Olney in London. I was the hands in the pictures in *The Good Cook* series for the first eight or nine books.

'Then I came back to America, did the Balboa Café in San Francisco, and then the Santa Fe Bar and Grill, which started the bar and grill craze.

'Four and a half years ago I sold that and started Stars. Now I have a new restaurant called Speedo 690, which is just starting in an old Speedo Carburetta building a block away: brick and exposed metal trusses.

'It's going to be the kind of food you always wanted at every tropical beach bar you ever went to in Mexico, Florida and Hawaii but never got: simple, grilled fish, very direct food. Spicy – but not very much – lots of lime juice, some Indian spices, some Thai spices, some Chinese techniques, but no identifiable dishes you know now. It's a mix we're developing.

'My philosophy on food is something I learned from Elizabeth David and Richard Olney. I believe totally in market place cuisine, which means more to a restaurateur than a housewife who goes shopping every day – or an American housewife who goes shopping every month!

'I believe that you don't go to the market place or the purveyors with a preconceived idea. You go and buy whatever is seasonal, best, freshest and ripest, come back and *then* figure out what you are going to do, rather than thinking: I'm a serious restaurateur, therefore I have to have Dover sole on the menu – I'm 8000 miles from the source of Dover sole, but I'll serve it, whatever happens.

'I say: absolute rubbish. You go down to the fishmonger's and pick up whatever is wonderful for the day. It's a major philosophical difference.

'The lunch menu here changes every day, except for the hamburgers; and the dinner menu changes every day, except that we always have a green salad.

'The menu isn't really fixed until about 4.30 p.m. It varies all day long depending on what comes in. I send things back, and drive the word-processor mad. But that's the way things are around here – totally flexible.

'I cook off the cuff and from the heart, but using principles that never vary. You buy the best possible ingredients and treat them as simply as possible – "simply" being a very complex word. When something looks totally effortless, it usually means it is very hard work.

'The ingredients should present themselves, and stand up for what they are. They should taste like what they are ... and then there should be a little flair and a little sex!'

☆

Into the kitchen for a breakfast glass of champagne – Fats Waller's liquid ham and eggs. We cook two kinds of prawns – Hawaiian Blue and Pink Santa Barbara Spots – sautée them in garlic, deglaze the pan with white wine, then serve the prawns with a sour cream and saffron sauce, garnished with broad beans and artichokes.

'Six years ago at a society dinner in San Francisco, they'd say: "Oh my God, he's a cook. What's he doing here?"' says Jeremiah. 'Some of my cooks were practically disowned by their parents.

'A lot of my waiters come from Eton. They're the best waiters I've ever seen. They're spectacular. The education system can be so wonderful and severe in England, they get awfully grown-up and they can coast for ever.

'But I think the English tend to peak a bit at 18, so I was glad to come back to America and get another jolt.

'I was a student here in the sixties, but everyone made fun of me because I was very aloof from all the rioting and teargas in the second half.

'I mean, there we were in Washington at the house of my best friend, whose father was with the FBI – staying in this huge mansion in Chevy Chase, going down to the riots and getting teargassed, coming back and having the maids take our coats at the back door, sending us up to showers and laying our clothes out on the bed.

'Then we'd go down to watch the news with his parents and their CIA and FBI friends, and watch us being teargassed on TV!

'I thought: this is the most decadent rubbish I've ever been through! I was very amused by it. I had a very European perspective on it.

'But they made so much fun of me that two years later, when the strike hit Harvard, I committed my only revolutionary act.

'I was in graduate school by this time – 29 years old, or so – and I gave a dinner party and we drank Dom Perignon and I filled up two of the bottles with gasoline and put a wick in them, and carried them in my shopping bag – probably a Bergdorf Goodman shopping bag! – over to the architecture building which was totally closed down.

'The whole inner campus was closed and surrounded by police. The students had burned a couple of buildings. It was pretty severe.

'I threw the first Molotov cocktail at the building, it bounced off it, across the lawn, hit the street, rolled down the gutter and disappeared down into the sewer, without anything happening.

'I left the other bottle in my shopping bag and that was the end of my revolution.

'These days my lifestyle is all about work. I live very modestly, except when I'm travelling. I rarely get away, but when I do, I'm incredibly extravagant with hotels. I've been doing my bit for everybody for so long that I want to go right to luxury and perfect service. That's why I go to the Savoy. They see me as demanding, but the Savoy loves that. They know exactly what to do about it.

'I have a room overlooking the river. In seconds I'm in the shower, and the champagne and smoked salmon sandwiches arrive.

'I dream about coming back to England and having perfectly cooked grouse or pheasant or woodcock. Smoked salmon, game birds, truffles, heavy linen sheets upstairs – and someone to share them with! That's my idea of heaven!'

☆

When the shadow of the grasshopper
Falls across the tail of the fieldmouse
On green slimy grass
And a red sun rises
Above the western horizon
Silhouetting a young and tautly muscled Indian
    warrior
Perched with a bow and arrow
Cocked and aimed straight at you . . .
Then it's time for another martini.

A wall, San Francisco

HIPPIES AND YUPPIES

The cab driver wore a flowered shirt, sunglasses and a pony tail.

'You want somewhere to eat? Try Hamburger Mary's – it's a great, great restaurant that started out about 15 years ago as a gay hippy place, and it gradually became known for good, wholesome food. They made their own bread, used all natural ingredients. Then it became a somewhat trendy place to go for Sunday brunch – you'd see families there, little old ladies ...

'Or go to Pasand, it's an Indian restaurant – part of a chain, but the other two have traditional sitar music. This guy hates Indian music – loves Indian food, but hates the music, so he has live jazz.

'Whoah child! [as we swerve] Another one of our drug-ridden, alcohol-ridden or just plain ill, homeless street people just fell off the sidewalk ...

'In California there was a policy about ten years ago, when Ronald Reagan was governor, of putting all the ambulatory mental patients out of the state hospitals and onto the streets.

'Various economic policies over the last eight years have put people out on the streets, with no way to get a home, and without a home and any stability it's hard to get a job.

'You have a serious drug problem in this country, and a lot of those people are on the streets. And, of course, in the last five years we've had the AIDS epidemic, which has put many people out on the streets, somewhat mentally deranged at times, because of the disease.

'Another significant portion of the homeless are veterans from the Vietnam war, who never recovered from their combat stress. Because of the horrors they experienced, they were just not able to stabilise their lives, hold down a job.

'There are probably more of them here, because we have a fairly liberal and caring government and population, and if you had a choice of being homeless and on the streets in this weather or in a place that was blistering hot in the summer and freezing cold in the winter, where would you hang out?'

Driving through Haight Ashbury, where the hippies were famous in the sixties and the shops on Haight Street still look like Portobello Road and Kensington Market used to.

'The hippy thing is competing fiercely with the uptight, rigid, materialistic yuppie,' says the cab driver. 'Twenty years ago the Haight Ashbury district was the home of the hippies, but in the last five to ten years, it has become increasingly upscale.

'The yuppies have gone into that area and bought the homes and put a lot of money into them, formed neighbourhood associations to improve the ambience of the neighbourhood, as it were.

'So you have the diehard hippies and the liberals, and the caring people in the neighbourhood who support the right of people to look and be the way they want – vying with the conservative upscales who don't want *those* elements in *their* area, because they don't want to subject *their* children to *that* type of environment . . . You can obviously tell where my sympathies lie!

'Recently we had a group of people in an organisation called Food Not Bombs – with a somewhat political, anti-war stance – saying that instead of spending billions of dollars for the Contras in Nicaragua and atomic weapons and B1 bombers, which cost millions of dollars apiece, why not take all that money and use it to feed and clothe and care for the homeless in this country? An absolutely stupid concept, you must agree! Why should we take care of the people in our country, when we can build bombers instead?

'So they were there giving out free food in the Golden Gate Park at the end of Haight Ashbury, and the neighbourhood association people really protested against this element gathering at the entrance to *their* park, where they wanted to take *their* children in designer toddlers' togs.

'So they got the police to go in and roust them up, because they didn't have a permit to give away free food . . .'

We pull up outside Hamburger Mary's Organic Grill.

FISHERMAN'S WHARF

Fisherman's Wharf looks like Weston-super-Mare on Bank Holiday Monday – except that its stalls are selling oysters, deep-fried shrimp and calamari, crab in sourdough rolls, and little bowls of hot clam chowder. But below the window of Alioto's Sicilian Fish Restaurant, looking away from the wharf, there are fat seals basking on a pontoon in the bay, with the Golden Gate Bridge behind; and as you squint up at the tiered flat-roofed houses you could be in the Middle East.

The Mexican chef, Juan Caravez, is cooking salmon Sicilian style, marinated in a sauce made from vinegar, onions, white wine and sugar, then baked.

Halibut – coated with breadcrumbs, cheese, garlic and spices – is baked for five minutes only and served with beurre blanc sauce: butter, shallots, white wine and vinegar.

There are mussels, shrimp, and calamari stuffed with crab and served with rigatoni.

Scampi is tossed in flour, fried in hot olive oil until it is browned but only half cooked, then finished in a sauce of butter, garlic, white wine, lemon juice and parsley – with an extra knob of butter added to make it rich and shiny.

A fillet of sole is served with pasta cooked *al dente*, and tossed in a sauce of olive oil, garlic, onions, fennel leaves, white raisins, tomatoes and pine nuts, sprinkled with toasted breadcrumbs.

A whole sole is broiled (grilled) with a lemon butter sauce, made with shallots, butter, lemon juice, white wine and white wine vinegar, reduced and cooked over a very low heat. Juan adds another knob of butter, seasons it, and puts in some chunks of fresh tomato, capers, fresh basil and bay leaf, then pours it over the fish.

Poached salmon is served in lemon butter sauce, too, but this time with salmon roe added at the last moment. Fresh roe and chives are arranged as a garnish.

My task is to make a crab cioppino – a kind of fish stew with tomato sauce, onions and carrots, cayenne pepper, parsley and thyme.

The Aliotos have been here for 60 years, since Giuseppe Alioto came over to America and sent for his six brothers to follow him. The current owner, Nunzio, is fourth generation. 'Myself and my cousin run the restaurant, but there are 16 of the family involved in the business,' he says.

'We really zero in on the regional cooking of Sicily, which is peasanty, very flavourful and spicy. Most of the recipes come from my grandmother and the old country.

'What happened in this city was people would say: let's open up an Italian restaurant and serve prosciutto and melon and tortellini and spaghetti with tomato sauce. But now specific, regional cooking is the in thing.

'We are even bringing over some chefs from a restaurant in Sicily, a two-star Michelin restaurant, because we have come as far as we can with what we learnt as children and from the family. Now they are going to teach us what they are doing there now.

'People in San Francisco are very fussy about their food because here they can have food from every country in the world. It is like a mini New York in that sense, but a bit cheaper. I think the standard of food is as high, if not higher – so everything you do has to be very good.

'In terms of food, San Franciscans are very spoilt.'

BACK IN THE CAB

They call this town Baghdad-by-the-Sea,' says the cab driver, heading past the Fairmont Hotel where limos pull up and the glass lift creeps up the outside wall to the roof restaurant, whisking well-heeled guests to cocktails by candlelight and dinner with a view.

'There was an earth tremor yesterday – you feel it? This is earthquake weather. I can't remember when it was so hot and humid . . .

'So where are you guys headed? Have you been to Rockin' Robin's on Haight yet? It's a fifties bar, where they have fifties shoes on the wall, and newspaper cuttings about American football and cars coming through the walls – a '56 Chevy, a '58 Buick . . . and it's all fifties and sixties music.

'What *is* wrong with this car? You know, they pair you up with a day driver. So they pair me up with Rasputin. The guy's a maniac. This'll be the third car the guy's messed up. Course, he weighs 280 pounds. He's insane. He's your basic 'Nam vet in a hunting jacket.

'By day I work at a bookstore. Sci-fi and fantasy. I just sit and read and occasionally sell a book. I'd like to be a writer, so I figure if I'm around books it might rub off.

'I'm gonna cut down this fare a little 'cos due to construction we're kinda goin' around the long way . . .

'You know, my wife's British. Scottish actually. She makes, like, bubble and squeak – fried cabbage or something? . . .'

Pulling up outside the San Francisco Brewing Company, with its pumps which look like enormous polished pepper mills, and its four real beers, brewed on the premises: Serpent Stout, Albatross Lager, Emperor Norton Lager, and a bitter which they call Pale Ale.

The owner, Allan Paul, used to brew lager in 5-gallon batches in his apartment on Telegraph Hill; then his friends persuaded him to do it for a living. So when the laws changed to allow brewers to sell their beer on their own premises, he raised 400 000 dollars and opened this place.

The Heath Robinson fan system is cooling overhead.

Outside on the streets of San Francisco the beautiful people of the eighties are coming out to play.

CHINATOWN

'Back in the late sixties, early seventies, we had a very terrible time with gang wars. Restaurants and shops closed as soon as it was dark. Now things are safer, and they're starting to open late again,' says Shirley Fong-Torres, fluttering like a brightly coloured butterfly through the bustling streets of Chinatown, flitting from cookie factory to tea emporium to dim sum palace, explaining, joking, greeting friends – half in Chinese, half in English – without drawing breath.

Past the take-away shops, like the best French delicatessens, laden with noodles, roasted ducks, and steamed salt chicken in re-chauffing dishes.

'A lot of the people here live in flats with six people sharing a common kitchen, so sometimes it's easier for them to come down here and buy precooked meat and then maybe steam some fresh vegetables, which is easy to do,' says Shirley.

Whole, huge, crispy-roasted pigs hang dripping over counters; there are ribs, tripe, tanks full of eel and carp ...; black 'thousand-year-old eggs' preserved in salt, lime and ashes; sesame balls – sticky and chewy, with sweet bean paste or fruit inside; and tamales – sticky rice, chicken, pork and shrimp wrapped in bamboo or lotus leaves and steamed so that the aroma permeates the rice.

Dim sum at the new Asia Restaurant is truly wonderful: fun rolls with chicken, shrimp bonnets and potstickers (little boiled dumplings filled with pork, cabbage, green onion, ginger and garlic); followed by almond bean pudding and steamed milk and egg cake. All piled high on trolleys driven by waitresses, weaving through the tables in one enormous room.

'Jeremiah was a bullfrog...' Sorry, chef! Cooking with Jeremiah Tower at Stars Restaurant, San Francisco.

'For God's sake Floyd, there's nothing to it! Look, you direct. I'll cook!'
David Pritchard rustling up a Clam Chowder by the Bay of San Francisco.

Outside, the Captain of the Central Police District has brought his team of Lion Dancers in our honour. The traffic stops, firecrackers chatter like machine-gun fire, the 'lion' with its 12-foot tail – dancers hidden inside – starts to move to Chinese music.

'The Lion Dance is very traditional. It scares away evil spirits,' says Captain Cairns. 'You use it when you open a new business, or a new house, at weddings ... The officers train twice a week for three hours, in their own time. It's a lot of work, but we've drawn ourselves closer to the community by doing this. We led the New Year's Parade, which was shown live throughout the United States. That was a great honour.

'The team is mostly Chinese with a few Caucasians. It's good public relations. This is a very busy area to police, but we have a low crime rate here in Chinatown. We keep it pretty much in control. The gangs have been pretty much subdued.

'Look – you'll see the lion waking up, the eyes will open, the ears will flutter. He'll start to stand up and lick his paws and dance. He'll 'eat' lettuce and spit it out. If you get hit by the lettuce, it's good luck ...'

In a herbalist's shop, with drawers and tubs full of gnarled and twisted roots, tree bark, ground shells, seeds and herbs, a Chinese doctor diagnoses problems behind screens, then mixes up a bag of roots and herbs, figuring out the cost on an abacus.

'You put the roots into a pot with water, reduce it, then drink it,' says Shirley. 'We believe in boiling the vitamins and proteins out of everything possible.

'Over there is shark's fin – a very exotic food item. It can cost up to 100 dollars a pound, or more. We use it for soup for exotic and important occasions, like weddings or birthdays, not just because we believe it is a healthy food, but because the colour is gold. And gold is a lucky colour for the Chinese people. It symbolises money.

'We Chinese are very superstitious. Numbers are very important and eight is the luckiest number in the Chinese culture, because it is never-ending. I was married on the eighth of the eighth, eighty-eight!'

☆

Through a doorway sheets of rice pasta, like shiny plastic, are being folded; through another a girl sits folding fortunes – processed on a computer far away – into fortune cookies, as the little circular pancakes made from flour, sesame, vanilla, eggs and sugar come round on a circular machine.

☆

A tea ceremony is being performed in a shop crammed with over 100 teas – three or four different grades for each kind of tea. 'As the quality goes up, so does the price, just like a good bottle of wine, or a good caviar,' says Shirley. 'It all depends on when the leaves are picked, and where. The most expensive is the King's Tea – a mixture of the best Oolong and Ginseng for 105 dollars a pound.

'I drink Ginseng tea – it gives me more energy. Some people say too much energy!

'We have tea ceremonies for special occasions. Like when a Chinese girl gets married. Afterwards she attends a tea ceremony at her mother-in-law's house and with each cup of tea she serves to a female relative, she gets in return jade, gold . . .

'Also it's a time when we get together, just to share each other's company.

'First you must approve the tea leaves. We always use a high-grade tea. Nothing cheap for our friends. If it wasn't good tea, it would be insulting.

'Then we pour hot water to clean the leaves. You must smell and approve them again. Then the cups are heated so that when you touch them they are not cold to your fingers, and when you drink there is no contrast between hot and cold.

'Tea is never served out of the teapot. The pot is only used for brewing. The tea pitcher is used for serving tea – that is so every cup is even in temperature and strength.

'We are not going to drink the tea yet. First you smell it again. Next I must propose a toast,' she says, raising her cup.

'I want to welcome you to America and tell you that I am so happy and honoured to be a part of the BBC.'

GOODBYE TO WASHINGTON SQUARE

In the Washington Square Bar & Grill Dennis O'Connor is mixing Picon Punch – Amer Picon liqueur in an Irish coffee glass over ice, topped up with soda, a float of Californian brandy and a twist of lemon.

'You can still get a march any time you want in this city,' he's saying. 'Any kind of cause you want, you can get 2000 people saying: let's go march. God bless 'em – just don't bug me! Hey, Mike, you wanna take this call? [hand cupped over phone] Somebody called Doreen – is she an ex-girlfriend? Do you owe her money?

'Here, try the Picon Punch. It looks harmless, tastes harmless. You can have four or five and from the waist up you can think, move and talk. But when you get up off that bar stool, you think you're paralysed!'

Ed Moose strolls in, jacket slung over his shoulder, happy from swapping stories and celebrating newspaper man Herb Caen's birthday, talking about plans for playing a softball game in Moscow with a KGB guy who came in here to eat.

'You know, there aren't too many good bars left in this city,' says Ed. 'People don't hang out in smoke-filled bars like they used to. There's been a whole revolution about health and drinking. People are worried about their jobs, so they go to work early ... what the hell's going on?

'You go into some of them and you see a bunch of really well-dressed, good-looking 6 foot 3 inch graduates watching basketball games on TV like it was the most important thing in the world ... Well, that's nice, but they don't know how to talk!

'That's not a great bar. You know, you really have to do some research now to find a great bar.'

Here's to the quest for knowledge, Ed!

CHAPTER EIGHT

EASTER IN SANTA FE

The sun is shining on the marzipan houses, the colour of red Devon earth.

J. J. is hopping around, being an Easter Bunny, delivering sweets and chocolate eggs.

'Floyd, you look scruffy,' she says, and gives me a haircut.

For two hours they have been playing back-to-back Beatles out-takes on a show called *Electric Brunch* on the local radio station.

The world is a bright, happy place.

☆

Yesterday, we drove the long, straight road from Albuquerque to Santa Fe, through the desert, where the colours are terracotta and palest lime green and buff, with mellow pinks and mauves. The scrub on the hills makes them look like mounds of green chocolate-chip cookies and in the distance the mountains are mauve-grey, capped with snow.

Past the Santa Ana and Santo Domingo Reservations, and a sign saying there are 193 restaurants in Santa Fe.

Billboards advertise abortion and cocaine hotlines, and there are Indian rugs for sale by the roadside. A lady in a bandana in a beaten-up Buick passes us.

Then into Santa Fe: sugartown, with pink adobe houses, one storey high, and shops spilling rugs and cushions, and turquoise and silver jewellery onto the pavements...

This morning's filming requires a Santa Fe outfit, I decide, heading for the Montecristi Custom Hat Works, where they cut, shape and steam a flat black hat over the spout of an old kettle and crown it with a hand-beaten silver band – all in half an hour – while David Pritchard waits and wonders.

'Have you been to Ten Thousand Waves yet?' asks Milton Johnson, 'the President' of Montecristi's, talking about the Japanese health spa in the mountains just outside Santa Fe, with its hot tubs and saunas and massage.

Where, yesterday, in a rare break from filming, we relaxed in a hot tub in the open air, with the snow on the mountains behind . . .

'It's even better when it's *actually* snowing,' he says.

Off next door, to buy a pure silk hand-made poncho in stunning shades of red, white and blue.

The look requires me to stand permanently in profile, with a long cigar . . .

SANTA CLARA

The Big Chief Sitting Bull crags are breathtaking – are they real or polystyrene, I wonder? After all, this is movie country. Where the likes of Clint Eastwood come to make Westerns.

The radio is playing Lou Reed's 'Walk on the Wild Side'. We are heading for the Santa Clara Indian Reservation, home of the Pueblo Indians.

We stop for a bowl of fabulous green chilli with deep-fried corn puffs, light and fluffy like good Yorkshire puddings, and iced bottles of pale yellow Mexican Corona beer – with slices of lime in the necks.

Santa Clara is like a housing estate, except for the enormous bell-shaped adobe oven outside the community centre, where women in brightly coloured dresses are making bread. Real Mother Earth bread. Warm and loving.

The people are real, too. Gentle, softly spoken and dignified, commanding your respect.

'We make the dough in the evening – 25 pounds or 50 pounds with lard and yeast, a handful of sugar, white flour and salt. We get up in the middle of the night and knead it, then we knead it again at five o'clock in the morning and we build our fire,' says an Indian lady called Janice.

'On the bottom of the oven are rocks, then a thin layer of mud, then tiny rocks, and another layer of mud. The little rocks keep the heat in.

'In the morning we put in chopped cedarwood and light it. We wait until it goes to white ash, then put more wood in. We put in a corn husk and if it turns a bit brown, the fire is ready. So we clean out all the ashes, and put the bread in. We put rags over the door to steam it. If it is cooking too quickly, we get paper sacks and open them and put them over the bread, so that it won't get more brown, and we open the door.

'We have regular stoves too, but we do this when we are having a feast or a dance, and we have to feed a lot of people,' says Laurie Vermillion – whose Indian name is Jo-Povi, or Cactus Blossom.

'We are called after the first thing we see, when we are taken outside as babies,' she says.

'On feast days I have a big, flat range outside, and I cook in great pots. We have services in the morning in the Catholic church, and afterwards everyone comes to eat, so the table is going all day.

'I make red chilli with pork or beef, and chicos – that is, white corn cooked with steam in the oven overnight and then hung up to dry. We take the corn off the husks and cook it with beef and onions. And we make posole – made with a type of corn, or hominy, cooked with pork and onion.

'We have potato salad. And bread pudding. We toast the bread, then in a dish we make layers of bread, cheese, nuts, raisins, sugar and cinnamon. Then we melt some sugar in a pan, brown it, and add water to make a syrup, pour it over the pudding and put it into the oven, just so that the cheese melts. It's very good.'

'And we drink Indian wild tea,' adds Elaine, whose Indian name is White Flower Lake. 'Alcohol is not allowed on the reservation. We have a problem among the Indians. Alcohol is bad for them, they don't know how to control it. They go wild and some of the teenagers turn into alcoholics.

'Each reservation has its own self-government, and ours bans alcohol.'

Elaine is married to a Navajo Indian – once famed for their warrior tendencies.

'The Plains Indians, like the Navajo and the Apaches, were the aggressive ones. They had tepees because they were always roaming from one site to the next. But the Pueblo Indians were a more peaceful tribe. They stayed in one place and kept mostly to themselves; farming, weaving baskets and clothes. They had a wheat mill here, they had their own irrigation system and roads.

'They lived in adobe buildings and were very family-orientated. They took care of one another and respected their elders. They only fought with other tribes, or with the Spanish, when it was absolutely necessary. It is still the main law of our tribe that we must respect our elders.

'Now there is a lot of intermarriage – but we cannot understand each other's language, so we have to speak in English. Here we speak Tewa, but there are many other Indian languages even in the Pueblo tribe.

'Not much of it is written down, and it saddens me that our children are no longer able to speak our language. I try to talk to my daughters in Tewa.'

Outside Elaine's house, where her sister is sewing beads on to a traditional white manta (dress) for a wedding, Laurie and I are cooking red chilli – the simplest, most delicious dish imaginable – over an open fire, in the shadow of the magic mountain, the Black Mesa, where the Indians held off the Spanish in 1694.

'The Indians knew a secret way down and they would come and get food and water in the night,' says Elaine. 'The Spanish couldn't understand how they could survive for so long with nothing to eat or drink.

'We believe the Black Mesa has great powers,' but we are forbidden to talk about such things.

'As Pueblo Indians we respect our mountains, our trees, the birds. Once we talked of the Great Spirit, now we say God – but we believe that He has given us these things and we should respect and care for them.

'If we go deer hunting, we have to say thank you to the deer for letting us kill them, and thank you to God for letting us have the food.

'When our medicine men go up to the hills to pick the roots and plants, they don't just go pick. They have to pray first.

'The body is sacred too. We try not to abuse it. That is why we are so worried about the younger generation, with alcohol and drugs. A lot of them are no longer taught the things that we were taught.

'Because we believe in respecting everything, dancing is one of our traditions. We have dances like the Deer Dance before and after hunting – to ask for good hunting, and to say thank you afterwards. And we still have the Buffalo Dance – where the men wear buffalo heads – even though there are no buffalo any more.

'We hunt for elks, duck and different birds, and we fish, but we always pray first. We never kill just to kill.

'We have other dances too, like the Rain Dance, the Pumpkin Dance and the Corn Dance. We're taught to dance when we are little kids. You'll see two-year-olds watching and waving their arms. Both men and women dance, but only the men play the drums and sing.

'You know,' says Elaine quietly, looking out at the Black Mesa, 'once all this land was ours. But we lost it. Part of it was taken by the Spanish, part of it by the government. I'm not going to say there is no bad feeling, but we have had to learn to live and work with both races, or we cannot expect to survive. What we have done is compromise. But when we look back we think about all the things we don't have any more. Like we don't have the geese, because they come and shoot them. They have no respect for nature or the land. We think: if they had just left the land with us, we could do better.

'Our parents told us: "Do not hold a grudge. Remember you have to live and work with these people ... but don't ever forget."'

☆

Debbie, the waitress at the hotel, used to teach ballet. Susie is an actress. She wants to get into TV. Mandy the barmaid has written three movie scripts. Her friend Belinda, sitting at the bar, says: 'I work in animation; right now I'm just reassessing my place in the universe.'

'I guess this town is a bit like a refugee camp for artists and actors and film producers,' says the bartender, mixing a Cape Cod – vodka and cranberry juice, with a dash of lime.

'But, see, they come for the atmosphere. It's quiet. It's beautiful. People walk around and say: "Gee. I'd like to stay here for a while." I used to work in films, but I've been here eight years, tending bar, waiting in restaurants, waiting for something to come along.

'The sky and the light are so beautiful, the air is so clear. There's so much collective energy here, it's hard to run against it.

'We have two communities here in Santa Fe: the second and third homers (people like Robert Redford who have places here), and the younger people who have a creative interest, who paint and work in bars and restaurants, and work in movies when they can. I think the two classes are interdependent, somewhat like the rhino and the tickbird ...'

GREEN CHILLI, RED CHILLI, RED CHILLI, GREEN...

'The reason we're all so healthy here in Santa Fe is 'cos we eat chilli morning, noon and night,' says Sam Pick, the town's gregarious Mayor. 'We make the best chilli you're ever gonna see.'

We are gathered at the Palace of the Governors for the great chilli cook-off. Me against the Mayor. And we're cooking real Santa Fe chilli. Not with minced beef and kidney beans, the way they serve it in London wine bars, but made like a rich stew with pork or beef – I'm using beef, Sam is using pork – potatoes, chillies and onions.

Of course I'm bound to lose – because all the judges are in the Mayor's pay!

'We eat chilli for breakfast – tortillas with eggs and potatoes and red or green chilli. Then at noon we might want to go ahead and diet a little bit, so we just have a bowl of green or red chilli, and at night, if we have people over, we have chilli in a big way, with enchiladas. We call them enchilada casseroles. You drink a little tequila – and you've had a great day in Santa Fe,' says Sam.

'Whenever I make a sandwich I put green chilli in it. I mix tuna fish with green onions and mayonnaise and green chilli and wrap it in a warm tortilla. Doesn't matter what it is: hamburgers, ham, grilled cheese – we always have green chilli in our house.'

'We do. We really do,' says Sam's delightful wife, Diane. 'We always have chopped green chilli in the fridge and we have a freezer full of it.

'When the chillies are harvested in September, the farmers bring them in in trucks from the country, and everyone looks for their own particular kind. The soil makes a difference to the taste and the amount of heat.

'Some are known for their blistering heat. Some are more mild. A lot of natives mix their chillies. We do. We have maybe one part hot to one part medium.

'When the green chilli trucks come in, they set up roasters and they'll roast you a bag for maybe 10 dollars for 50 pounds of raw chilli. Then you take them home and peel them, and put them in the freezer.

'But most people like to make a big thing about roasting the chillies at home. You take the fresh green chillies, wash the pods, then put them on racks in the oven at about 350 degrees for about 15 minutes, turning once, until the skin turns brown and pops.

'When they come out they're very hot and very limp. You put them in a large bowl or a pan and then douse a clean kitchen towel in cold water, wring it out very well and put it over the top of the pan to steam for about 15 minutes.

'Then you peel the chillies, put them in bags and store them in the freezer – that's us fixed for the whole winter.

'Red chillies are green chillies, dried. When you go out into the farm and valley lands in the fall, you'll see these amazing splashes of red, which are the chillies tied on a string, called the ristra.

'If you want to make paste to make red chilli, you take these pods, wash them in warm water, toss out all the yellow seeds – because they make the peppers very, very hot – and put the pods in a blender, with maybe two cups of water and make a paste. We put it into plastic containers and freeze that too.

'You know, we have a lot of wonderfully healthy old people in Santa Fe – because we all eat chillies. They're so good for you. It's a fact that they have lots of calcium in them.

'We literally eat chilli all day. If we go away, we're so desperate for a chilli fix that when we get back we sometimes have to stop off in Albuquerque on the way back from the airport!

'In the morning we fix blue corn tortillas, fry them in an inch or so of cooking oil, for a minute or two. Then we have the red chilli bubbling away, and we dip the tortillas in it, put a little chopped onion and grated cheese on top, and build it up in layers, with as many tortillas as you want.

'When the kids were small, they'd have one, as they got older they'd have two. Dad has always been a three-tortilla man!

'You put a little more red chilli on the top, then put the tortillas in a moderate oven for about 15 minutes. While they're in the oven you fry up a nice fresh egg, and serve it on top. Then you've got yourself a great New Mexico breakfast.

'Lunch might be a bowl of green chilli, or a corn tortilla, deep-fried with a layer of chopped lettuce and tomato, some hot re-fried beans: pinto beans mashed with a little bit of salt and a little bit of garlic and shredded cheese, some shredded chicken and some green chilli.

'If you were coming to our house for dinner, we'd start with a big pitcher of margaritas, some sangria and a bottle of tequila on the side, with salt and lime, if you just want straight shooters. And we'd have some good Mexican beer.

'We'd have some nice white corn chips and guacamole: mashed avocado with chopped green onion and garlic, a little green chilli and lime juice and some finely chopped tomatoes. And we'd have salsa: freshly chopped tomatoes, chillies and onions.

'Then for our entrée we'd have enchilada casserole. We'd make the enchiladas the same way as for breakfast, except we'd have beef and chicken fillings, with bowls of pure red chilli and chopped green chilli. We'd also have a nice big pot of green chilli stew and flour tortillas on the side. And you could make your own tacos, with various fillings, and lettuce, onion, tomato, shredded cheese topped with salsa and sour cream, or guacamole.

'Or we might have cabrito baby goat, which we roast in the ground in a pit. We stuff it with garlic cloves like a leg of lamb, and have it with red chilli and tortillas.

'It makes a marvellous sandwich the next day, with some green chilli, wrapped in a nice fresh, hot flour tortilla.

'We haven't yet put chilli in puddings – I must think on that! We're not big sweet-eaters here, but we have special cookies, called biscochitos, made with flour, lard, sugar and eggs, and aniseed.

'And we have flan – like a crème caramel – or natillas, which is a little richer, with lots of cooked egg whites and custard, and cinnamon and sugar dusted on top.

'I guess we like bland custards and puddings, because it takes the edge off all that chilli!'

A hush descends on the proceedings, Sam and I mop our brows, and I sprinkle a little parsley on to my chilli. I'm feeling very proud of it. But Sam has a confident twinkle in his eye.

The judges file in solemnly. Dishes of chilli are placed in front of them – of course, they have no idea whose is whose!

'And the winner,' says their spokeswoman, 'is the Mayor!'

☆

'I need a typical Santa Fe dish that's colourful and will impress an artist,' I say to Rod Clark, the brilliant young chef at the St Francis Hotel.

'How about my fritatta? It's an omelette I make with artichoke and onions and peppers, but it is simple and colourful,' he says, dashing into his kitchen to bring me fresh herbs and vegetables . . .

The Pink Adobe Restaurant has walls 3 feet thick and windows high up the wall to keep the arrows out.

175

Rosalea Murphy, the owner, is the painter in question, and she's really from New Orleans, but she came to Santa Fe in 1940, and opened the Pink Adobe four years later.

'I started with hamburgers and apple pie and French onion soup. I introduced onion soup to Santa Fe,' she says. 'In those days I did all the cooking. I had a dish washer and a waitress. The restaurant became my monster, so I gave up painting. Now I have 74 employees, so I can go back to my painting. And everyone from President Bush to Cher eats here.

'We do a mixture of South-Western and New Orleans cooking. One of today's specials is an oyster loaf – in New Orleans they call them oyster po-boys.

'We don't emphasise chilli *that* much here – though we're famous for our steak Dunigan, which is sirloin steak covered with green chilli and mushrooms. I named it after a friend of mine, 30 years ago – because he always wanted green chilli on his steak. It's become a favourite dish all over the country.

'The other dish everyone comes for is gypsy stew, with chicken – and I'm afraid that's with chillies too!

'Painting and food go together. I never met a good artist that wasn't a good cook, and vice versa. It's a matter of mixing flavours, colours...

'Santa Fe is a wonderful place for artists,' she says as I admire a painting of a cockerel. 'The light is so wonderful, and the colours – there's no blue quite like this sky. And the attitude is so relaxed.'

Rod's fritatta doesn't let me down – I have red peppers, green peppers, yellow peppers, red ... splashed against the creamy yellow of the eggs and the pale ivory artichokes...

☆

The breakfast menu offers huevos rancheros – eggs with red or green chilli and blue corn tortillas; huevos borrachos – scrambled eggs with serrano chilli, tomato, onion, cilantro (coriander) and chorizo (Mexican sausage); Santa Fe omelette, with green chilli and cheese...

'I would like one egg over hard, two side orders of bacon, and some ketchup, please.'

'Aren't you with the BBC?' says the waiter. 'I used to work for a video company ... this is a great place to make movies, they shoot a lot of Westerns here. We have a lot of locals who look like cowboys, and a lot of 'wait' people who are hoping to get jobs as extras . . .

'About two months ago there was a rumour that Steven Spielberg was in town. There were probably 200 people waiting to knock on his door . . . now, can I get you another round of coffee?'

The ketchup arrives – lots of it – in little individual pots! Alleluia!

But then the tea plates start arriving, hundreds of them, with just one egg on each, or strips of bacon, or slices of toast. Until the table looks like a dim sum party.

☆

Afternoon tea in the charming St Francis Hotel is an event. A lady with bobbed hair and striped stockings, looking as though she has just stepped off the film set of *The Great Gatsby*, wafts in, and a circle of friends rush over to greet her.

Outside, a man in a pigtail strolls by in the sunshine. Santa Fe has to be the male pigtail capital of the world: smart middle-aged men have them; young ones, tall ones, elderly ones have them; they are grey, blond, bleached, dyed . . . all pulled back into hand-worked leather pigtail holders.

FLOYD FAILS TO GRASP AMERICAN FOOTBALL . . . AGAIN

Tomasita's on Guadalupe, near the old railway station, is my kind of place, with simple, unpretentious food – a mix of Mexican and American – carefully prepared. I order a hamburger and issue a whole range of instructions to the waiter: burnt on the outside, rare in the middle, no top bun, no lettuce and tomato . . . and it arrives perfectly cooked.

Happy, I pour another round of margaritas from the pitcher.

'I used to play rugby at Princeton,' says the Mayor's Public Relations Officer. She is fresh-faced and long-legged, like an antelope.

'Really?' This makes a change from acting, dancing or movie directing . . .

'Sure. Fly half. It was fun, totally wild. We were the Ivy League champions the year I scored against Yale in the last game of the season.

'It was an all-female league, but sometimes we'd have co-ed scrimmages. We had one woman who was the number one sprinter for the track team. Her coach was furious that she was playing rugby, but she could outsprint all of the guys.

'The best women's team was Smith – they've always been all-women's colleges. They never went co-ed. There's no one on their team shaped like me. All of the women were 6 foot and 200 pounds.

'We all wear mouthguards, but in the scrum one time, one of them took hers out and bit the thigh of one of our players!

'The best part was the rugby songs. We were very creative – we had one called "Birth Control", to the tune of "Yesterday." Every Thursday after practice we'd sit around the beer keg singing rugby songs – sometimes with the guys – until the keg was finished, or someone passed out.

'My family is very competitive in sports – like my husband's family. I have a whole set of cousins in Florida who are tennis pros and our family would always go down there and challenge them. They're a wild family, totally insane. They have wild goats and pigs they keep in their house. We'd go down there and our family would always lose at tennis. That's one of the reasons I married John – I brought in a ringer!

'He's a good oarsman too, like my brothers. And we go mountain biking. I play soccer in the summer too – co-ed. When I was in Washington, I played on the co-ed softball team, and I worked in England, in Oxford, for a while, and I was on the Oxford Women's Basketball team.'

'I don't suppose you could explain the rules of American football?' I venture . . .

'Well, there are four quarters, two halves, and a certain amount of time for the halves. Everyone can take time off . . .'

'Never mind . . .'

'When John and I got married in St Louis,' she says, 'we had four days of sports. My mother organised the whole wedding: all we had to do was show up and compete!

'We started off on Wednesday night at the basketball game – my dad had tickets for the St Louis Cardinals. On Thursday we had a big cook-out. Friday morning was the golf tournament, Friday afternoon was the practice for the tennis tournament. Saturday morning, before the wedding, we had the tennis tournament. I wasn't nervous about the wedding, but I was nervous about the tennis game.

Baking with the Pueblo Indians, Santa Clara Reservation, New Mexico.

Swapping kitchen gossip with Chef Rod Clark at the St Francis Hotel, Santa Fe.

I told wardrobe a Lone Ranger suit – not Sloane Ranger!

'John and I got into the finals, but my aunt from Florida was against us, and she's really competitive. She was teamed up with a friend who was really good – so they beat us. Everybody was real mad at them for it.

'The wedding was at 6.30 p.m. and at 5.30 p.m. they were all out on the basketball court, playing this really gruelling, physical basketball game. I wasn't there – I was getting my hair done! But I think my husband was. I guess he stopped early, though...

'Everyone was totally exhausted from all the sports, they could hardly walk down the aisle.

'On the Sunday there was another basketball game, so several people missed their planes home, they were so wrapped up in it. We'd gone off to Hawaii for our honeymoon. It's great, there's lots of sports – scuba diving, snorkelling...

'Of course, when I came to Santa Fe, I was going to be a painter. Then I got into radio. What I'd really like to be is a famous writer...'

PLAYING COWBOYS

'Three beers,' I said to the barman, in a laconic drawl, one hand hovering restlessly over my holster. I was feeling mean. And, besides, you couldn't be too careful in this town.

The beers came sliding down the bar – one, two three. Too fast. I caught them one-handed and decided to let it go – this time.

I moseyed over to a table in the corner of the saloon, where Boots and Al were toying with the plates of pork and beans I'd just rustled up over an open fire. Al's Colt 45 lay close to his shooting hand. If they didn't like the food, there could be trouble...

'Cut,' said David Pritchard. 'Now what we need is some real action here...'

Forget yuppy war games, forget therapy groups ... If you want to lose your inhibitions and exorcise your frustrations, a day in a cowboy town, playing Clint Eastwood, is the way to do it...

Floyd in best pinstripe suit, eyes watering from the smoke of the fire beneath the cauldron, mixing a cowboy *roux* of blue cornflour, crushed chillies and black bean juice beside the chuckwagon.

The crew are trying to make the tumbleweed bowl down the deserted street, past the saloon, past the hangman's noose where a body swings in the wind.

Boots, mending a wheel on the wagon, scratches his head and grins. 'We spent hundreds of years tryin' to get rid of that stuff. Now all you want to do is put it back . . .'

Al is showing the way to do a quick draw, 'an' all that fancy twirling stuff'.

He's J. W. Eaves, the owner's right-hand man – 'everything they want for a picture: horses, cattle, wagons, cowboys, rattlesnakes . . . I get it for 'em. If they want stunts, we do them . . .

'I guess I draw a gun in about a second,' he says. 'I've always liked guns. I've been around them since I was little. To me a gun is like a good-looking woman – you wanna reach out and hold it.

'When you practise the fast draw, you end up with your fingers all cut up, you shoot your leg . . . In the days when they used guns, they didn't really aim, they'd just draw and fire. The real fast guys had holsters that snapped open.'

This town was built in 1969, for the film *The Cheyenne Social Club* with Jimmy Stewart and Henry Fonda, and since then they've made some 30 Westerns. Clint Eastwood and John Wayne have filmed here, Kirk Douglas and Johnny Cash made *A Gunfight* here.

'I remember when John Wayne was here, he was quite old, and the horse was so high they got a stool for him to get up on his horse. It sure threw me to see John Wayne, the cowboy image of the world, needing a stool to get on his horse . . .' says Al.

'Clint Eastwood is very good on horseback, but I double for some of the guys who don't know how to ride . . . And I do things like have buildings falling down on me, or getting dragged by horses. Sure, its dangerous, but they can't afford for the actors to do it.

'Being dragged by a horse is probably the most dangerous thing. You can get your head caved in on the corner of a building, or something like that. And jumping on to another rider, dragging him off his horse and starting fighting – all that stuff – you can get caught in the stirrup real easy.

'You gotta be alert, you can't be hung over, you gotta pay attention and you gotta be fit. I've broken a few arms, had a few bruises. But that's part of the game. Play with fire, and you'll get burnt sooner or later.

'It's good money, but it has to be because of the risk you're taking. There are stuntmen who can probably earn up to 7000 dollars a day on big, heavy, hairy stuff like car crashes and jumping off cliffs.

'I've done 79 motion pictures, and I've done spaghetti Westerns in Europe, and sometimes I feel like I really lived those days in some other life. When I start to do a Western everything comes so naturally, it's real funny...

'They were rough, tough times. You couldn't be a lightweight. Some of those guys used to be on the cattle trail for 300 to 500 miles. They got up early, they went to bed early. They had their own bed rolls, they used their saddles for pillows and covered themselves with horse blankets.

'Once in a while they'd go into town and live it up, shoot it up, find some ladies and have a good time. They'd only be there overnight – how long was it gonna be before they'd get to another town? It could be months.

'They probably never took a bath until they came to a river, probably wore the same clothes for months...

'There are still cowboys now, but they don't drive cattle like they used to.

'In the old days on the cattle drives they'd have their cook travelling with them in the chuckwagon – "chuck" is a slang word for eating. He'd carry his own water can on the side, because you didn't know how many miles you'd have to travel to find water.

'They'd carry beans, and flour and beef jerky (dried beef), mostly dried foods that wouldn't spoil, and they'd make their own whisky – "home brew" – and wine. They'd gather wood and make camp and they'd make bread and biscuits and cook up beans with the jerky and whatever vegetables they could find.

'But the beans were the staple, they were good and nourishing. They must've been – some of those cowboys were 80, 90 years old and still riding trails. The food was bland, but I reckon it was good and healthy ... and those cooks were pretty clever...'

☆

I guess they just didn't like my food. Al came from behind, but I was ready for him. He lay in the dust outside the saloon doors. I kicked him aside, dusted myself off and walked away. No one was on the streets. But somewhere a curtain twitched.

I heard the scuffle behind me long before Al had pulled himself up and reached for his shotgun. I went for my holster. He didn't stand a chance. I blew softly across the barrel and left him where he fell.

But I knew I had to get out of town. Fast.

I jumped on to a wagon tied up by the saloon, gave the horses the rein, and on three wheels, in a cloud of dust, I rode off into the sunset.

THE FAREWELL BREAKFAST

'Good morning, sir, and what can I get you this morning? It's your last morning isn't it?'

'Yes it is. And since it is, I'd like some cereal . . .'

'Wheat puffs, bran chips, flaked wheat with raisins, golden nuggets, honey-coated corn puffs . . . ?'

'Just some cornflakes, please! And one egg over hard, a side of bacon. And some ketchup . . .'

'Yes, sir. Have a nice day . . .'

'You know, Floyd, basically human beings are weak,' says J. J. 'They don't have a clue, they just wander around. So if you can just blast right through, like we've done, and have fun while you're doing it, it's like, it's just like . . . well . . . do I have to finish? Could you finish it?'

'I could try . . .'

'Can I get you anything else today, sir?'

'Some ketchup, please.'

'Sure. I'll get it on the next round. I'll be right back . . .'

'You know, I'm really going to miss you guys. I love you all . . .'

'We love you too, J. J.'

'Here you are, sir,' says the waitress, bringing the cornflakes with the egg, and the bacon on a separate plate. 'It's been great having you, sir. Now can I get you anything else?'

'Could I have some ketchup, please?'

Epilogue

When I was leavin' the bay
I saw three ships a-sailin'
They were all heading my way
I asked the captain what his name was
And how come he didn't drive a truck
He said his name was Columbus
I just said, 'Good luck.'

Bob Dylan

Some Recipes I thought were Quite Good

Florida

☆ # PICKLED SHRIMP ☆

Or prawns, as we would say.

SERVES 3–4

16 fl oz (475 ml) white wine vinegar
½ teaspoon ground allspice
½ teaspoon mustard powder
1 teaspoon dill seed
1 teaspoon dried red chilli peppers
1 teaspoon paprika
4 lb (1.8 kg) uncooked prawns, peeled and washed
2 teaspoons chopped fresh parsley
1 large onion, thinly sliced
2 limes, thinly sliced

Put the vinegar into a large pan. Add the spices and simmer for about 30 minutes. Add the prawns, bring to the boil and cook for another 5 minutes. Transfer the prawns to a bowl and leave to cool. Stir in the parsley and arrange onion and lime slices over the top. Serve chilled.

EVANDER PRESTON'S
CRABMEAT FRITTERS

☆   ☆

Evander's secret ingredient is Aunt Jemima's Complete Pancake Mix – but since this may not be available from your local grocer I've suggested an alternative.

SERVES 8–10

Batter
1 egg
3 oz (75 g) flour
A little milk

1 small green pepper, finely chopped
1 small onion, finely chopped
1 lb (450 g) crab meat (fresh or frozen)
1 pickled jalapeño or any other hot chilli pepper, finely chopped
Peanut or vegetable oil for deep-frying
Cocktail or chilli sauce to serve

First make the batter by beating the egg into the flour and gradually adding enough milk until the mixture has the consistency of thick cream. Leave to stand for 1 hour.

Place the green pepper and onion in a sieve and blanch for 1 minute in boiling water. Refresh under cold running water and drain thoroughly. Add to the crab meat, together with the jalapeño, and mix thoroughly, adding water if the mixture is too stiff. Leave to cool and set for 30 minutes. With a small scoop, or your hands, make balls of about 1 inch (2.5 cm) in diameter and coat them in the batter. Heat the oil to 350°F (180°C) and deep-fry the fritters, a few at a time, until deep golden in colour. Serve with cocktail or chilli sauce.

☆ FLOYD'S DESERT ISLAND ☆ LIME SAUCE

Fresh, juicy limes are so abundant in Florida that it's no wonder they crop up in recipe after recipe, from the famous Key Lime Pie (page 200) to simple fish dishes. Not to be outdone, I made up my own tangy lime sauce to go with the grouper I caught on Captain Jack's boat and later barbecued over an open fire on a desert island – and I must say it's a pretty good sauce, too. In fact it goes well with any white fish.

SERVES 3-4

1 tablespoon olive oil
2 oz (50 g) plus 1 knob of butter
2 oz (50 g) shallots, finely chopped
2 oz (50 g) flour
1½ glasses white wine (preferably Californian)
Juice and finely grated rind of 2 limes
Salt and freshly ground pepper
Lime wedges and dill sprigs to garnish

Heat the olive oil and butter in a pan. Add the shallots and fry gently until soft. Stir in the flour to make a *roux*, then add the wine, followed by the lime juice, and cook, stirring, until thickened. Let the juice simmer for 4 minutes. Beat in a knob of butter and stir in the grated lime rind. Season to taste with salt and pepper. Pour the sauce over the fish of your choice and garnish with wedges of lime and sprigs of dill.

☆ BAKED GROUPER ☆

This is another way of combining lime with fish. You can substitute any firm white fish for the grouper.

S E R V E S 3–4

3 lb (1.4 kg) grouper or any whole firm white fish, cleaned
1 small onion, thinly sliced
1 teaspoon salt
$\frac{1}{2}$ teaspoon pepper
4 oz (110 g) butter, melted
$\frac{1}{2}$ teaspoon thyme leaves
4 tablespoons lime juice
1 tablespoon soy sauce

Pre-heat the oven to gas mark 4, 350°F (180°C). Butter a baking dish. Make cuts at regular intervals along the sides of the fish and insert slices of onion. Mix all the other ingredients together and brush over the inside and outside of the fish, retaining a little of the sauce for basting. Bake in the oven for about 30 minutes, basting occasionally with the reserved sauce.

☆ GROUPER IN COCONUT AND LIME ☆

As you've guessed by now, grouper is a big favourite in St Pete's Beach, Florida – but, again, this recipe will work for any firm white fish.

S E R V E S 6

3 lb (1.4 kg) grouper or any other firm white fish fillets
Juice of 1 lime
2 medium onions, chopped
1 clove garlic, crushed
Salt and freshly ground pepper
Oil for frying
At least 8 fl oz (250 ml) coconut milk
2 tablespoons butter
2 tablespoons flour

Place the fish in a non-metallic dish, pour over the lime juice, add the onions, garlic and a large pinch of pepper, cover and leave to stand for about 30 minutes (a little longer won't hurt). Then heat the oil in a frying-pan, remove the onions and garlic from the marinade and sauté them in the oil. Add the coconut milk. Put the fish into the pan and cook over a medium heat, basting regularly with the coconut milk and pan juices, for about 30 minutes or until cooked through. Remove the fish from the pan and keep warm. Make a *roux* with the flour and butter and beat into the liquid to thicken the sauce, seasoning to taste with salt and pepper. Pour over the fish to serve.

☆ MULLET WITH LIME ☆

SERVES 6

3 lb (1.4 kg) red mullet fillets
1 small onion, finely chopped
2 oz (50 g) butter
1 tablespoon lime juice
1 teaspoon salt
Large pinch of freshly ground pepper

Pre-heat the oven to gas mark 4, 350°F (180°C). Place each fish fillet on a square of aluminium foil. Mix together the other ingredients and pour over the fish. Bring up the edges of each foil square and seal to make a parcel. Bake in the oven for 20–30 minutes or until the fish is just cooked.

☆ EVANDER PRESTON'S ☆ HUSH PUPPIES

The story goes that these little balls of fried cornbread got their name during the Civil War, when the people of the Deep South cooked them around the campfire and threw them at their dogs to shut them up if they heard Yankee soldiers approaching. Evander Preston prefers to eat his, Florida-style, with freshly caught catfish (see the following recipe).

SERVES 4–6

10 oz (275 g) cornmeal
2 teaspoons baking powder
1 teaspoon salt
1 teaspoon freshly ground black pepper
16 fl oz (475 ml) milk
4 fl oz (120 ml) water
1 large onion, finely chopped
Oil for deep-frying

Sift the dry ingredients together and add the milk and water. Stir in the chopped onion. Add more cornmeal or milk if necessary to form a soft but workable dough. With your hands make pieces of dough into pones (oblong cakes) about 5 inches (12.5 cm) long, 3 inches (7.5 cm) wide and $\frac{3}{4}$ in (1.5 cm) thick. Deep-fry in oil until golden-brown.

☆ DEEP-FRIED CATFISH ☆

Serve this fish with Evander Preston's Hush Puppies (see the preceding recipe).

SERVES 2–4

3 catfish fillets
3 oz (75 g) cornmeal or wholewheat flour
Salt and freshly ground pepper
Oil for deep-frying
Lime or lemon quarters to garnish

Cut each fillet into the size you prefer. Season the cornmeal or flour with salt and pepper and dredge the fish with it. Deep-fry for 5–10 minutes or until crisp and brown. Garnish with lime or lemon quarters.

☆ FLOYD'S SUNSHINE ☆ CHICKEN

This sunny, fruity dish, made with lovely, plumptious, little raisins, juicy pineapples and fresh limes, celebrates my impression of Florida as a place of plenty – and since I made it on the day that Salvador Dali died, I was inspired to do a little painting on a plate.

SERVES 4

Juice of 6–8 limes
1 clove garlic, crushed
Salt and freshly ground pepper
4 boneless chicken breasts
Flour for dusting
Cornmeal for dusting
1 oz (25 g) butter
Dash of rum
1 stick celery, diced
2 tomatoes, peeled, quartered and de-seeded
5 oz (150 g) fresh pineapple, cubed
Good dash of Budweiser beer
1 tablespoon raisins to garnish

Accompaniment
Wild, brown and white rice
Knob of butter
Good pinch of curry powder
Good pinch of saffron

Combine the lime juice, garlic and a pinch of salt and marinate the chicken in the mixture for about 2 hours. Drain the chicken, reserving the marinade. Mix together roughly equal quantities of flour and cornmeal, season with salt and pepper and dip the chicken in the mixture to coat thoroughly. Heat the butter in a frying-pan and fry the chicken breasts until brown. Flame the chicken with rum. Add the celery, tomatoes, reserved marinade, pineapple cubes and a good dash of Budweiser. Bubble gently for 20 minutes until the pineapple is soft and the sauce has reduced.

Meanwhile, boil the rice in water to which you have added a knob of butter and a good pinch each of curry powder and saffron.

Remove the chicken from the pan and liquidise the sauce to a purée. Pour the sauce on to 4 warmed serving plates and place the chicken on top. Arrange the rice on the plates also and garnish the whole dish with raisins – as flamboyantly as you can manage!

☆ BARBECUED CHICKEN ☆ WINGS

S E R V E S   A B O U T   6

5 lb (2.3 kg) chicken wings
3 teaspoons paprika
Salt to taste and 2 teaspoons freshly ground black pepper
4 fl oz (120 ml) corn oil plus extra for brushing the chicken wings
8 fl oz (250 ml) tomato ketchup
3 oz (75 g) honey
1 tablespoon crushed garlic
6 tablespoons white wine vinegar
2 tablespoons Worcestershire sauce
1 teaspoon Tabasco sauce
1 teaspoon Dijon mustard
4 tablespoons butter
1 bay leaf

Pre-heat the oven to gas mark 6, 400°F (200°C). Sprinkle the chicken wings with 2 teaspoons of the paprika, salt to taste and the black pepper, pour over half the oil, coating the wings well, and cook in the oven for 15 minutes. Mix together the rest of the ingredients, including the remaining oil and 1 teaspoon paprika, bring to the boil in a saucepan, then brush some over the wings. Turn them over, brush the other side with sauce and return to the oven to cook for a further 15 minutes. Repeat this process twice more, until the wings have been cooked for an hour.

Grouper in coconut and lime (page 192); Key lime pie (page 200)

☆ EVANDER PRESTON'S ☆
ROAST QUAILS WITH BLACK-EYED PEAS

SERVES 6

1 lb (450 g) dried black-eyed peas
12 oz (350 g) salt pork or bacon in a piece
12 oz (350 g) onions, chopped
3 bay leaves
1 teaspoon thyme leaves
3 tablespoons chopped garlic
Chicken stock
Salt and freshly ground pepper
Bacon rashers
12 quails
Boiled quails' eggs to garnish

Cover the peas generously with water and leave to soak overnight. Drain. Sweat the salt pork in a pan until the fat runs, then add the onions, herbs, garlic and drained peas. Mix thoroughly, cover with chicken stock and season to taste with pepper and salt if necessary. Simmer gently for about 2 hours or until the peas are tender. Lay bacon rashers over the quails and roast in the oven at gas mark 7, 425°F (220°C), for 15 minutes or until cooked through and golden-brown. Serve on top of the drained black-eyed peas, nap with some of their cooking juice and garnish with quails' eggs.

☆ EVANDER PRESTON'S ☆
ROAST SADDLE OF VENISON WITH
BLACKJACK SAUCE

SERVES ABOUT 12

1 saddle of venison
8 oz (225 g) salt pork or bacon, cubed

Pickled shrimp (page 189); Sunshine chicken (page 195);
Roast quails with black-eyed peas (page 199)

Butter for frying
Salt and freshly ground pepper
16 fl oz (475 ml) Jack Daniels bourbon
Juice of 4 lemons
A few sassafras leaves (optional)
12 oz (350 g) dark molasses
$1\frac{3}{4}$ pints (1 litre) stock or water
Flour

Bone the saddle of venison and brown the bones in the oven. In a heavy flameproof casserole fry the salt pork with a little butter until it releases its fat. Remove the pork and sauté the venison in the fat until brown on all sides. Season with salt and pepper, then transfer the casserole to the oven pre-heated to gas mark 4, 350°F (180°C). Cook for about 15 minutes per lb (450 g) plus 15 minutes. Remove when the meat is medium rare to medium and set aside to keep warm, reserving the fat. Pour the Jack Daniels into the casserole, taking great care as it will flame up. When the flames go out, add the lemon juice, sassafras leaves (if using) and molasses, together with the browned bones. Cover with the stock or water and simmer for 30 minutes. Strain the stock and adjust the seasoning if necessary. Make a *roux* with the reserved fat and a little flour. Mix into the sauce and heat, stirring, until thickened. Slice the venison. Pour some sauce on to each of 12 plates and arrange the meat on top.

☆ EVANDER PRESTON'S KEY LIME PIE ☆

Ideally this should be made with Key limes from the Florida Keys or the Caribbean, which have a wonderful strong tart flavour.

SERVES 6–8

Crust
4 oz (110 g) softened butter
6 oz (175 g) Graham crackers or digestive biscuits, crumbled
$\frac{1}{4}$ teaspoon vanilla essence

Filling
6 egg yolks
1 × 14 oz (400 g) tin sweetened condensed milk
6 fl oz (175 ml) Key lime juice
2 teaspoons grated lime rind

Meringue
6 egg whites
1 teaspoon vanilla essence
1 teaspoon cream of tartar
$\frac{1}{4}$ teaspoon salt
8 oz (225 g) caster sugar

Make the crust by blending the softened butter with the cracker or digestive biscuit crumbs and vanilla essence. Spread and press the mixture around the bottom and sides of a 9 inch (23 cm) pie dish. Make the filling by blending the egg yolks with the condensed milk. Add the lime juice. Put the filling into the pie shell. Bake for 15 minutes at gas mark 4, 350°F (180°C). To make the meringue, beat the egg whites until frothy. Add the vanilla essence, cream of tartar and salt and beat slightly. Add the sugar gradually, beating well. Continue beating until the mixture forms stiff peaks. Swirl over the pie filling and bake in the oven at gas mark 6, 400°F (200°C), for about 7–10 minutes or until the meringue is browned. Allow to cool and refrigerate before serving.

☆ TONY BELMONT'S ☆ FLORIDA ORANGE PIE

According to Tony Belmont, the man who would be King of Rock and Roll, this is a 'real cute pie'.

SERVES 6–8

Filling
8 fl oz (250 ml) orange juice
1 medium orange, peel and pith removed, cut in pieces
2 tablespoons grated orange rind
7 oz (200 g) sugar
5 tablespoons cornflour
3 egg yolks
2 tablespoons lemon juice
2 tablespoons butter
1 quantity Meringue (see above)

Pastry
8 oz (225 g) flour
1 teaspoon sugar
6 tablespoons chilled butter
3–4 tablespoons iced water

First make the pastry. Sift the flour and sugar together. Cut the butter into small pieces and work into the flour with your fingertips until the mixture resembles fine breadcrumbs. Stir in enough water to make a firm but unsticky dough, form into a ball and refrigerate for 1 hour. Roll out to line a 9 inch (23 cm) flan tin and bake blind in the oven at gas mark 6, 400°F (200°C), for 10 minutes.

To make the filling, combine the orange juice, segments and grated rind, sugar and cornflour in a saucepan. Cook over a low heat, stirring, until clear. In a bowl beat the egg yolks, stir in a little of the hot mixture, then add to the saucepan. Cook for about 5 minutes. Remove from the heat. Add the lemon juice and butter. Beat together and pour into the baked pie shell if it is still warm; if the pie shell has cooled, allow the mixture to cool also before pouring it in. Cover the mixture with meringue and bake at gas mark 4, 350°F (180°C), until slightly browned.

☆ MANGO CHEESECAKE ☆

SERVES 6–8

Biscuit Crust
8 oz (225 g) digestive biscuits, crushed into crumbs
1 oz (25 g) caster sugar
4 oz (110 g) melted butter

2 mangoes, chopped
2 teaspoons lime juice
3 oz (75 g) sugar
1 sachet gelatine powder
12 oz (350 g) cream cheese
6 fl oz (175 ml) soured cream
1 teaspoon vanilla essence
Mango slices to decorate

First make the biscuit crust by throughly combining all the ingredients and lining a 9 inch (23 cm) flan tin with the mixture.

Mix together the chopped mango, lime juice and sugar. Cover and refrigerate for about 30 minutes. Drain off the liquid and place it in a bowl over hot water. Add the gelatine and allow to dissolve, then add this to the mango mixture. Beat the cream cheese, stir in the soured cream and vanilla and fold in the mango mixture. Spoon into the biscuit crust and refrigerate until firm. Decorate with fresh mango slices before serving.

☆ EVANDER PRESTON'S ☆ SUNSHINE BISCUITS

M A K E S   A B O U T $2\frac{1}{2}$ lb (1.25 kg) B I S C U I T S

16 fl oz (475 ml) milk
Butter
1 teaspoon salt
1 teaspoon margarine
1 tablespoon sugar
1 small packet powdered yeast
2 fl oz (50 ml) lukewarm water
1 lb 14 oz (750 g) flour
1 egg, well beaten

Place the milk, 1 tablespoon butter, salt, margarine and sugar into a double boiler and whisk together. Let the mixture cool until it is lukewarm, then dissolve the yeast in the lukewarm water and stir into the mixture. Leave to cool again, then add 12 oz (350 g) of the flour and mix to a stiff batter. Add the egg and leave in a warm place to rise. After about 5 hours, knead, using the rest of the flour. When the dough can be handled easily, roll out to a thickness of $\frac{1}{2}$ inch (1 cm). Cut with a biscuit cutter, butter the tops of biscuits, then arrange them in pairs, placing one on top of the other to form a double biscuit. Arrange them on a baking sheet so that they do not touch each other. Bake in the oven for about 15 minutes at gas mark 6, 400°F (200°C).

Louisiana

☆ Eggs Sardou ☆

S E R V E S 2

Hollandaise Sauce
8 oz (225 g) unsalted butter
2 egg yolks
1 tablespoon water
Salt
Pinch of cayenne pepper
1 tablespoon lemon juice

4 eggs
4 artichoke bottoms, cooked
4 tinned anchovy fillets
4 tablespoons finely chopped cooked ham

To make the hollandaise sauce, melt the butter in a bowl set over a pan of simmering water. Remove the white foam from the top and discard. Allow to cool; use only the yellow liquid, discarding the milky solids that sink to the bottom. Beat the egg yolks and water together in another bowl over simmering water, add the butter and beat until the mixture has the texture of thin mayonnaise. Mix in salt and cayenne to taste and the lemon juice.

Poach the eggs. Put 2 artichoke bottoms on to each of 2 heated plates. Arrange 2 anchovy fillets in a cross over the contents of each plate and place a poached egg on each artichoke bottom. Spoon 1 tablespoon hollandaise sauce over each egg. In a frying-pan heat the ham and sprinkle over the top of each egg.

☆ CRAB CHOWDER ☆

SERVES 4-6

5 tablespoons butter
5 tablespoons flour
1 pint (570 ml) milk
16 fl oz (475 ml) chicken stock
1 oz (25 g) onion, finely chopped
6 oz (175 g) fresh or frozen crab meat
1 × 12 oz (350 g) tin sweet corn, drained
Salt and freshly ground pepper
Large pinch of cayenne pepper
4 fl oz (120 ml) double cream

In a saucepan melt 4 tablespoons of the butter and beat in the flour. Add the milk and stock, whisking all the time. Cook for about 10 minutes, stirring constantly. In a separate saucepan melt the remaining 1 tablespoon butter, add the onion and cook until soft. Put in the crab meat, corn and seasoning. Heat through and add to the sauce. Stir in the cream. Bring to simmering point and simmer very gently for about 5 minutes.

☆ CHEF EUGENE'S ☆ SHRIMP CLEMENCEAU
DOOKY CHASE'S, NEW ORLEANS

For this recipe, get the biggest prawns (or shrimps, as the Americans call them) you can find.

SERVES 1

Butter for frying
12 large prawns, peeled
1 clove garlic, crushed
4 mushrooms, sliced
1 oz (25 g) fresh peas (shelled weight)
8 oz (225 g) potatoes, chopped and pre-fried until just golden

Salt and freshly ground pepper
$\frac{1}{2}$ oz (10 g) parsley, chopped
Pinch of paprika

Melt the butter in a frying-pan and sauté the prawns in it for 1 minute or until coloured. Add the garlic, mushrooms and peas. Cook for another minute. Add the potatoes, salt and pepper to taste and the parsley. Cook for another minute. Sprinkle with paprika and serve.

☆ LEAH CHASE'S ☆ OYSTER PO-BOY
DOOKY CHASE'S, NEW ORLEANS

'You ain't been to New Orleans till you've had an oyster po-boy,' says Leah Chase.

SERVES 6

2 thick French loaves
A little butter
4 dozen oysters, shelled
Cornmeal for dusting
Salt and freshly ground pepper
Oil for deep-frying
Tabasco sauce
Dill pickle (pickled gherkins), sliced

Cut the loaves in half lengthways. Toast each half and spread with a little butter. Dust the oysters in cornmeal, salt and pepper, and deep-fry in hot oil for a few minutes. Make a sandwich with the toast, oysters, sprinkled with Tabasco sauce, and sliced dill pickle.

☆ Ed Moise's Seafood ☆ Brochettes with Meunière Sauce

HILLERY'S AT THE GAZEBO. NEW ORLEANS

This dish may be served with potatoes and a steamed vegetable. Scallops and mussels may be used instead of the suggested shellfish. For a plainer dish, omit the eggwash and coating and simply brush the bacon and seafood with oil and cook under the grill.

S E R V E S   2

2 × 8 inch (20 cm) rashers bacon
4 medium oysters
4 large prawns
Peanut or vegetable oil for deep-frying
2 toasted bread croûtes, each cut into 4 triangles

Eggwash
3 eggs, beaten
8 fl oz (250 ml) milk

Coating
4½ oz (130 g) cornflour
1 tablespoon salt
1 teaspoon cayenne pepper
1 tablespoon chopped garlic

Meunière Sauce
4 oz (110 g) butter
2 fl oz (50 ml) red wine vinegar
1 tablespoon lemon juice
Grated rind of 1 lemon

With an 8 inch (20 cm) skewer pierce one end of a bacon rasher, then slip an oyster on to the skewer. Being careful to keep the bacon whole, pierce it again, then add a prawn to the skewer, piercing it twice. Continue to alternate in this way with a second oyster and prawn, so that the bacon forms a double 'S' shape around the seafood (if this proves too difficult, cut the rasher into squares and skewer them individually). Prepare the second brochette in the same way.

In a shallow dish make the eggwash by combining the beaten eggs and milk. On a plate combine the ingredients for the coating. Dip the brochettes first in eggwash and then in coating, pressing gently to hold them together. Heat the oil and deep-fry the brochettes for 5–7 minutes, or until they begin to float. Remove and drain. Place a clean teatowel on top of each brochette in turn and, holding it firmly, remove the skewer with a quick twist and pull.

Meanwhile, make the meunière sauce. Melt the butter in a pan, add the vinegar, lemon juice and rind and heat, stirring, until thoroughly blended.

To serve, place the brochettes on the croûtes and nap with meunière sauce.

☆ PAUL PRUDHOMME'S ☆ CRAWFISH PIE

SERVES 6

Crusts
12 oz (350 g) unsalted butter, at room temperature
5 oz (150 g) sugar
$1\frac{1}{2}$ teaspoons vanilla essence
$\frac{1}{2}$ teaspoon salt
3 eggs
4 fl oz (120 ml) milk
About $1\frac{1}{4}$ lb (550 g) flour

Filling
2 fl oz (50 ml) vegetable oil
About 1 oz (25 g) flour
8 tablespoons very finely chopped green peppers
5 tablespoons very finely chopped onions
4 tablespoons very finely chopped celery
16 fl oz (475 ml) double cream

Seasoning Mix
1½ teaspoons salt
1 teaspoon paprika
½ teaspoon ground white pepper
¼ teaspoon onion powder
¼ teaspoon garlic powder
¼ teaspoon mustard powder
¼ teaspoon ground red pepper (preferably cayenne)
¼ teaspoon ground black pepper
¼ teaspoon filé powder (optional)
⅛ teaspoon dried thyme
⅛ teaspoon dried basil

6 oz (175 g) unsalted butter
12 tablespoons finely chopped spring onions
1 teaspoon crushed garlic
1½ lb (700 g) peeled crawfish (freshwater crayfish) tails

First make the crusts. You will need at least 6 individual oval ovenproof pie-dishes, each about 12 fl oz (350 ml) capacity.

In a large bowl combine the butter, sugar, vanilla and salt; stir until creamy and smooth. Stir in the eggs and milk. Gradually add 1 lb 2 oz (500 g) of the flour and stir until it is all mixed in.

On a surface floured with the remaining flour, knead the dough for 1 minute. Place in a bowl, cover and refrigerate at least 1 hour. Then divide the dough into 6 equal portions. Re-flour the surface and roll each piece into an oval shape about ¼ inch (0.5 cm) thick. Place a pie-dish face down over each piece of dough. With a knife cut around the shape of the dish, leaving an additional ½ inch (1 cm) border. (You will have enough dough scraps left to make an extra crust, or you can use the scraps to make decorative strips to put across the tops of the pies.) Flour the dough's surface lightly, fold into quarters, and carefully place the dough so that the corner of the fold is centred in the ungreased dish. Unfold the dough and line the dish with it, pressing it firmly against the bottom and sides. The dough should come slightly over the dish top. Place an empty dish of the same size (or use baking beans) on top to hold the dough in place while baking. Bake in the oven at gas mark 4, 350°F (180°C), for 25 minutes. Remove the top dish or baking beans. Reduce the oven temperature to gas mark 2, 300°F (150°C), and continue baking for about 40 minutes more or until the sides and bottom of the crust are browned (the baking time may vary by about 10–15 minutes depending on what you used to weigh down the dough). Remove from the oven and cool slightly; then remove the crusts from the dishes and set aside.

Now make the filling. In a large, heavy saucepan heat the vegetable oil until it begins to smoke. With a long-handled metal whisk or a wooden spoon, gradually stir in about 1 oz (25 g) flour and cook, whisking constantly or stirring briskly, for about 2–3 minutes or until the *roux* is a dark red-brown; remove the pan momentarily from the heat if the *roux* is browning too quickly for you to keep it from burning (be careful not to splash it on your skin). Remove from the heat and immediately add the peppers, onions and celery. Continue whisking constantly for about 3 minutes or until the mixture cools. Set aside.

In another saucepan heat the cream to a quick simmer over a high heat, whisking almost constantly. Gradually add the *roux*, stirring until dissolved between each addition. Bring to the boil, whisking constantly so that the mixture does not burn. Remove from the heat and set aside.

Thoroughly combine the seasoning mix ingredients in a small bowl and set aside.

In a large frying-pan combine the butter with the spring onions and garlic; cook over a low heat until the butter melts, stirring occasionally. Add the crawfish (reserving a few tails to garnish the finished dish) and $1\frac{1}{2}$ tablespoons of the seasoning mix; turn the heat to high and sauté for about 3 minutes or until the crawfish are hot, stirring almost constantly. Stir the cream mixture into the crawfish mixture.

Fill each crust with the resulting mixture and garnish with a few crawfish tails.

☆ PAUL PRUDHOMME'S ☆ BLACKENED REDFISH

This is the dish Paul Prudhomme 'invented'.

Redfish and pompano are ideal for this method of cooking. If using tilefish, you may have to split the fillets in half horizontally to obtain the proper thickness. If you cannot get any of these fish, salmon steaks or red snapper fillets can be substituted. In any case, the fillets or steaks must not be more than $\frac{3}{4}$ inch (1.5 cm) thick.

SERVES 6

12 oz (350 g) unsalted butter, melted
6 × 8–10 oz (225–275 g) fish fillets (preferably redfish, bass, pompano or tilefish), cut about $\frac{1}{2}$ inch (1 cm) thick

Seasoning Mix
1 tablespoon paprika
$2\frac{1}{2}$ teaspoons salt
1 teaspoon onion powder
1 teaspoon garlic powder
1 teaspoon ground red pepper (preferably cayenne)
$\frac{3}{4}$ teaspoon ground white pepper
$\frac{3}{4}$ teaspoon ground black pepper
$\frac{1}{2}$ teaspoon dried thyme
$\frac{1}{2}$ teaspoon dried oregano

Heat a large, heavy, cast-iron frying-pan over very high heat for at least 10 minutes or until it is beyond the smoking stage and you see white ash in the bottom (the pan cannot be too hot for this dish).

Meanwhile, pour 2 tablespoons of the melted butter into each of 6 small ramekins; set aside and keep warm. Heat 6 dinner plates in the oven.

Thoroughly combine the seasoning mix ingredients in a small bowl. Dip each fish fillet in the remaining melted butter so that both sides are well coated; then sprinkle the seasoning mix generously and evenly on both sides of the fillets, patting it in by hand. Place as many fillets in the hot frying-pan as will comfortably fit in one layer and pour 1 teaspoon melted butter on top of each one (be careful, as the butter may flame up). Cook, uncovered, over the same high heat for about 2 minutes or until the underside of the fish looks charred (the time will vary according to the fillets' thickness and the heat of the pan). Turn the fish over and again pour 1 teaspoon butter on top; cook for about 2 minutes more or until the fish is done. Repeat with the remaining fillets. Serve each fillet while piping hot.

To serve, place one fillet and a ramekin of butter on each heated plate.

☆ KING CREOLE FISH ☆

S E R V E S   6

6 tablespoons butter
1 onion, thinly sliced
12 oz (350 g) chopped mixed green and red peppers
1 teaspoon chopped garlic
Salt and freshly ground black pepper
4 tablespoons finely chopped parsley
10 oz (275 g) tomatoes, peeled
Dash of tomato purée
Dash of Tabasco sauce
Pinch of dried basil
2 tablespoons capers
6 fish fillets (bass, cod, hake or any other firm white fish)

Melt half the butter in a saucepan and sauté the onion in it until soft. Add the peppers and garlic and season to taste with salt and pepper. Add the parsley, tomatoes, tomato purée, Tabasco, basil and capers. Cover and cook for 15 minutes, then remove the lid and cook for another 5 minutes.

Pre-heat the oven to gas mark 8, 450°F (230°C). Grease a baking dish with 1 tablespoon butter to which you have added salt and pepper, and put in the fish fillets. Dot with the remaining butter, pour over the sauce and bake in the oven for about 15 minutes.

Paul Prudhomme and I cooked this recipe and his Sunshine Vegetable Medley (page 222) together in his restaurant, K-Paul's Louisiana Kitchen, in New Orleans.

☆ PAN-FRIED TROUT IN CREAMY ☆ SAUCE

This recipe uses Louisiana smoked ham, called tasso, which is spicy and sweet, but you can substitute any smoked ham you can buy locally.

S E R V E S   3

Flour for dusting
2 teaspoons Paul Prudhomme's Cajun Magic or barbecue spice
1 egg, beaten
8 fl oz (250 ml) milk
6 trout fillets
Oil for frying

Sauce
2 oz (50 g) butter
2 oz (50 g) tasso or other smoked ham, chopped
1 bunch spring onions, chopped
10 fl oz (300 ml) fish stock
2 fl oz (50 ml) cream

On a plate combine some flour with the Cajun Magic or barbecue spice. In a bowl mix the egg and milk. Coat the fish fillets in the flour, dip them into the egg and milk mixture and then in the flour again. Heat some oil in a frying-pan and fry the fish for 1–3 minutes on each side or until just cooked through. Drain and keep warm. To make the sauce, heat the butter in a pan and add the smoked ham and onions. Pour in the stock, bring to the boil and continue boiling to reduce until it is of a shiny, creamy consistency. Stir in a knob of butter and the cream.

☆ PAUL PRUDHOMME'S ☆ RABBIT TENDERLOIN WITH MUSTARD SAUCE

S E R V E S 6 A S A S T A R T E R

6 × 2–3 oz (50–75 g) boneless rabbit tenderloins
$2\frac{1}{2}$ oz (65 g) flour
Vegetable oil and unsalted butter for frying

Seasoning Mix
1 teaspoon salt
$\frac{3}{4}$ teaspoon garlic powder
$\frac{1}{2}$ teaspoon onion powder
$\frac{1}{4}$ teaspoon ground red pepper (preferably cayenne)
$\frac{1}{4}$ teaspoon ground black pepper
$\frac{1}{4}$ teaspoon dried basil
$\frac{1}{8}$ teaspoon ground white pepper
$\frac{1}{8}$ teaspoon ground coriander

Mustard Sauce
4 fl oz (120 ml) double cream
4 fl oz (120 ml) soured cream
6 tablespoons Creole or other sweet strong mustard
2 teaspoons Worcestershire sauce
$1\frac{1}{2}$ teaspoons English mustard
$\frac{1}{2}$ teaspoon salt
$\frac{1}{4}$ teaspoon ground black pepper
$\frac{1}{8}$ teaspoon ground white pepper
$\frac{1}{8}$ teaspoon ground red pepper (preferably cayenne)
$\frac{1}{8}$ teaspoon dried basil

First make the Mustard Sauce. Combine all the ingredients in a saucepan over medium-low heat. Simmer, stirring constantly, for about 15–20 minutes or until thickened. Cool to room temperature. You should have about 8 fl oz (250 ml) sauce.

Continued on page 217

Oyster po-boy (page 206)

Peel any membrane from the rabbit and discard. Combine the ingredients of the seasoning mix, mixing well; sprinkle the rabbit lightly and evenly with about $1\frac{1}{2}$ teaspoons of the mix and combine the remaining seasoning with the flour in a medium-sized bowl or a plastic bag.

Pour $\frac{1}{4}$ inch (0.5 cm) oil into a large frying-pan and heat to about 350°F (180°C). Add about one third that amount of butter, being careful as the butter will sizzle briefly. Meanwhile, coat the rabbit with the seasoned flour, shaking off the excess. Immediately add the rabbit to the pan and fry for about $1\frac{1}{2}$ minutes on each side or until golden-brown. Drain on kitchen paper. Serve immediately.

To serve, cut each tenderloin diagonally into slices $\frac{1}{4}$ inch (0.5 cm) thick and arrange in a crescent around the edge of a salad plate. Pour about 2 tablespoons Mustard Sauce in the centre of each plate.

☆ FLOYD'S GUMBO ☆

Gumbo is a kind of spicy soup-cum-stew, served in bowls with a little rice, which can be eaten as a starter or a hearty main course, depending on the quantity you make. Its name was imported by the Africans in the dreadful days of slavery, and some people reckon that a traditional gumbo should have okra, or ladies' fingers, in it; however, I don't go along with that theory, and mine doesn't! It does contain filé powder, made from sassafras leaves which turns into a kind of stringy substance in the pot ('filé' means 'string' in Cajun), but filé is not essential for gumbo and it's OK to omit it if you can't get it.

Like jambalaya, gumbo is the perfect example of what my good friend Joe Cahn at the New Orleans School of Cooking likes to call 'cooking with jazz': once you have a rough idea of the tune, you can give it your own interpretation. Play it by ear, with plenty of heart and soul. Here's my variation on a theme . . .

I used a rather special fish *boudin* – a sausage made from minced crawfish (freshwater crayfish) and rice, with herbs, onions and red pepper – which I spotted at dawn in the French market in New Orleans. Naturally

Sunshine vegetable medley (page 222); Crab chowder (page 205);
Red beans (page 220)

it isn't essential, but do shop around, because some delicatessens in the UK are making fish *boudins* these days, and I think it is an interesting addition to this dish. You could also make your own fish *quenelles* – dumplings, formed into a sausage shape – and add those.

Traditionally Louisiana chefs prepare a *roux* for this dish: not the European kind in which you add flour to melted butter to thicken sauces, but a darker one in which flour and oil are cooked together for some time (you must stir constantly) until the desired colour is achieved. Some recipes call for a light- or medium-coloured *roux*, others for a dark one. However, since this is *my* jazz solo, I'm being very European about things and leaving out the *roux* completely.

SERVES 4 AS A MAIN COURSE

Fish Stock
Fish heads, tails and trimmings
1 onion
2 carrots
1 stick celery
1 leek
1 bay leaf
2 sprigs parsley
Black peppercorns
Prawn shells and heads

Oil for frying
10 oz (275 g) onions, chopped
8 oz (225 g) green peppers, chopped
2 sticks celery, chopped
1 oz (25 g) andouille or other spicy sausage, sliced
1 oz (25 g) smoked pork or bacon, cubed
1 teaspoon crushed garlic
$\frac{1}{2}$ teaspoon dried oregano
$\frac{1}{2}$ teaspoon dried thyme
1 bay leaf, crumbled
1 teaspoon salt
$1\frac{1}{2}$ teaspoons cayenne pepper
$1\frac{1}{2}$ teaspoons paprika
$\frac{1}{2}$ teaspoon freshly ground black pepper
$\frac{1}{2}$ teaspoon freshly ground white pepper

3 tablespoons filé powder (optional)
1 tablespoon Tabasco sauce
10 fl oz (300 ml) puréed fresh tomatoes, strained
Crab shells to flavour (optional)
1 lb (450 g) large prawns (reserve the shells and heads for the stock)
1 dozen oysters
8 oz (225 g) crab meat
6 freshwater crayfish
2 *boudins*
About 2 oz (50 g) cooked rice per person to serve

Place all the ingredients for the stock in a large saucepan and cover with about 3 pints (1.7 litres) cold water. Simmer for as long as possible – 4 hours if you can manage it – and strain. Set aside.

Heat the oil in a large pan, add the onions, green peppers and celery and let them sweat for a few minutes. Add the spicy sausage and smoked pork. Stir in the garlic, herbs, salt, spices and finally the filé powder, if using. (Some people like to add filé at the end, but to my European way of thinking it should go in at the beginning.) Add the Tabasco sauce, puréed tomatoes and 2 pints (1.1 litres) of the fish stock. Simmer for at least 45 minutes. Add crab shells, if you have them, to give a little extra flavour and colour, the prawns, oysters, crab meat, crayfish and finally the *boudins*. Simmer for another 10 minutes. To serve as a main course, place about 2 oz (50 g) cooked rice per person in each bowl and top up with Gumbo.

☆ CAJUN CHRIS'S JAMBALAYA ☆
JOE CAHN'S NEW ORLEANS SCHOOL OF COOKING

This kind of Cajun risotto is traditionally the one-pot meal made at the end of the week from whatever is left in the larder – and since the Cajun people fish and hunt for their food along the bayou, that often includes things like alligator and racoon. As it's tricky to get these at Sainsbury's, you can make do quite happily with chicken and some good spicy sausage, such as chorizo. Or you could add some diced pork or ham, or even some seafood. It's really up to you. Provided you keep to the Cajun 'trinity' of onion, celery and green pepper, which provide the basic flavouring, you can experiment as much as you like.

S E R V E S   6

1 fl oz (25 ml) oil
12 oz (350 g) spicy sausage (such as chorizo), sliced
6 chicken breasts, boned and cut into small pieces
Salt and freshly ground pepper
5 oz (150 g) onions, chopped
4 sticks celery, chopped
8 oz (225 g) green peppers, chopped
$\frac{1}{2}$ tablespoon chopped garlic
1$\frac{1}{4}$ pints (700 ml) stock
Cayenne pepper
1 bouquet garni
14 oz (400 g) white long-grain rice
5 oz (150 g) spring onions, chopped

Heat the oil in a large, heavy saucepan and add the sausage. Season the chicken with salt and pepper and add to the pan. Fry them together until browned, then add the 'trinity' of onions, celery and green peppers together with the garlic. Cover with the stock, add salt and cayenne pepper to taste and the bouquet garni. Bring to the boil and add the rice. Cover tightly and simmer for 10 minutes. Turn off the heat and leave for 20 minutes to allow the rice to finish cooking. Serve the dish garnished with the chopped spring onions.

☆ LEAH CHASE'S RED BEANS ☆
DOOKY CHASE'S, NEW ORLEANS

S E R V E S   4-6

1 lb (450g) dried red kidney beans
12 oz (350 g) onions, chopped
2 oz (50 g) bacon dripping or vegetable oil
8 oz (225 g) spicy sausage (such as chorizo), sliced
8 oz (225 g) smoked ham, cubed
4 oz (110 g) green pepper, chopped
$\frac{1}{2}$ teaspoon thyme leaves
1 tablespoon chopped garlic
2 tablespoons chopped parsley

1 bay leaf
1 tablespoon salt
1 tablespoon ground black pepper

Soak the beans overnight in plenty of cold water. Drain and place in very large saucepan. Cover with fresh water and add the onions. Bring to the boil and continue to boil for about $1\frac{1}{4}$ hours or until the beans are tender. Heat the dripping or oil in a frying-pan. Add the sausage and ham and sauté for about 10 minutes. Add the green pepper and cook for about 5 minutes, stirring regularly. Add the contents of the frying-pan to the beans. Stir well. Add the thyme, garlic, parsley, bay leaf, salt and pepper. Simmer for about 20 minutes or until the beans are creamy, adding more water if the mixture is too thick. Serve over rice.

☆ PAUL PRUDHOMME'S DIRTY RICE ☆

SERVES 6 AS A SIDE DISH

Seasoning Mix
2 teaspoons ground red pepper (preferably cayenne)
$1\frac{1}{2}$ teaspoons salt
$1\frac{1}{2}$ teaspoons ground black pepper
$1\frac{1}{4}$ teaspoons paprika
1 teaspoon mustard powder
1 teaspoon ground cumin
$\frac{1}{2}$ teaspoon dried thyme
$\frac{1}{2}$ teaspoon dried oregano

2 tablespoons chicken fat or vegetable oil
8 oz (225 g) chicken gizzards, minced
4 oz (110 g) minced pork
2 bay leaves
8 tablespoons finely chopped onions
8 tablespoons finely chopped celery
8 tablespoons finely chopped green peppers
2 teaspoons crushed garlic
2 tablespoons unsalted butter

16 fl oz (475 ml) chicken or pork stock
5 oz (150 g) chicken livers, minced
5 oz (150 g) uncooked rice (preferably converted)

Combine the seasoning mix ingredients in a small bowl and set aside.

Place the chicken fat, gizzards, pork and bay leaves in a large frying-pan over high heat; cook for about 6 minutes, stirring occasionally, until the meat is thoroughly browned. Stir in the seasoning mix, then add the onions, celery, green peppers and garlic; stir thoroughly, scraping the pan bottom well. Add the butter and stir until melted. Reduce the heat to medium and cook for about 8 minutes, stirring constantly and scraping the pan bottom well (if you are not using a heavy-bottomed pan, the mixture will probably stick a lot). Add the stock and stir until any mixture sticking to the pan bottom comes lose; cook for about 8 minutes over a high heat, stirring once. Then stir in the chicken livers and cook for about 2 minutes. Add the rice and stir thoroughly; cover the pan and turn the heat to very low; cook for 5 minutes. Remove from the heat and leave to stand, covered, for about 10 minutes or until the rice is tender. (The rice is finished in this way so as not to overcook the livers and to preserve their delicate flavour.) Remove the bay leaves and serve immediately.

☆ SUNSHINE VEGETABLE ☆ MEDLEY

You can make any amount of this: just make sure that you have equal quantities of each type of vegetable.

Butter
Paul Prudhomme's Cajun Magic or barbecue spice
Louisiana or other spicy sausage, finely diced
Chicken stock

Equal quantities of the following
Onions
Red, yellow and green peppers, chopped
Okra
Tomatoes, chopped

Heat some butter in a pan. Sauté the onions, peppers and okra. Season with Cajun Magic or barbecue spice to taste and stir well. Put in the spicy sausage, the chicken stock and tomatoes, bring to simmering point and let the dish bubble away for 35 minutes.

☆ JOE CAHN'S ☆
BREAD PUDDING WITH WHISKEY SAUCE

SERVES 16–20

10 oz (275 g) breadcrumbs made from stale French bread

$1\frac{1}{2}$ pints (900 ml) milk

14 oz (400 g) sugar

8 tablespoons melted butter

3 eggs

2 teaspoons vanilla essence

$5\frac{1}{2}$ oz (165 g) raisins

$3\frac{1}{2}$ oz (90 g) desiccated coconut

4 oz (110 g) pecan nuts, chopped

1 teaspoon ground cinnamon

1 teaspoon grated nutmeg

Sauce

4 oz (110 g) butter

$10\frac{1}{2}$ oz (285 g) caster sugar

2 egg yolks

About 4 fl oz (120 ml) bourbon or other American whiskey

Combine all the pudding ingredients in a large bowl: the mixture should be moist but not soupy. Transfer to a buttered baking dish approximately 9 × 12 inches (23 × 30 cm) in size and bake in the oven at gas mark 4, 350°F (180°C), for about $1\frac{1}{4}$ hours or until the top is golden-brown.

To make the sauce, cream the butter and sugar together in a pan over medium heat until all the butter is absorbed. Remove from the heat and blend in the egg yolks. Gradually add the bourbon to your own taste, stirring constantly. Allow the sauce to cool a little before serving – it will thicken as it does so. Serve warm over the warm pudding.

☆ Joe Cahn's Pralines ☆

M A K E S   U P   T O   5 0   (D E P E N D I N G   O N   S I Z E)

7½ oz (210 g) pecan or similar nuts
10½ oz (285 g) granulated white sugar
5 oz (150 g) light brown sugar
4 fl oz (120 ml) milk
6 tablespoons butter
1 teaspoon vanilla essence

Spread the nuts out on a baking sheet and roast in the oven at gas mark 1, 275°F (140°C), for 20–25 minutes or until slightly browned and aromatic, then chop roughly. Combine all the praline ingredients and heat, stirring constantly, until the mixture reaches the 'soft ball' stage (that is, like soft toffee). Remove from the heat and continue to stir until the mixture thickens, becoming creamy and cloudy, and the pecans (if using) no longer sink but remain suspended. Spoon portions of the required size on to a sheet of aluminium foil and leave to cool.

☆ FLOYD'S MEMPHIS SOULFOOD ☆
CHITLINS, CANDIED YAMS, BLACK-EYED PEAS
AND TURNIP GREENS

Mississippi caviar – that's what the folks around here call chitlins (or chitterlings, as we know them). When I was a boy in Somerset, they were big news, but it's years and years since I ate them, so when I was asked to cook my idea of a Memphis meal for the Reverend Cutter, I thought it would be fun to cook up some chitlins.

First of all I asked around to find out how they cook them in Memphis. Since I can't in all honesty pretend that the aroma of chitlins during the early stages of cooking is very sweet, the best piece of advice I got was to do it with the window open and a bottle of Jack Daniels handy!

Memphisonians differ on how to cook chitlins. The traditional way is to boil them with onions and peppers for 3 to 4 hours and then serve them in their own juices. One cook, however, suggested boiling them with garlic powder, barbecue sauce and cayenne pepper, then dipping them in waffle batter, deep-frying them in peanut oil and serving them with Louisiana hot sauce.

Eventually I decided to boil them in the traditional way then deep-fry them and make up my own spicy tomato and pepper sauce to go with them.

CHITLINS

1 lb (450 g) or more chitlins
1 medium onion, chopped
1 green pepper, chopped
Flour for dusting
Oil for deep-frying

Sauce
1 medium onion, chopped
1 green pepper, chopped
1 clove garlic, crushed
A little oil
Dash of tomato purée
Pinch of cayenne pepper
$\frac{1}{2}$ teaspoon paprika

Clean and cut up the chitlins. Blanch for about 3 hours in gently simmering water with the onion and green pepper. The chitlins should then look like little pieces of squid. Strain, dry them with kitchen paper and set aside.

To make the sauce, sauté the onion, green pepper and garlic in a little oil in a frying-pan until soft. Add the tomato sauce, cayenne and paprika and simmer gently for 20–30 minutes. When the sauce is just ready, dust the chitlins with flour and deep-fry for a few minutes in hot oil until crisp. Serve with the sauce.

CANDIED YAMS

I borrowed this recipe from Buntyn's Restaurant in Memphis.

1½ lb (700 g) yams (sweet potatoes)
2 teaspoons butter

4 oz (110 g) sugar
1 teaspoon cornflour mixed with a little water
1 teaspoon grated nutmeg
1 teaspoon vanilla essence

Peel the yams and cut into slices 1 inch (2.5 cm) thick. Boil in water for about 20 minutes like ordinary potatoes until just cooked. Strain off most of the water, then add the butter, sugar, cornflour and water mixture, nutmeg and vanilla essence and mix gently but thoroughly. Simmer for 5–6 minutes.

BLACK-EYED PEAS

8 oz (225 g) dried black-eyed peas
7 oz (200 g) smoked or salted fat pork, diced

Soak the peas overnight in plenty of cold water. Drain. In a hot pan fry the pork until the fat runs. Add the peas. Cover with water and simmer for about 1½ hours or until the peas are tender.

TURNIP GREENS

In England we would throw away greens like this or give them to the animals – but in Southern cooking they are highly regarded.

1 lb (450 g) smoked or salted fat pork, diced
2 lb (900 g) turnip greens
Salt (optional)

In a hot pan fry the pork until the fat runs. Add the turnip greens and stir (they will shrink, rather like spinach). Then add about 16 fl oz (475 ml) water and salt if you like – but remember that the greens are quite bitter. Simmer for about 40 minutes or until the greens are tender.

☆ OYSTER STEW ☆
MRS HUBERT K. REESE

'This is a meal in itself and should be used as such,' says Mrs Hubert K. Reese.

SERVES 4–6

Parsley
4 small white onions
4 celery hearts
4 small carrots
2 turnips
6 tablespoons butter
2 heaped tablespoons flour
16 fl oz (475 ml) hot milk
2 dozen oysters, shelled
Salt and freshly ground pepper
16 fl oz (475 ml) double cream

Chop the parsley, onions, celery, carrots and turnips. Put 2 tablespoons of the butter in frying-pan, add the vegetables and sauté until golden brown. Make a white sauce in a double boiler by melting 2 more tablespoons of the butter and stirring in the flour and milk until thickened. Keep warm. Place the oysters and their juice in an enamel pan with the remaining 2 tablespoons butter, some pepper and a little salt. When ready to serve, heat the oysters until the edges curl. Add the chopped vegetables to the white sauce, then add the heated cream, and then the oysters with a little of their juice. Omit the parsley from the vegetable mixture if desired and instead sprinkle it on top of the dish before serving.

☆ BARBECUED CHICKEN IN A PAPER BAG ☆

MRS JOHN H. TERRY

S ERVES 4

3 tablespoons tomato ketchup

2 tablespoons vinegar

1 tablespoon lemon juice

2 tablespoons Worcestershire sauce

4 tablespoons water

2 tablespoons butter

3 tablespoons brown sugar

1 teaspoon salt

1 teaspoon mustard

1 teaspoon chilli powder

1 teaspoon paprika

$\frac{1}{2}$ teaspoon cayenne pepper

1 × 3 lb (1.4 kg) chicken, jointed

Pre-heat the oven to gas mark 8, 450°F (230°C). Mix together all the ingredients except the chicken and bring to the boil in a saucepan. Grease the inside of a roasting bag and place it in a lidded oval roaster. Dip the chicken pieces into the hot sauce to coat well and place in the bag. Pour the remaining sauce into the bag also and carefully fold over the top so that it will not leak. Put the lid on the roaster and cook in the oven for 15 minutes, then lower the heat to gas mark 4, 350°F (180°C), and cook for a further $1\frac{1}{4}$ hours. Do not open the bag until the end of the cooking time.

☆ IRENE CLEAVES'S ☆
SOUTHERN FRIED CHICKEN
FOURWAYS GRILL, MEMPHIS

As an alternative to gravy, you could serve this chicken with my Memphis Sauce (see the recipe following this one).

SERVES 4

Flour for dusting
Salt and freshly ground black pepper
2 eggs, beaten
A little milk
1 × 3 lb (1.4 kg) chicken, jointed
Oil for frying

Gravy
A little flour
Salt and freshly ground black pepper

Season the flour with salt and pepper and combine the eggs and milk. Dust the chicken pieces with flour and then dip in the eggwash. In a large frying-pan heat the oil and fry the chicken gently to begin with, raising the temperature until it is as brown as desired and cooked through – this will take about 10–15 minutes. Remove from the pan and keep warm.

To make the gravy, add a little flour to the oil in the pan and brown slowly. Add cold water, stirring, until the gravy is of the required thickness, plus salt and pepper to taste. Simmer for a few minutes, then pour over chicken.

☆ FLOYD'S MEMPHIS SAUCE ☆ FOR SOUTHERN FRIED CHICKEN

Tampering with Southern Fried Chicken can be a dangerous thing in this part of the world, where it is practically a national institution. Traditionally it is served dry, which, I think, is a bit boring, or with the kind of simple yet delicious gravy that Irene Cleaves makes at the Fourways Grill. I decided to take my life in my hands and go one step further, so I invented this bacon-flavoured little number with sweetcorn and some crunchy spring onions to counteract the creaminess. I don't think it's on the menu at the Fourways Grill yet, but I did live to pass on the recipe!

SERVES 4

Butter
1 oz (25 g) smoked bacon, diced
2 shallots, finely chopped
1 tablespoon finely diced red pepper
1 tablespoon finely diced green pepper
2 tablespoons sweet corn
Chicken stock
American or other mild mustard
Paprika or chilli powder
Jack Daniels bourbon
Cream
Salt and freshly ground black pepper
Chopped spring onions to garnish

Melt a little butter in a pan and add the bacon. Add the shallots, peppers and corn. Pour in some chicken stock. Turn up the heat and let the sauce bubble for 3–4 minutes. Add a little mustard, a dash of paprika or chilli powder and a knob of butter, plus a little Jack Daniels bourbon to taste. If the sauce tastes bitter, bubble up again to get rid of the alcohol and add a little more butter if necessary. Stir in a little cream, season with salt and pepper, garnish with chopped spring onions and serve instead of gravy with Irene Cleaves's Southern Fried Chicken (see preceding recipe).

On my arrival in Memphis, I was presented with a copy of *The Memphis Cookery Book* – a collection of recipes handed down through American homes. These are a few which caught my fancy.

☆ JELLIED BEEF LOAF ☆
MRS HENRY H. HAIZLIP

SERVES 8

2 lb (900 g) good-quality braising steak, cut into 1 inch (2.5 cm) cubes
1 onion, sliced
2 sticks celery, chopped
1 carrot, chopped
3 cups boiling water
Few sprigs parsley
1 cup tomato juice
1 tablespoon vinegar
2 teaspoons salt
$1\frac{1}{2}$ tablespoons gelatine powder
$\frac{1}{8}$ teaspoon pepper
$\frac{1}{4}$ teaspoon mustard powder
$\frac{1}{2}$ teaspoon Worcestershire sauce
1 teaspoon creamed horseradish
$\frac{1}{2}$ teaspoon vinegar
$\frac{3}{4}$ teaspoon salt

Place the first nine ingredients in a saucepan, bring to the boil and simmer, covered, for 2 hours. Drain, reserving the liquid. Chop the meat roughly. Cool 4 fl oz (120 ml) of the cooking liquid and soak the gelatine in it for 5 minutes. Dissolve this in the remaining liquid, boiling hot. Add the remaining ingredients. Chill the mixture until it begins to thicken, add the meat, pour into a mould and chill in the refrigerator until firm. Serve with creamed horseradish.

Candied yams (page 226); Black-eyed peas (page 227);
Chitlins (page 226); Turnip greens (page 227)

☆ OQUREE'S CORNBREAD ☆
BUNTYN'S RESTAURANT, MEMPHIS

MAKES ABOUT 25

8 oz (225 g) cornmeal
3 tablespoons strong white flour
1 teaspoon salt
2½ tablespoons sugar
2 tablespoons baking powder
16 fl oz (475 ml) buttermilk
3 tablespoons oil
2 eggs, beaten

Pre-heat the oven to gas mark 8, 450°F (230°C). In a bowl mix together the cornmeal, flour, salt, sugar and baking powder. Mix in the buttermilk, then add the oil and finally the eggs. Continue to mix until smooth. Brush small skillets or muffin tins with oil and heat in the oven. Transfer the mixture to the skillets or tins and bake in the oven for about 15–20 minutes or until brown on top and cooked through.

☆ OQUREE'S COCONUT PIE ☆
BUNTYN'S RESTAURANT, MEMPHIS

SERVES 6–8

9 tablespoons sugar
3 egg yolks
16 fl oz (475 ml) milk
2 tablespoons cornflour
2 oz (50 g) butter
4–6 oz (110–175 g) fresh coconut, grated
1 teaspoon vanilla essence
1 × 9 inch (23 cm) part-baked pastry shell (see page 202)

Southern fried chicken with Memphis sauce (page 230);
Peach cobbler (page 236); Cornbread (page 235)

Meringue
4 egg whites
$3\frac{1}{2}$ oz (90 g) sugar

First make the pie filling. Stir together the sugar and egg yolks. Add the milk. Put into a double boiler and bring to the boil. Meanwhile mix the cornflour with a little water, add to the egg mixture and stir until thick. Add the butter, coconut (reserving 1 tablespoon) and vanilla. Pour into the pastry shell and leave to cool.

Make the meringue by beating the egg whites until stiff but not dry. Fold in the sugar. Pile on top of the pie. Sprinkle with the reserved coconut and bake in the oven at gas mark 5, 375°F (190°C), for about 10 minutes or until the meringue is lightly browned.

☆ # IRENE CLEAVES'S ☆
PEACH COBBLER
FOURWAYS GRILL, MEMPHIS

SERVES 4-6

8 medium peaches, peeled, stoned and sliced
7 oz (200 g) sugar
2 oz (50 g) butter
Pinch of grated nutmeg

Crust
2 tablespoons lard
5 oz (150 g) flour
Pinch of salt
A little butter

Pre-heat the oven to gas mark 5, 375°F (190°C). Place the peaches, sugar, butter and 4 fl oz (120 ml) water in an ovenproof dish and sprinkle with nutmeg. Make the crust by rubbing the lard into the flour and salt with your fingers. Add enough cold water to make a soft dough – but not so moist that it sticks to your hands. Roll out as thinly as possible and cut into 1 inch (2.5 cm) strips. Line the rim of the dish with a continuous strip, joining as necessary, and place the remaining strips over the peaches lengthways and widthways to make a lattice pattern. Melt a little butter and pour over crust. Bake in the oven for about 30 minutes or until brown.

☆ NEW ORLEANS-STYLE ☆
CHOCOLATE WALNUT BREAD PUDDING
SLEEP OUT LOUIE'S, MEMPHIS

Sleep Out Louie's is a cosy little joint with a roaring fire in winter, where you can get wonderfully comforting things like a bowl of beef stew with a side order of cheese on toast and a bourbon on the rocks pretty late into the night – well, late for America where, surprisingly, many restaurants close at around 9pm. Sleep Out Louie's even does 'half' hamburgers for wimps who can't manage the lot! But best of all is this chocolate bread pudding, which is served with bourbon sauce – and they don't stint on the bourbon either! They're a bit secretive about how the sauce is made, but since this is an adaptation of a New Orleans recipe anyway, you can use Joe Cahn's recipe for Whiskey Sauce on page 223.

This recipe makes a vast amount, but it is the principle that counts, so just reduce the quantities to suit yourself – or cook the full amount for a large party.

SERVES A PARTY

8 pints (4.5 litres) milk
1 lb 5 oz (595 g) sugar
3 teaspoons salt
3 teaspoons vanilla essence
1 tablespoon ground cinnamon
5 teaspoons grated nutmeg
$1\frac{1}{2}$ lb (700 g) plain chocolate, broken into pieces

12 eggs
Butter
6 loaves French bread, cut in $\frac{1}{4}$ inch (0.5 cm) thick slices
10 oz (275 g) walnuts, chopped
Whiskey Sauce to serve (see page 223)

Heat the milk to boiling point. Add the sugar, salt, vanilla, spices and chocolate. Stir and allow the chocolate to melt. In a large bowl beat the eggs and add the milk mixture slowly, stirring constantly. Butter the slices of bread and arrange some in a layer, one slice deep, in a large, greased baking tin. Sprinkle some of the walnuts over the bread. Continue to layer the bread and walnuts until they are all used up. Pour the chocolate mixture over and leave for 45 minutes to allow it to soak into the bread. Cook in a pre-heated oven at gas mark 5, 375°F (190°C), for about 1 hour or until a knife blade inserted in the centre of the pudding comes out clean. Serve with Whiskey Sauce.

☆ PECAN OR PEANUT ☆
BRITTLE

Once I discovered this, I couldn't stop eating it.

MAKES ABOUT $1\frac{1}{4}$ lb (550 g)

14 oz (400 g) sugar
1 tablespoon butter
8 oz (225 g) pecan nuts or peanuts (unsalted)
$\frac{1}{2}$ teaspoon bicarbonate of soda

In a heavy skillet or frying-pan cook the sugar until it caramelises, being careful not to let it burn. Add the butter, nuts and baking soda and mix well. Lightly oil a baking sheet and smooth the mixture evenly and thinly over it. Leave to cool completely and then break into pieces.

Texas

☆ <u>FLOYD'S CEVICHE</u> ☆

This dish uses very fresh, raw fish, tenderised in a spicy Mexican marinade. I used scallops, halibut and fresh prawns, but you can use salmon or any fish you like.

SERVES 4

6 tomatoes, peeled, halved and de-seeded
2 fresh chilli peppers, chopped
Dash of Tabasco sauce
Juice of 3 lemons and/or limes
Good dash of tomato ketchup
1 small onion, finely chopped
1 tablespoon chopped coriander leaves
12 scallops
8 oz (225 g) halibut fillet, thinly sliced
12 prawns

Combine the tomatoes, chillies, Tabasco, lemon and/or lime juice and tomato ketchup in a blender. Stir in the onion and coriander. Pour over the raw fish and leave to marinate in the refrigerator for 3 hours. Serve with crusty bread or corn chips.

☆ FLOYD'S MEXICAN BEEF ☆

SERVES 4–6

3 medium red potatoes
4 tablespoons vegetable oil
1 large green pepper, de-seeded and chopped
1 large onion, chopped
1½ lb (700 g) beef tenderloin, cubed
2 large tomatoes, peeled and chopped
A little beef stock
Salt and freshly ground black pepper
Chopped coriander leaves to garnish

Par-boil the potatoes in water for about 5 minutes. Peel and cut into cubes. Heat the oil in a frying-pan, sauté the potatoes until browned and set aside. In the same pan sauté the green pepper and onion briefly, add the beef and tomatoes, and, when the meat has browned, add the potatoes and a little beef stock and bubble for about 20 minutes until the meat is tender and the sauce is reduced. Season to taste with salt and pepper and sprinkle with coriander just before serving.

☆ JAILHOUSE CHILLI ☆

This is chilli cooked with no added liquid. Unfortunately, the quantities would have fed the inmates of the Caldwell County Jail for months – if you fancy trying it, you'll have to do some long division.

SERVES A WHOLE JAIL!

50 lb (23 kg) minced beef
1 lb (450 g) garlic, crushed
8 oz (225 g) red chilli powder
4 oz (110 g) paprika
1 lb (450 g) ground cumin
4 tablespoons crushed red chilli peppers (optional)

Cook in a pan roughly the size of a dustbin, covered with a lid, over a medium heat for about 1 hour, stirring regularly.

☆ BEEF RIBS ☆

S E R V E S   A B O U T   4

3 lb (1.4 kg) beef ribs
2 fl oz (50 ml) oil
1 medium onion, chopped
2 sticks celery
1 clove garlic, crushed
2 fl oz (50 ml) white wine
4 fl oz (120 ml) soy sauce
$\frac{1}{4}$ teaspoon chilli powder
$\frac{1}{4}$ teaspoon freshly ground pepper
8 oz (225 g) tomato ketchup
8 carrots, peeled and chopped
4 potatoes, peeled and chopped

Pre-heat the oven to gas mark 3, 325°F (170°C). In a flameproof casserole brown the ribs in the oil. Then mix all the other ingredients and pour over. Bake in the oven for 2 hours.

☆ FLOYD'S TEXAS ☆ BARBECUE SAUCE

This is good with barbecued steak or any other meat.

S E R V E S   4–6

1 onion, finely chopped
1 clove garlic, crushed
4 oz (110 g) butter
1 tablespoon sugar
2 teaspoons mustard powder
2 teaspoons chilli powder
8 fl oz (250 ml) tomato ketchup
4 fl oz (120 ml) vinegar
1 tablespoon Worcestershire sauce

In a large skillet or frying-pan, sauté the onion and garlic gently in the butter. Combine all the other ingredients in a bowl with 4 fl oz (120 ml) water, then add to the pan. Bring to the boil and simmer for 5 minutes or until the sauce thickens.

☆ # FIRST MAKE YOUR ☆
TORTILLA

All Mexican cookery starts with the tortilla. Buying them ready-made is simpler, but if you fancy having a go at making them yourself and can find some corn masa (speciality shops should have it), here's how to do it.

MAKES ABOUT 12

10 oz (275 g) corn masa
8 fl oz (250 ml) plus 2 tablespoons warm water

Mix the masa or wholewheat flour and water in a bowl until they form a dough that holds together. Divide into 12 pieces and roll each between your hands to form a ball. Place each in turn between 2 sheets of firm plastic, flatten with the palm of the hand, then roll out with a rolling pin, turning the dough over, still inside the plastic, until it is about 6 inches (15 cm) in diameter. Gently peel away the plastic and, using a sharp cutter about 5 inches (12.5 cm) in diameter, cut the dough into a round. Heat a griddle or a frying-pan and cook each tortilla quickly for about 30 seconds on either side, keeping it flat with a spatula, until it is speckled in appearance. Then either turn the tortilla again or flash it under a hot grill until it puffs up.

☆

Once you have your tortillas, you can make a complete Mexican feast:

☆ NACHOS ☆

These crispy triangular corn chips are great for dipping into spicy dips, or salsas, at parties or as a prelude to a meal.

Tortillas
Oil for frying

Cut the tortillas into quarters and fry in hot oil until crisp. Keep warm until you are ready to serve them with guacamole or a salsa like the one following or the one on page 261.

You can make cheese nachos by placing a thin slice of cheese on each one, topping with thin slices of hot chilli pepper and grilling quickly, so that the cheese melts.

SALSA RANCHERA

SERVES 4–6

About 5 small green chilli peppers, de-seeded
A pinch of salt
5 fl oz (150 ml) vinegar
$2\frac{1}{2}$ fl oz (65 ml) cold water
1 lb (450 g) tomatoes, skinned and very finely chopped

Lightly blend the peppers, salt, vinegar and water. Mix with the tomatoes.

☆ TACOS ☆

To make tacos, fry tortillas one at a time in about 1 inch (2.5 cm) hot oil, folding them in half over a spoon almost immediately to keep the 'envelope' open. Fry until crisp, turning once.

These shells can then be filled with cooked shredded chicken, minced beef chilli or guacamole, topped with shredded lettuce, chopped tomato and a little hot chilli sauce. Or you can make up your own filling.

☆ SOFT TACOS ☆

Instead of frying the tortillas crisply, fry them in about $\frac{1}{2}$ inch (1 cm) oil, making sure that they stay soft, for about 30 seconds, turning once. These 'pancakes' can then be stuffed with the filling of your choice (see preceding recipe) and topped with this tomato sauce:

1 small onion, chopped
1 clove garlic, crushed
1 tablespoon oil
1 lb (450 g) tomatoes, skinned and chopped
$\frac{1}{2}$ teaspoon salt

Sauté the onion and garlic in the oil, add the tomatoes and salt and simmer for about 10 minutes.

☆ CHICKEN ENCHILADAS ☆

Enchiladas are tortillas soaked in chilli sauce.

SERVES 6

2 green peppers, chopped
1 onion, chopped
$2\frac{1}{2}$ oz (65 g) butter
1 × 14 oz (400 g) tin tomatoes
16 fl oz (475 ml) tomato ketchup
$\frac{1}{4}$ teaspoon chopped garlic
$\frac{1}{2}$ teaspoon fresh oregano leaves
$\frac{1}{4}$ teaspoon freshly ground pepper
2 tablespoons flour
2 lb (900 g) cooked chicken, cut into thin strips
Vegetable oil
12 corn tortillas
6 oz (75 g) goat's cheese, crumbled
Chopped parsley to garnish

Sauté the peppers and onion in $\frac{1}{2}$ oz (10 g) of the butter until soft. Add the tomatoes, ketchup, garlic, oregano, pepper and 4 fl oz (120 ml) water and simmer for 20–30 minutes. In a food processor blend the remaining butter, the flour and 4 fl oz (120 ml) water with 4 fl oz (120 ml) of the tomato mixture. Whisk into the rest of the tomato mixture and cook for another 10 minutes. Thin with more water if necessary. Stir the chicken into 4 fl oz (120 ml) of the sauce and set aside. Heat the oil in a frying-pan, put in the tortillas and soften for a few seconds on each side. Drain on kitchen paper. Dip the tortillas into the tomato sauce, fill with the chicken mixture and roll up like pancakes.

Place, seam downwards, in a dish, pour over the rest of the sauce and bake in the oven at gas mark 4, 350°F (180°C), for 10–15 minutes. Remove from the oven. Sprinkle with cheese, then return to the oven for another 2–3 minutes. Garnish with parsley before serving.

☆ CHICKEN FAJITAS ☆
SEIS SALSA, AUSTIN

This is delicious on its own or wrapped in a soft taco.

SERVES 4

4 chicken breasts, cut into strips $\frac{1}{2}$ inch (1 cm) wide
Oil for frying

Marinade
6 green peppers, blanched and de-seeded
5 cloves garlic
$\frac{1}{4}$ teaspoon ground cumin
$\frac{1}{4}$ teaspoon dried oregano
$\frac{1}{4}$ teaspoon freshly ground black pepper
$\frac{1}{2}$ teaspoon salt
2 tablespoons vinegar

Garnish
2 chilli peppers, blanched and de-seeded
1 medium white onion, chopped
1 bunch spring onions, coarsely chopped

Put all the marinade ingredients into a blender with 16 fl oz (475 ml) water and whizz to a consistency that will stick to the chicken (add more water if necessary). Coat the chicken in the mixture and leave to marinate for 30 minutes. Heat the oil in a frying-pan and quickly sear the strips of chicken for a couple of minutes on each side. At the same time, in another pan, heat more oil and fiercely and quickly fry the garnish ingredients. Tip this sizzling mixture over the strips of cooked chicken and serve.

☆ CHILLI RELLENOS ☆ (STUFFED CHILLIES)

SERVES 4

12 large poblano chillies
4 oz (110 g) cheese, grated
1 small onion, chopped
Oil for deep-frying

Batter
2 eggs, separated
2 tablespoons flour
Pinch of salt
$\frac{1}{2}$ teaspoon baking powder

First make the batter. Beat the egg whites until they are stiff; beat the yolks until thick. Sift the flour and salt and baking powder and mix into the egg yolks, then fold in the whites.

Peel the chillies if you wish, but leave the stems on. Slit each one lengthways from tip to stem and remove the pith and seeds. Combine the cheese and onion and carefully stuff the chillies with the mixture. Dip each chilli into the batter to coat well and deep-fry in hot oil until golden-brown.

☆ GINGER COOKIES ☆

MAKES MASSES

$1\frac{1}{2}$ lb (700 g) molasses
8 oz (225 g) lard
1 tablespoon ground ginger
$\frac{1}{2}$ teaspoon salt
1 teaspoon bicarbonate of soda
10 oz (275 g) pecan nuts or walnuts, finely chopped
$2\frac{1}{2}$ lb (1.25 kg) flour

Bring the molasses to the boil in a pan, add the lard, ginger and salt, and mix well. Dissolve the bicarbonate of soda in 1 tablespoon hot water and add to the pan. Stir, then leave to cool.

Pre-heat the oven to gas mark 4, 350°F (180°C). Add the pecan nuts or walnuts to the cooled mixture. Stir in the flour to make a stiff dough. Roll out and cut into shapes of your choice. Place on a greased baking sheet and bake in the oven for about 10 minutes or until set and golden-brown.

☆ PECAN PIE ☆

SERVES 6–8

1 × 9 inch (23 cm) part-baked pastry shell (see page 202)

Filling
3 eggs, lightly beaten
8 fl oz (250 ml) corn syrup
1 teaspoon vanilla essence
7 oz (200 g) sugar or to taste
Pinch of salt
2 tablespoons melted butter
4 oz (110 g) pecan nuts, broken or halved

Pre-heat the oven to gas mark 6, 400°F (200°C). Mix together all the filling ingredients and pour into the pastry shell. Bake in the oven for 15 minutes, then reduce the heat to gas mark 4, 350°F (180°C), and bake for another 30 minutes or until set and golden-brown on top.

☆ Jeremiah Tower's ☆ San Franciscan Prawns
STARS RESTAURANT, SAN FRANCISCO

This being California, we used Hawaiian blue and pink Santa Barbara spot prawns (which are about the size of langoustines), but you can substitute large Mediterranean prawns.

S E R V E S   2

4–6 uncooked Mediterranean prawns
1 teaspoon chopped garlic
Butter
Couple of small sprigs thyme
Couple of small sprigs rosemary
1½ glasses white wine
1 tablespoon chopped parsley
Pinch of powdered saffron
2 tablespoons soured cream
Salt and freshly ground pepper
4–5 oz (110–150 g) broad beans, cooked and peeled
2 artichoke hearts, cooked and quartered

Sauté the prawns and garlic in a little butter in a frying-pan. Add the thyme and rosemary. Remove the prawns from the pan and keep warm. De-glaze the pan with some white wine. Add the chopped parsley, reserving a little to garnish the finished dish. Mix the saffron into the soured cream, stir into the pan juices and season to taste with salt and pepper. Add the cooked beans and artichoke hearts and warm through. Pour some sauce on to each plate, dividing the vegetables evenly between them, place the prawns on top and sprinkle with the reserved parsley.

☆ JEREMIAH TOWER'S ☆ BLINIS WITH SMOKED STURGEON AND CAVIAR

Another favourite from Stars Restaurant, a bit of unashamed luxury from Jeremiah Tower, one of San Francisco's most innovative chefs. It follows his principle of buying only the best ingredients and treating them as simply as possible.

S E R V E S 8

1 lb (450 g) butter plus 2 tablespoons melted butter
5 oz (150 g) yellow cornmeal
½ teaspoon salt
2 eggs
8 fl oz (250 ml) milk
3 oz (75 g) flour, sifted
8 tablespoons soured cream
8 tablespoons salmon caviar
8 teaspoons black caviar
24 thin slices smoked sturgeon

First clarify the 1 lb (450 g) butter. Melt it over a very low heat and leave in a warm place for 15 minutes. Skim the foam from the top, spoon off the clear, yellow, clarified butter and discard the milky liquid in the bottom. Set aside.

Now mix the cornmeal and salt. Stir in 16 fl oz (475 ml) boiling water. Cover and leave to stand for 10 minutes. Beat in the eggs, one at a time, then add the milk, stirring slowly. Mix in the flour and the 2 tablespoons melted butter and beat until the mixture is smooth. The batter should be the consistency of double cream. If necessary, thin it with a little more milk.

Brush a crêpe pan with warm clarified butter and heat. Pour in about 3 tablespoons batter and tilt the pan to spread the batter evenly. Cook for about 2–3 minutes or until the underside is browned. Turn and cook the other side for 1–2 minutes. Remove from the pan and keep warm. Make 7 more blinis in the same way.

To serve, place each blini on a hot plate and pour 3 tablespoons clarified butter over the top. Put 1 tablespoon soured cream in the centre of each, then 1 tablespoon salmon caviar on top and 1 teaspoon black caviar in the centre of that. Place 3 slices smoked sturgeon around each blini. Serve immediately.

☆ JEREMIAH TOWER'S ☆ CUCUMBER AND CRAYFISH CREAM VICHYSSOISE

SERVES 4

1 small onion, finely chopped
16 fl oz (475 ml) chicken stock
1 sprig fresh tarragon
2 large cucumbers, peeled, de-seeded and finely chopped
12 fl oz (350 ml) whipping cream
Salt and freshly ground pepper
4 sprigs chervil to garnish

Crayfish Essence
4 oz (100g) cooked crayfish shells
1½ pints (900 ml) fish stock

First make the crayfish essence by putting the shells into a food processor and grinding just enough to break them up. Put in the bowl of an electric mixer, fitted with a dough hook or paddle. Add 8 fl oz (250 ml) of the fish stock and mix for a further 40 minutes at a low speed until the shells are completely broken up and the stock is red-coloured. Put the mixture into a saucepan. Add the rest of the fish stock, bring to the boil, then simmer for 15 minutes. Strain, reserving the liquid, and set aside.

Continued on page 255

Opposite: Pak choy with scallops and prawns (page 258); Various kinds of Dim sum (page 256); Overleaf: Beef ribs (page 241); Chilli rellenos (page 246)

Put the onion, 2 tablespoons of the chicken stock and the tarragon into a saucepan, cover and sweat over very low heat for 10 minutes. Add the cucumbers and cook, covered, for a further 5 minutes. Then add the remaining chicken stock, bring to the boil and remove from the heat. Mix 2 fl oz (50 ml) crayfish essence into 4 fl oz (120 ml) of the cream and leave to stand for 30 minutes. (Freeze the remainder of the crayfish essence for use in other dishes.) Purée the cucumbers with their cooking liquid and stir in the remaining cream. Put into the refrigerator and leave until cold. Whip the crayfish cream for about a minute, season the soup and serve in chilled bowls with the crayfish cream swirled on top. Garnish each bowl with a sprig of chervil.

☆ FLOYD'S ☆
SAN FRANCISCAN CIOPPINO

This old Sicilian dish is really a kind of seafood stew, not unlike the French *bouillabaisse*. Down on Fisherman's Wharf in San Francisco it's a favourite at Alioto's Restaurant – but this is my version.

SERVES 8

2 large onions, chopped
3 carrots, chopped
3 cloves garlic, crushed
4 fl oz (120 ml) olive oil
$1\frac{1}{2}$ pints (900 ml) puréed fresh tomatoes plus a little tomato purée
2 fl oz (50 ml) dry white wine
6 heaped tablespoons chopped parsley
$1\frac{1}{2}$ teaspoons chopped thyme
1 tablespoon chopped basil
Pinch of cayenne pepper
1 lb (450 g) uncooked prawns

Previous page: Ginger cookies (page 247); Pecan pie (page 247);
Opposite: San Franciscan prawns (page 248); Salad; Barbecued lamb with Meyer lemon
sauce (page 262)

2 lb (900 g) white fish fillets
3 lb (1.4 kg) clams in shells, carefully scrubbed
2 crabs in shells, cooked and with shells cracked
Fish stock
Salt

Sauté the onions, carrots and garlic in the olive oil until the onions are soft. Add the puréed fresh tomatoes, tomato purée, wine, parsley, thyme, basil and cayenne pepper. Partially cover and simmer for 15 minutes. Add the prawns, white fish and unshelled clams and crabs, cover with fish stock and simmer for 15–20 minutes, adding a little salt if necessary.

Dim sum in San Francisco's Chinatown is a favourite event with Shirley Fong-Torres, the delightfully zany, ginseng-fuelled food critic, cooking instructor and tour director who whizzed us around *her* Chinatown. Here are a couple of her own recipes.

☆ SHIRLEY FONG-TORRES'S ☆ <u>'GOOD YEAR SHRIMPS'</u>

MAKES 16

5–6 oz (150–175 g) medium prawns, peeled and de-veined
4 tablespoons cooked ham
3–4 fresh or tinned Chinese water chestnuts
4 tablespoons finely chopped spring onions
8 rashers bacon
1 quantity Batter (see page 190)
Oil for deep-frying
Chinese hot mustard to serve

Seasonings
1½ teaspoons soy sauce
1 teaspoon Chinese rice wine

256

2 teaspoons cornflour
$\frac{1}{2}$ teaspoon sesame oil
Pinch of white pepper

First 'de-fat' the bacon. Either cook in a microwave oven for 3 minutes on HIGH or place on a baking sheet and bake in the oven at gas mark 4, 350°F (180°C), for 2 minutes (do not allow to brown). Drain well and pat dry. Cut each rasher in half and trim into 2 × 2$\frac{1}{2}$ inch (6 cm) lengths.

Now coarsely chop the prawns, ham and water chestnuts and mix together. Add the spring onions and stir until well blended. Place in a medium-sized bowl. Add the seasonings and mix well. Shape into little balls and place each one on a half-rasher of bacon; roll up and secure with a wooden cocktail stick. Dip into the batter to coat, shake off the excess batter and deep-fry in oil over a medium heat until golden-brown (approximately 4 minutes on each side). Drain well before serving with the Chinese hot mustard as a dip.

☆ SHIRLEY FONG-TORRES'S ☆ POTSTICKERS

These little dumplings are shaped like Cornish pasties and made with flour dough 'wrappers' which you can buy in Chinese supermarkets.

MAKES ABOUT 30

1 lb (450 g) potsticker wrappers
Oil

Filling
8 oz (225 g) lean minced pork
8 oz (225 g) cabbage, cored and finely chopped
1 spring onion, finely chopped
1 clove garlic, finely chopped
1 teaspoon finely chopped fresh root ginger
1 tablespoon soy sauce
1 tablespoon dry sherry
1 tablespoon cornflour
1 teaspoon sesame oil
Pinch of white pepper

Prepare the filling by mixing the pork, cabbage, spring onion, garlic and ginger together in a bowl. Add the soy sauce, sherry, cornflour, sesame oil and pepper. Refrigerate at this point if necessary, until ready to use.

To assemble the potstickers, spoon 1 tablespoon of the filling into the centre of each potsticker wrapper. Fold the dough over to make a half-circle and moisten the bottom half-circle with a small amount of water. Pleat the edges firmly, forming 3–4 pleats on the top half-circle. Set each potsticker upright on a platter, so that a flat base is formed.

To cook the potstickers, heat a large non-stick frying-pan and put in 1 tablespoon oil. Place the potstickers, close to one another, around the pan but not touching. Brown them for about 30 seconds. Pour in enough hot water to cover the potstickers half-way. Cover with a lid and let cook over a moderate heat for 5–6 minutes. After the water has evaporated, swirl in 1 teaspoon oil. Tip the pan to ease the potstickers out of the pan. Remove very carefully with a spatula. Turn each potsticker over, dark side up, and place on a platter to serve, accompanied by little dishes of chilli oil, vinegar, soy sauce and sesame oil, which the diners mix according to individual taste.

☆ FLOYD'S PAK CHOY ☆ WITH SCALLOPS AND PRAWNS

A-wok-bop-a-loo-wok ... my contribution to Chinatown. (And sorry, but you do need to get to a Chinese supermarket for the ingredients to make it.)

SERVES 4

8 oz (225 g) chicken, diced
1 tablespoon black bean sauce
Oil for frying
1 teaspoon chopped fresh root ginger
$\frac{1}{2}$ teaspoon chopped garlic
5 oz (150 g) spring onions, chopped
6 scallops
6 prawns, peeled

4 oz (110 g) Chinese broccoli, cut into thin strips
2 oz (50 g) baby pak choy
2 oz (50 g) choy sum
2 tablespoons Chinese chives
1 tablespoon Chinese yellow chives
8 fl oz (250 ml) chicken stock
1 teaspoon cornflour
Couple of dashes of soy sauce
Finely chopped lemon grass

Marinate the chicken in the black bean sauce for 1 hour. Heat some oil in a wok until very hot and put in the ginger, garlic, spring onions and chicken. Stir-fry briefly, then add the scallops and prawns and continue to cook. Add the broccoli and pak choy, followed by the choy sum and chives, and stir-fry for a further minute or two. Pour in the chicken stock. Mix the cornflour with a little water and add to the wok to thicken the sauce. Flavour with soy sauce to taste, add the lemon grass, stir-fry briefly and serve.

☆ JEREMIAH TOWER'S ☆ STEAK TARTARE

SERVES 4

8 fl oz (250 ml) mayonnaise
1 lb (450 g) lean sirloin steak
2 eggs, hard-boiled
1 medium green chilli pepper
1 medium yellow chilli pepper
1 medium red chilli pepper
$\frac{1}{2}$ teaspoon Tabasco sauce
2 tablespoons lemon juice
Salt and freshly ground pepper
4 tablespoons capers, rinsed
4 tablespoons chopped parsley

Chilli Purée
About 10 ancho (or large, dried, mild) chilli peppers
1 tablespoon lime juice
4 fl oz (120 ml) olive oil
Salt

First make the chilli purée. Put the ancho chillies into a bowl, cover with water and weight them down with a plate so that they are all submerged in the water. Leave overnight, drain, then remove the stems and seeds. Purée the chillies in a blender or food processor with the lime juice and whisk in the olive oil. Season with salt to taste. This makes about 8 fl oz (250 ml) – more than you need for this recipe, so store the remainder in the refrigerator for later use.

Now mix 2 fl oz (50 ml) chilli purée with the mayonnaise and leave to stand for 1 hour. Trim the steak and cut into 1 inch (2.5 cm) cubes, then mince in a food processor or chop finely. Separate the yolks from the whites of the hard-boiled eggs and sieve separately. Slice the chilli peppers into thin strips and discard the seeds. Mix the Tabasco, lemon juice and salt and pepper to taste. Add the steak and mix well. To serve, place a portion of steak mixture in the centre of each plate, top with some chilli mayonnaise and 1 tablespoon capers and arrange with the egg yolks, whites and chopped parsley decoratively around it.

☆ # JEREMIAH TOWER'S STUFFED CHILLIES ☆

SERVES 4

8 fresh poblano (or large, dried, mild) chilli peppers
2 fl oz (50 ml) oil
6 oz (175 g) white goat's cheese
4 tablespoons grated Fontina or Gruyère cheese
4 tablespoons finely grated Parmesan cheese
6 tablespoons double cream
$\frac{1}{2}$ teaspoon freshly ground black pepper
Coriander sprigs to garnish

Black Bean Sauce
4 tablespoons fermented salted Chinese black beans
4 fl oz (120 ml) chicken stock
4 oz (110 g) unsalted butter, cut into pieces
Freshly ground black pepper

Jeremiah Tower's Salsa
10 oz (275 g) tomatoes, skinned, de-seeded and chopped
1 small red onion, finely chopped
1 serrano or other hot chilli pepper, de-seeded and finely chopped
4 tablespoons chopped coriander
$\frac{1}{2}$ teaspoon salt
1–2 tablespoons lime juice
$\frac{1}{2}$ tablespoon olive oil

First make the black bean sauce. Rinse the beans and soak them in cold water for 2–3 hours, depending on how strong you want the sauce to taste. Change the water twice during the soaking time. Drain and rinse under cold running water. Put the beans in a blender, add the stock and blend to a fine purée. Put this into a saucepan, bring to the boil, then reduce the heat and simmer for 5 minutes. Remove from the heat and whisk in the butter, a piece at a time. Season with pepper and set aside.

Make the salsa by mixing the tomatoes, onion, serrano chilli and coriander in a bowl. Add the salt and half the lime juice. Mix, taste and add the rest of the lime juice if necessary. Leave for 1 hour before using. If the salsa becomes too watery, strain it. Stir in the oil just before serving.

Pre-heat the grill. Coat the poblano chillies with the oil, place them in the bottom of the grill pan and grill them, turning often, until the skin is browned and the flesh is just tender. Remove, cover and leave to stand for 15 minutes. Peel, slit lengthways and remove the seeds. Pre-heat the oven to gas mark 6, 400°F (200°C). Mix the cheeses, cream and black pepper in a bowl and stuff the chillies with this mixture. Place on an oiled baking sheet and bake in the oven for about 15 minutes or until the cheese begins to melt. Meanwhile, heat the black bean sauce in a double boiler. Pour the sauce on to 4 hot plates, place the stuffed chillies on top and garnish with coriander sprigs and salsa.

☆ FLOYD'S BARBECUED LAMB ☆ WITH MEYER LEMON SAUCE

I'm quite proud of this simple little dish, created entirely on the spur of the moment from an abundance of glorious ingredients offered to me by our genial hosts at the Iron Horse Vineyard in Sonoma County. Its special flavour comes from the Meyer lemons – little Californian delights which are a sort of cross between a lemon and a tangerine. Sadly, unless you're planning a trip to Sonoma County, the closest you can probably get is to use a mixture of lemon and orange juice. Similarly I used wonderful little golden mushrooms called cinnamon caps – but you can substitute small button mushrooms.

SERVES 2

8 cinnamon cap or button mushrooms
4 baby asparagus
Raspberry vinegar
Olive oil
4 kumquats
Garlic
Sage leaves
6 scollops of loin of lamb
4 baby leeks

Sauce
Juice of 2 Meyer lemons or 1 lemon and 1 orange
2 egg yolks
4 oz (110 g) melted butter

Marinate the mushrooms and asparagus in raspberry vinegar and olive oil for 10 minutes. Make mini-brochettes, alternating the mushrooms, kumquats, garlic cloves and sage leaves. Brush the lamb with oil and barbecue or grill until charred on the outside and pink in the middle. Barbecue or grill the marinated asparagus and baby leeks, and the mini-brochettes. Make the sauce by putting the lemon or mixed fruit juice into a double boiler. Add the egg yolks and whisk quickly. Add the melted butter and continue to whisk until thickened. Pour some sauce on to each plate, place the lamb on top and garnish with the young vegetables and fruit.

On my travels, I picked up a brilliant book called *White Trash Cooking* by Ernest Matthew Mickler (published by Ten Speed Press), which is full of whacky culinary concoctions. Here are a few I just couldn't resist including – although I have not cooked them, so beware!

☆ FREDA'S FIVE-CAN ☆ CASSEROLE

In glorious contrast to Jeremiah Tower's sophisticated cuisine, how about this!

1 small can boneless chicken
1 can cream of mushroom soup
1 can Chinese noodles
1 can chicken with rice soup
1 small can evaporated milk
1 small onion, finely chopped
8 tablespoons diced celery
2 oz (50 g) flaked almonds

Mix all the ingredients together and place in a casserole. Bake in the oven at gas mark 4, 350°F (180°C), for 1 hour.

☆ CHICKEN STEW (BROWN) ☆

$3\frac{1}{2}$ oz (90 g) bacon fat or oil
$3\frac{1}{2}$ oz (90 g) flour
1 bunch spring onions, chopped
1 bunch parsley, chopped
1 chicken, jointed
Salt, pepper and Tabasco sauce

Put the drippins (bacon fat) or oil in a Dutch oven (heavy, cast-iron, lidded pan) and heat. Add the flour and cook until it is a rich brown, stirring constantly. Add the onions and parsley and a little more fat or oil if it's too stiff to stir. Cook for a few minutes and add the chicken pieces and enough water barely to cover. Put in salt, pepper and Tabasco to taste and mix everything real good. Put the lid on it and cook until the meat is just before leaving the bone. Serve over rice with corn and greens.

This is very good with half-dollar-size dumplings made in the stew. You may need more liquid. If you do, just go ahead and add it.

☆ BRUNSWICK STEW ☆

This one is so deliciously over the top!

5 lb (2.3 kg) beef
5 lb (2.3 kg) chicken
2½ lb (1.25 kg) pork
5 lb (2.3 kg) Irish potatoes
4 lb (1.8 kg) onions
1½ lb (700 g) lima beans
2½ lb (1.25 kg) tomatoes
4 × 12 oz (350 g) tins sweet corn
2 lb (900 g) okra
1 × 10 fl oz (300 ml) bottle Worcestershire sauce
¼ teaspoon ground allspice
Juice of 6 Sunkist lemons
1 tablespoon sugar
1 hot chilli pepper or 1 teaspoon Tabasco sauce (more if you want it real hot)
2 bottles tomato ketchup
1 tablespoon prepared mustard
¼ teaspoon ground cloves
2 fl oz (50 ml) white vinegar
1 tablespoon liquid hickory smoke (speciality shops should have it)
1½ gallons (7 litres) chicken-and-meat stock

Put the beef, chicken and pork in a very large pan, cover with water and cook gently until tender. Let cool. Mince the meat. Mince the potatoes and onions and add to the meat and its stock. Cook for 30 minutes. Add the other ingredients as listed. Mix well. Cook for $1\frac{1}{2}$ hours, stirring often. If canning, cook for only 30 minutes. Place in jars. Process 60 minutes at 15 lb (6.75 kg) pressure or 90 minutes at 10 lb (4.5 kg) pressure. If freezing, let cool, place in containers and freeze. Or serve hot with rice and corn pone (corn bread).

Good for a family reunion or church supper.

☆ AUNT ROSIE DEATON'S ☆ ALL-AMERICAN SLUM-GULLION*
THE BEST (SO THEY SAY!)

Cook some elbow macaroni – plenty. Brown minced onion (the stronger, the better), hamburger and/or bacon in a skillet. Add 1 can tomatoes, salt, pepper and all the macaroni you got. Simmer till you can't stand it any more, then take it off the fire and dive in. This is especially good when you're in a hurry-up day, like when there's a funeral, an auction, or a flag-burning at the Legion Hall.

---

* 'Slum-gullion' is a term first used by miners in the California Gold Rush to denote unpleasant or makeshift food.

And here are three gravies, probably best avoided!

☆ Mamma's Brown Gravy ☆

Leave enough grease in the skillet after frying meat (pork, beef, or chicken) and add 3 or 4 heaping tablespoons of flour on medium-to-high heat and stir constantly with a fork until dark golden-brown. Then add water and cook until it just will run out of a spoon. Also, leave the crispies in the grease from the fried meat because they add a lot of rich flavour. Salt and black pepper to taste. Serve over hot rice, grits (finely ground, dried, hulled corn kernels) or mashed potatoes.

☆ Yankee Cream Gravy ☆

$2\frac{1}{2}$ oz (65 g) flour
8 fl oz (250 ml) milk
Salt and pepper

To avoid lumps, put the flour and milk in a jar and shake it vigorously until blended. After you have fried some green tomatoes, remove them from the pan and pour in the mixture of flour and milk. Stir constantly until it thickens and serve on top of the green tomatoes.

This will go with just about anything.

☆ Red Eye Gravy ☆

After cooking the breakfast meat (bacon, ham, or sausage), remove it from the iron skillet and put it aside. To the drippins add $2\frac{1}{2}$ fl oz (65 ml) strong coffee and stir while continuing to heat. Pour over hot grits (finely ground, dried, hulled corn kernels) or sop up with hot biscuits.

New Mexico

☆ ROD'S FRITATTA ☆
ST FRANCIS HOTEL, SANTA FE

New Mexicans eat this Italian-inspired omelette for breakfast – when they're not tucking into chillied eggs and tortillas, that is!

Potatoes, diced
Olive oil for frying
Onion, chopped
Red, green and yellow peppers, chopped
Pinch of oregano (preferably fresh)
Pinch of basil (preferably fresh)
Pinch of rosemary (preferably fresh)
Pinch of chopped parsley
Cooked artichoke hearts, chopped
2 eggs per person, beaten
Salt and freshly ground pepper
Parmesan cheese, grated

Cook the potatoes in boiling water. Heat the olive oil in a frying-pan and sweat the onion and peppers. Add the potatoes and herbs and continue to cook until the potatoes are golden-brown. Add the artichoke hearts, eggs and salt and pepper to taste. Stir until the eggs congeal and either flip over the omelette or brown the top under the grill until it puffs up. Sprinkle with a little Parmesan cheese and serve immediately.

☆ THE CHILLI FILE ☆

FLOYD'S CHUCK WAGON PORK AND BEANS

SERVES 4–6

6 oz (175 g) dried black beans
$\frac{1}{2}$ teaspoon salt
2 bay leaves
$\frac{1}{2}$ teaspoon freshly ground pepper
$\frac{1}{2}$ teaspoon cumin seeds
$\frac{1}{2}$ teaspoon dried oregano
2 tablespoons vegetable oil
$1\frac{1}{2}$ lb (700 g) pork shoulder, cubed
2–3 jalapeño or other chilli peppers, chopped
1 onion, chopped
2 cloves garlic, finely chopped
3 tablespoons crushed red chilli peppers
2 tablespoons blue cornmeal or cornflour
2 tablespoons honey

Soak the beans overnight in plenty of cold water. Drain, then boil for 2 hours with the salt, bay leaves, black pepper, cumin and oregano. Strain, reserving the liquid, and set aside. Heat the oil in a pan (preferably a cauldron hung over a wood fire, wood mark 3!) and add the pork, jalapeños, onion and garlic. In a bowl mix the red chillies, cornmeal or cornflour and the cooking liquid from the beans to make a kind of cowboy *roux* and stir this into the pan. Add the beans and finally the honey. Simmer for about 2 hours. Serve as the sun goes down around an open fire, with a bottle of Kentucky Fried Gentleman and someone playing guitar.

Mayor Sam Pick's Green Chilli

Ok, so the Mayor of Santa Fe beat me in our great chilli cook-off – but I'm magnanimous enough to pass on his recipe. I'm sorry to say that it's excellent!

Serves 2–4

1 lb (450 g) pork
2 tablespoons lard
1 tablespoon flour
6–7 green chilli peppers, de-seeded and chopped
1 onion, chopped
2 large potatoes, chopped
1 tomato, chopped
1 clove garlic, crushed
Salt

Put the pork into a pan with 4 fl oz (120 ml) water and cook for about $1\frac{1}{2}$ hours or until tender. Leave to cool, then strain, reserving the cooking liquid. Trim any fat off the meat and discard; shred the lean finely with your hands. In the same pan make a *roux* with the lard and flour, cooking it gently and stirring all the time until it browns. Add the cooking liquid from the pork, the pork itself, the chillies, onion, potatoes, tomato and garlic. Cover with *cold* water. Bring to the boil and simmer until the potatoes are cooked. Add salt to taste.

Floyd's Green Chilli

And now for *my* green chilli … actually I borrowed it from my pal Rod, our chef at the St Francis Hotel in Santa Fe – who assured me that we would beat the mayor hands down! The proportions of this dish are one part onion to two parts beef, one part carrot to two parts onion, and equal quantities of potatoes and beef. Use at least four chilli peppers if you like your chilli hot.

Beef (preferably sirloin), cut into $\frac{1}{2}$ inch (1 cm) cubes
Oil for frying
Onions, chopped
Carrots, chopped

Potatoes, cut into chunks
Cloves garlic, crushed
Jalapeño or other chilli peppers, diced, retaining seeds
Beef stock
Bay leaf
Dried oregano
Butter
Flour
Parsley, chopped

Sauté the meat in the oil. Add the onions, carrots and potatoes and continue to cook for a few minutes. Add the garlic and chillies and cover with stock, then add the bay leaf and oregano to taste. Bring to the boil and simmer for about $1\frac{1}{2}$ hours or until the meat is tender. Mix the butter and flour together and stir a knob or two into the stew to thicken the sauce. Stir in the parsley and leave to stand for a few minutes before serving.

Pueblo Indian Red Chilli

This is very fiery stuff! Cut down on the chilli powder if you think you can't take the heat.

Serves 2–4

1 lb (450 g) beef, cubed
1 small onion, diced
1 clove garlic, crushed
3 tablespoons chilli powder
1 tablespoon blue cornmeal or wholewheat flour

Put the beef into a pan, cover with water and simmer for 30 minutes on top of the stove. Then transfer to a casserole, add the onion and garlic and continue cooking in the oven at gas mark 4, 350°F (180°C), for about $1\frac{1}{2}$ hours or until the meat is tender. Mix the chilli powder with a little cornmeal or wholewheat flour, mix into a paste with water, and stir into the stew to thicken. Cook for a further 30 minutes or so.

Mayor Sam Pick's green chilli (page 269); Floyd's green chilli (page 269);
Steak Dunigan (page 273)

☆ ROSALEA MURPHY'S ☆ STEAK DUNIGAN
PINK ADOBE, SANTA FE

This was named after its inventor, Pat Dunigan, who insisted on adding green chillies to his steak. There was soon such a demand for it that Rosalea had to put it on the menu.

SERVES 2

4 large mushrooms, thinly sliced
4 tablespoons butter
Hickory-smoked salt (Spice Island or Schilling is best), available from speciality shops, to taste
2 × 14–15 oz (400–425 g) top-grade New York cut (sirloin) steaks

Green Chilli Sauce
1 medium onion, finely chopped
2 tablespoons olive oil
2 × 4 oz (110 g) tins green chilli peppers, drained and chopped
$\frac{1}{4}$ teaspoon dried oregano
$\frac{1}{4}$ teaspoon chopped fresh coriander
$\frac{1}{4}$ teaspoon salt
1 teaspoon Tabasco sauce or chopped jalapeño pepper

First prepare the Green Chilli Sauce. Sauté the onion in the oil. Add the remaining sauce ingredients and cook for 5 minutes. Keep warm.

Sauté the mushrooms in the butter for approximately 5 minutes or until soft. Remove from the pan and keep warm. Shake the hickory salt on both sides of the steaks. Fry or grill until cooked as desired (10–15 minutes for rare; 15–20 minutes for medium), turning once.

Transfer the steaks to a platter. Divide the mushrooms over the top of the steaks. Cover each with Green Chilli Sauce.

Fritatta (page 267)

☆ ROSALEA MURPHY'S ☆ GYPSY STEW

PINK ADOBE, SANTA FE

On his travels in Spain with the gypsies, Vicente Romero, the world-famous flamenco dancer, discovered this marvellous gypsy chicken stew. Vicente has improved upon the quality and taste by adding green chillies.

SERVES 10-12

1 × 3 lb (1.4 kg) whole chicken, plus 4–5 extra breasts
6 yellow onions, quartered
15 cloves garlic, halved
2 pints (900 ml) cocktail sherry
1 × 15 oz (425 g) tin chicken soup
About 20 roasted and peeled large fresh green chilli peppers or 9 × 4 oz (110 g)
tins whole green chilli peppers
4 × 14 oz (400 g) tins tomatoes
2 teaspoons salt or to taste
1 lb (450 g) Monterey Jack cheese or mild Cheddar

Put the chicken, onions, garlic, half the sherry and the soup into a large, heavy pan or Dutch oven. If the liquid isn't enough to cover the other ingredients, add more soup or water. Cover the pan and simmer *slowly* for 1–1½ hours or until the chicken is cooked. Never boil this stew: boiling will ruin it because all the sherry will cook out. On the other hand, if it's not cooked enough it will taste bitter.

Cut the chillies into chunks. Using 2 forks, tear the tomatoes apart and place in a large bowl with the chillies and all of their juices, to mingle together while chicken is cooking.

Remove the cooked chicken from the pan and let cool enough so that you can pick the meat off the bones. Add the chillies, tomatoes, remaining sherry, salt and chicken to the liquid in the pan. Cover and simmer *slowly* for about an hour.

Cut the cheese into cubes and place in the bottom of 10–12 individual serving bowls. Pour some stew into each bowl; the heat will melt the cheese. Serve with tortillas (see page 242) and a side dish of guacamole or beans.

☆ ROD'S PINON PIE ☆
ST FRANCIS HOTEL, SANTA FE

SERVES 6–8

3 oz (75 g) plain chocolate, coarsely chopped
5 oz (150 g) pinons (pine nuts) or pecan nuts, walnuts, almonds or a mixture of
any of these

Dough
12 oz (350 g) flour
8 oz (225 g) chilled unsalted butter, cut in small pieces
2–3 tablespoons sugar
4 oz (110 g) ground almonds
Pinch of salt
1 egg, lightly beaten
1 teaspoon vanilla essence

Syrup
3 eggs, beaten
3 oz (75 g) sugar
Pinch of salt
2 fl oz (50 ml) dark corn syrup
2–3 tablespoons dark rum

First make the dough. With your fingers or using a food processor, blend the flour, butter, sugar, almonds and salt until you have a fine mixture. Add the egg and vanilla and work in until the dough holds together – you may need another $\frac{1}{2}$ egg or 2 tablespoons water to achieve the required consistency. Chill the dough for at least 1 hour, then roll out to fit a 9 inch (23 cm) cake tin. Bake blind for 15–20 minutes in the oven at gas mark 4, 350°F (180°C). Leave to cool.

Put the chocolate chips in the pastry shell followed by the nuts. Mix together the syrup ingredients and heat gently. Pour into the pastry shell. Bake in the oven at the same temperature as before for another 30–45 minutes or until the pie filling is browned and springy.

☆ CAPE COD ☆

Fill a highball glass with ice, add a measure of vodka and top up with cranberry juice. Add a dash of orange juice to make a **Madres**, or grapefruit to make a **Sea Breeze**.

☆ LIME DAIQUIRI ☆

Put some ice in a blender, add two measures of rum, one measure of fresh lime juice and half a teaspoon of sugar syrup (or more, to taste). Blend until smooth. Decorate the glass with slices of lime.

☆ MARGARITA ☆

In a jug mix equal parts of tequila (preferably José Cuervo Gold) and Triple Sec. Top up with freshly squeezed lime juice (or a mixture of lemon and lime juice). Chill. Serve over ice in glasses with salted rims. (Dip the rims of the glasses first into a saucer of lime juice, then into a saucer of salt.)

☆ MINT JULEP ☆

Fill a glass with ice, add a good sprig of mint, and a teaspoon of sugar. Pour over two measures of bourbon. If you like, top up with soda.

☆ MISSISSIPPI MILK SHAKE ☆

Shake one measure of brandy, a pinch of nutmeg, some sugar syrup to taste with ice and enough milk to fill up a highball glass.

☆ TEQUILA SUNRISE ☆

Pour a measure of tequila over ice. Nearly fill the glass with fresh orange juice, then pour over a little grenadine.

☆ WHISKY SOUR ☆

Shake two measures of whisky or bourbon with one measure of fresh lemon juice and half a teaspoon of sugar.

Italic page numbers refer to colour illustrations

ACKNOWLEDGEMENTS

The author and publishers are grateful to the following for permission to reproduce recipes in this book: Dell Publishing Group Inc. for Gypsy Stew (page 274) and Steak Dunigan (page 273) from *The Pink Adobe Cookbook* by Rosalea Murphy; Shirley Fong-Torres for Good Year Shrimps (page 256) and Potstickers (page 257) from *Wok Wiz Chinatown Tour Cookbook*; Harper and Row Publishers Inc. for Blinis with Smoked Sturgeon and Caviar (page 249), Cucumber and Crayfish Cream Vichyssoise (page 250), Steak Tartare (page 259) and Stuffed Chillies (page 260) from *Jeremiah Tower's New American Classics*; The Junior League of Memphis for Barbecued Chicken (page 229), Jellied Beef Loaf (page 232) and Oyster Stew (page 228) from *The Memphis Cookbook*; and William Morrow and Co. Inc. for Blackened Redfish (page 211), Crawfish Pie (page 208), Dirty Rice (page 221) and Rabbit Tenderloin with Mustard Sauce (page 214) from *Paul Prudhomme's Louisiana Kitchen*.

PICTURE CREDITS

All pictures in the travelogue section taken by Sheila Keating, excluding pages 18 and 126 (Tim White) and pages 71 *top and bottom*, 89 *top*, 90 *bottom*, 143, 144, 161, 162 and 179 (Andy MacCormack).

Every effort has been made to contact copyright holders for the use of the material in this book but, if copyright material has been used inadvertently without permission, the publishers would be delighted to hear from those concerned.